Please return this item to any Poole library
by the due date.
Renew on (01202) 265200 or at
www.boroughofpoole.com/libraries

Student Finance **For Dummies**®

Published by: **John Wiley & Sons, Ltd., The Atrium, Southern Gate, Chichester,**
www.wiley.com

This edition first published 2016

© 2016 by John Wiley & Sons, Ltd., Chichester, West Sussex

Registered Office

John Wiley & Sons, Ltd., The Atrium, Southern Gate, Chichester, West Sussex, PO19 8SQ,
United Kingdom

For details of our global editorial offices, for customer services and for information about how
to apply for permission to reuse the copyright material in this book, please see our website at
www.wiley.com.

Designations used by companies to distinguish their products are often claimed as trademarks. All
brand names and product names used in this book are trade names, service marks, trademarks or
registered trademarks of their respective owners. The publisher is not associated with any product
or vendor mentioned in this book.

LIMIT OF LIABILITY/DISCLAIMER OF WARRANTY: WHILE THE PUBLISHER AND AUTHOR HAVE
USED THEIR BEST EFFORTS IN PREPARING THIS BOOK, THEY MAKE NO REPRESENTATIONS
OR WARRANTIES WITH RESPECT TO THE ACCURACY OR COMPLETENESS OF THE CONTENTS
OF THIS BOOK AND SPECIFICALLY DISCLAIM ANY IMPLIED WARRANTIES OF MERCHANTABILITY
OR FITNESS FOR A PARTICULAR PURPOSE. IT IS SOLD ON THE UNDERSTANDING THAT THE
PUBLISHER IS NOT ENGAGED IN RENDERING PROFESSIONAL SERVICES AND NEITHER THE
PUBLISHER NOR THE AUTHOR SHALL BE LIABLE FOR DAMAGES ARISING HEREFROM. IF
PROFESSIONAL ADVICE OR OTHER EXPERT ASSISTANCE IS REQUIRED, THE SERVICES OF A
COMPETENT PROFESSIONAL SHOULD BE SOUGHT.

For general information on our other products and services, please contact our Customer Care
Department within the U.S. at 877-762-2974, outside the U.S. at 317-572-3993, or fax 317-572-4002. For
technical support, please visit www.wiley.com/techsupport.

Wiley publishes in a variety of print and electronic formats and by print-on-demand. Some material
included with standard print versions of this book may not be included in e-books or in print-on-
demand. If this book refers to media such as a CD or DVD that is not included in the version you
purchased, you may download this material at http://booksupport.wiley.com. For more
information about Wiley products, visit www.wiley.com.

A catalogue record for this book is available from the British Library.

ISBN 978-1-119-07585-1 (pbk); ISBN 978-1-119-07587-5 (ebk); ISBN 978-1-119-07586-8 (ebk)

Printed and Bound in Great Britain by TJ International, Padstow, Cornwall.

10 9 8 7 6 5 4 3 2 1

Contents at a Glance

Table of Contents

Part IV: Finding Financing from Other (Non-Statutory) Sources........................... 187

Chapter 11: Finance From Universities 189

Chapter 12: Trying Out Educational Trusts and Charities 203

Introduction

● ●

*I*f you're looking for an overview of the student finance system in the UK, you've opened the right book! My aim is to give you a sufficient level of detail to inform you of the variety of support available in each of the four nations of the UK through the provision of student loans, grants and other sources of financial support such as educational trusts and charities.

You'll find information about eligibility for support, how and when to apply, how your support is assessed and paid to you and what you need to pay back. My intention is to provide a guide to how the student finance system functions so you can gain a better insight when navigating the system during your studies. I provide you with enough information to understand how student finance should work for you – so that you can quickly resolve any difficulties, or identify where to turn to for assistance should any difficulties arise.

The government's student finance system is not perfect in terms of meeting all the needs of all students, and there is a realistic chance that you may need to supplement your student finance with income from other sources. A wide range of options including part-time work, discretionary funding, effective money management and even credit are discussed – with the intention of raising your awareness of the various options you have available to you to make your student finance work for you as effectively as it can.

Good luck with your studies!

About This Book

This book aims to provide you with a realistic representation of how the student finance system operates, to help inform your use of it and hopefully enable you to have an effective and positive experience of it.

Wherever possible, I have taken the opportunity to break information down into easily accessible and identifiable sections, so that you are able to quickly find the topic you wish to read about. Sections are designed to stand alone and to be read in whatever order you find useful, and to dip into on a need-to-know basis.

Some sections may never apply to you during your studies. For instance, some material is subject specific, or concerns regional info or personal circumstances which do not apply to you. Nor should you be concerned with trying to remember all the information contained here – the book is intended to act as a quick resource for you to refer to no matter how frequently. Think of it as your friendly guide to understanding the student finance system, always ready to assist you with what you want to know.

The majority of the book uses the student finance system in England as the 'default' version. The reason for this being that the majority of students access the English student finance system. Every effort has been made to signpost the exceptions relevant to the Scottish, Welsh and Northern Irish systems, so you should find the important information you require wherever you're studying, and whichever of the UK's student finance systems you're making an application through.

At the time of writing, the only rates of student finance which have been confirmed for 2016/17 are those for England. The latest information has been used for Wales, Scotland and Northern Ireland, but this may change during the months leading up to September 2016/17. The online information supporting the book includes links to the funding websites for each of the nations, so reference to these resources will provide the equivalent rates for 2016/17 once they are released.

You may notice that some web addresses break across two lines of text. If you're reading this book in print and want to visit one of these web pages, simply key in the web address exactly as it's noted in the text, pretending that the line break doesn't exist. If you're reading this as an e-book, you've got it easy – just click the web address to be taken directly to the web page.

Foolish Assumptions

To help me focus on giving you the information you need, I've made a few assumptions about the 'average' reader (no, of course you're not one of those *average* readers, you're in the top percentile . . .).

The majority of information is relevant to undergraduate students, although some sections target specific postgraduate studies as well.

I don't expect you to have any advanced mathematical skills or in-depth knowledge of financial products in order to use this book as an effective resource. On the contrary, the book aims to simplify the various aspects of student finance so that you can gain a thorough understanding of the various options and entitlements available to you, and to help explain the more complex elements of the system.

Finally, the info I provide assumes that you may be one of the majority of students experiencing the responsibility for managing their money for the very first time, and so the emphasis is very much upon presenting student finance in as straightforward a way as possible. I make no assumptions that you've already gained financial experience in order to provide you with strategies for the effective management of whatever finances you have available.

One final point worth noting is that I cannot see into the future, so the detail contained within these pages is as up to date as it can be at the time of writing.

Icons Used in This Book

Across the pages of this book, you'll find icons sitting in the margin. These are designed to highlight key items of information which you might find particularly useful.

The Tip icon aims to give you a helpful insight into information which you may not already know. Tips ensure you are in a position to make effective use of the information provided, often with practical experience in mind.

The Remember icon ensures that you're able to bear in mind key facts or requirements that require emphasis. You're advised to pay attention to these icons because they often seek to explain more complex pieces of information that may be important to you.

 Some aspects of the student finance system can be more problematic, and may lead to difficulties for you. Wherever any potential pitfalls are identified, the Warning icon is used to warn you of the issues you need to be aware of. Be sure to read them – forewarned is forearmed!

 All of the details within this book are relevant to *someone* – it's just that someone may not be you! Additionally, some people like more financial detail (and number crunching) than others. This icon highlights information that you may find useful or of interest, but you also have my express permission to skim over paragraphs with this icon should they not be offering you the cup of tea you desire.

Beyond the Book

In addition to the material in the print or e-book you're reading right now, this product also comes with some access-anywhere goodies on the web found at www.dummies.com/extras/studentfinanceuk.

Check out the free Cheat Sheet at www.dummies.com/cheatsheet/studentfinanceuk for helpful funding-related tips, pointers for tackling common problems that can arise, and a few words on where to turn to for advice if you can't find the answer you're searching for.

Where to Go from Here

Remember that you can dip into this book at any point – any section gives you a useful overview of the topic it describes.

Whilst the majority of the information in this book is centred around the student finance system, and related subjects such as financial capability (using your money wisely), you may find the following prompts useful:

✔ If you're on a course leading directly to a subject such as teaching, social work or an NHS career, refer to the sections in Part III in the first instance.

✔ For information on getting started with student finance, Part II gives immediate access to the elements of the student finance system across all UK nations.

✔ Part IV provides a useful introduction to additional sources of student funding – some of these need you to do some research before your course begins, so you should dip into this section even before you start your course.

✔ If you'd like information about how to use your money so that it works for you, Part V gives some practical information on common sense tips and how to's in order to make your money go further and maximise your income.

Don't forget to check online for additional information – particularly for updated rates for student finance in Wales, Scotland and Northern Ireland once they are published by the respective governments. These are published annually.

Part I

Wading into the Funding Pool

In this part . . .

✔ Build your understanding of the basic features of the student finance system: the loans you have to pay back and the grants you don't!

✔ Discover the basics of how to make an effective application for student finance, and what to do if it goes wrong.

✔ Get an introduction to how student finance looks in different parts of the UK.

✔ Get prepared for your studies by planning your finances and identifying sources of income.

✔ Get acquainted with the other sources of funding that might help you in your studies.

Chapter 1

Who Needs Student Finance?

In This Chapter

▶ Introducing student finance

▶ Learning some useful jargon

▶ Finding sources of student finance

'*S*tudent finance' is a term which covers a wide variety of funding schemes across the UK. Student finance differs across the four nations of the UK, and describes a number of different models of funding, including grants, loans, bursaries and scholarships. In addition to the various items of funding available, 'student finance' also covers the notion of financial capability – or how you can look after your money so that it can work for you (and not against your studies). This includes making strategies for budgeting and looking after the money that you have, as well as being careful to make informed choices about credit.

In this chapter, I provide an introduction to the various forms student finance can take, along with suggestions for the next chapters to read depending on your personal interest in finance.

Paying for Your Education and Making It Pay

Your higher education study is likely to give you a truly transformational experience, opening your horizons to opportunities for life-enriching experiences in terms of your academic, social and personal development. Higher education can also be an opportunity to develop your financial capability, and for many higher education students, time spent studying a degree is also time spent learning to manage personal finances for the very first time.

The time you begin to consider higher education study is also the ideal time for you to begin considering the practicalities of the financial side of studying, and to begin making preparations for it if at all possible.

You may not have had any previous contact with the world of student finance, particularly if you're the first in your family to enter higher education, so finding out how you can manage your money is really important. You also need to understand how you can afford to pay for the experience of taking your education to the next level.

The UK government introduced the concept of students paying towards the cost of their tuition fees in 1998. Since then, government-subsidised loan schemes have been available to meet the cost of tuition fees. The loan scheme allows students to *defer* the cost of their education, not needing to repay until they have both finished their time in higher education and have entered into employment earning a sufficient level for the loan to be repaid.

These basic principles of the funding system remain in place today, and although some other aspects of the system have been 'tweaked', you can still enter your studies safe in the knowledge that you haven't a thing to repay whilst you're studying, and usually only need to make repayments once your personal taxable income has reached a required threshold.

Whilst tuition fee loans have been around since 2006 (prior to that tuition fee contribution grants had been in place since 1998), student loans for maintenance (living costs) were introduced back in 1990. Since then they have become an increasingly major part of the student finance package – and now you may even find a student loan is the sole source of student finance available to you (particularly if you're ordinarily resident in England).

Being aware of the student finance available to you, understanding it and accessing it is only part of the story when it comes to making your finances work for you during your studies. You also need to develop your capability in terms of ensuring that you make the most of what money is available to you, avoiding unnecessary costs and realising as many economies as you can. Every little saving you can identify is the best means towards safeguarding your financial situation during your studies (read Chapters 15 and 16 for more tips on looking after your money once you have it). You should also seek to maximise the opportunities for securing funds to help make managing your situation far easier.

Building Your Funding Vocabulary

The UK student finance system has terminology you may not have encountered until you come to use it.

If you get a chance, start reading some online resources which describe the student finance system – particularly for courses that you're interested in studying. The more you read, the sooner you become familiar with the various phrases and terms used. Check out the sidebar, 'Speaking the lingo', to get off to a flying start.

Loans versus grants

You probably require at least one student loan of some kind (maintenance and/or tuition fee) during your studies. You can usually expect to have to repay at least some of any loan you take out at some point during your career, but if you're eligible to receive a grant, you must take every step to ensure you get it paid to you, as grants don't have to be repaid and are effectively 'free money'.

You can view a grant as being your 'entitlement' and as long as you meet the criteria for a grant to be payable, you should ensure that you apply for and obtain the money available to you.

Speaking the lingo

Here's a quick checklist of terms to get you started:

✓ **Bursary:** Usually this is an amount of money your course provider pays to you if you meet eligibility requirements. The amount you receive varies between course providers and often between types of course as well. You need to check your course provider's access agreement (in England) or website for more details of what is available and how to apply. Some courses have statutory bursary schemes (which are usually non-repayable) available to them, such as NHS courses and courses for Initial Teacher Education.

✓ **Grant:** Grants may be available to you depending on your circumstances. They can assist with general living costs, costs associated with caring for a child (including childcare), costs associated with having someone else financially dependent upon you, and additional costs associated with study if you have a disability.

✓ **Income-assessed:** Several items of student finance depend upon your household income situation – generally speaking, you're likely to be eligible to receive more student finance if your household income is lower. The lower income threshold for maximum financial support varies among the UK nations. An alternative phrase is 'means-tested', which is applied to NHS funding and sometimes to welfare benefits.

✓ **Maintenance Loan:** An amount available to you during your study in order to help your general costs whilst you study, such as course materials, accommodation, household and other living costs. You may be required to repay the loan in part or in full once you have finished your time in education and once you're earning at a sufficient level from employment.

✓ **Non income-assessed:** This phrase is usually associated with tuition fee support and grants for students with a disability – both of which require basic criteria to be met in order for the financial support to be paid to you. The phrase also refers to the basic package of support available to students whose household income is too high to be considered for additional income-assessed financial support. 'Non means-tested' is an alternative phrase which is applied to NHS funding, and sometimes to welfare benefits.

✓ **Scholarship:** A scholarship may be very similar to a bursary – usually because it's available from your course provider, but it's more likely to have some more complex eligibility criteria, perhaps based on your academic achievements to date or your subject of study. Scholarships are usually non-repayable.

✔ **Student Finance England (SFE):** The agency responsible for processing student finance applications if you're ordinarily resident in England.

✔ **Student Finance Northern Ireland (SFNI):** This actually is the name only of the website representing the Education Library Boards, which still process student finance applications at local level in Northern Ireland.

✔ **Student Awards Agency for Scotland (SAAS):** The agency responsible for processing student finance applications if you're ordinarily resident in Scotland.

✔ **Student Finance Wales (SFW):** The agency responsible for processing student finance applications if you're ordinarily resident in Wales.

✔ **Student loan:** This usually refers to a loan available from the UK government, paid to you by the Student Loans Company. There are four agencies which assess entitlement to loans in each of the four UK nations.

In Scotland, you may only have access to a Maintenance Loan if you're a Scottish student studying in Scotland, as the Scottish government covers the cost of your tuition fees — but you can get a Tuition Fee Loan if you choose to study elsewhere in the UK.

Whilst student loans are very much defined as being either for tuition fees or general living costs, grants can be available for wider, more specific purposes, for example:

✔ Students who are parents (Parent's Learning Allowance; Lone Parent's Grant; Childcare Grant)

✔ Disabled students (Disabled Students' Allowances)

✔ Students studying abroad or on NHS dental/medical courses (Travel Grant)

If you'd like to find out more about specific examples, check out Chapters 5 and 6.

If you think you have some special circumstances which may mean you require grant assistance, discuss these with the advice service at your course provider. Even if there isn't a specific grant available to assist you with your studies, you may find some other sources of discretionary support are available which can assist. Flick through to Chapters 11 and 12 for more advice on special circumstances.

Tuition and maintenance

The two main categories of student finance are those sources which meet the cost of your tuition fees and those which meet the cost of your maintenance, or living costs.

Student loans are available to meet the cost of both your tuition fees and living costs, but you need to apply for separate loans for each purpose. Limited opportunities exist for grants for tuition fees, but these are primarily found in Wales, Scotland and Northern Ireland – and in some cases only for part-time study. Some grant-based fee support still exists in England – the PGCE for Early Years Teaching Status being one example (funded by the National College for Teacher Education).

Tuition Fee Loans are non income-assessed and only rely on the most basic eligibility criteria for funding (for example, personal eligibility, course provider and programme of study). Tuition Fee Loan support is available to you if you've been ordinarily resident in the UK for three years before the start of your course, or if you're an EU national who has been ordinarily resident in the European Economic Area for an equivalent three-year period.

Maintenance support is intended to contribute toward all costs you may encounter except your tuition fees. Your accommodation, food, household expenses, utility bills, clothing, travel and course-related costs (books/materials/computer consumables) are all included in the range of costs which maintenance support is intended to assist with.

Maintenance support is more complex in so far as non income-assessed and income-assessed elements of student finance are available. A 'basic' non income-assessed loan is available to you if you're ordinarily resident in the UK and have been so for the qualifying three-year period (the usual requirements around course provider and programme of study also apply). In addition to the non income-assessed loan, higher amounts are available if you undergo an assessment of your household income. Find out more in Chapter 5.

Bursaries, scholarships and all the rest

Bursaries and scholarships are almost always available on a non-repayable basis, so they are well worth investigating as a meaningful additional source of income to support your studies.

With the exception of the NHS Bursary, Social Work Bursary and National School of Teaching and Leadership Training Bursaries (for PGCE and non-salaried School Direct courses), bursaries are provided by your course provider.

In England, the provision of bursaries is largely governed by the Office for Fair Access, with course providers charging over £6,000 a year for a course being required to have an Access Agreement in place, which often includes provision for bursary and scholarship schemes. Bursaries and scholarships are available in other nations of the UK (but are not governed by OFFA).

You need to check with your course provider to find out what bursary and scholarship schemes it offers, and what eligibility criteria are used, to determine entitlement. A variety of criteria is used, with income assessment being an extremely common factor. However, other methods can apply, such as your academic achievement to date, your performance on the course you're studying (which determines the release of future payments), the subject you study and your address where you usually live outside term time (some course providers seek to encourage applicants from their local community, or from areas with little participation in higher education).

Further sources of financial support may also be available from your course provider – discretionary funds are often available if you can provide evidence of any financial hardship you are facing, or costs associated with your own children, or travel costs – all of these are common factors which can lead to additional financial support becoming accessible to you.

You may also wish to do some additional research to find out if there are any educational trusts or charitable funds in your area, or associated with your area of study which may be available to you. I recommend that you do this well in advance of the start of your course so that you can make a note of requirements such as application deadlines. For more info on trusts and charitable funds, please read Chapter 12.

Getting Funds from the Government

Statutory student finance is likely to be the main source of funding you will access to support your studies. Undergraduate student finance is well established, but from 2016/17 there are plans to introduce a system of postgraduate student loans for taught masters and research degrees as well.

The advantage of using government funding systems is that non-repayable grants are available if your circumstances make you eligible to receive one (grants are effectively your entitlement to 'free money') and the available loans are heavily subsidised in terms of the low rates of interest attached to them, together with the fact that the repayment terms may mean that you don't need to repay the full amount owing under the loan agreement.

You may be aware of the availability of government funding, but researching how to apply and how to maximise the funding available to you is crucial. Be aware of the deadlines for making an application and also find out when the funding application cycle opens – find out more in Chapter 4.

The online application form can supposedly be completed in around 30 minutes, but experience of using it with students suggests you're probably better off setting an hour aside to be sure of completing the form in one sitting. Chapter 4 talks you through the form.

Once you have registered and created your online student finance account, make sure that you keep your details safe and secure because you'll need to refer back to your account when applying for funding for later years of your course.

The geography of funding

There are several versions of the statutory student finance system operating in the UK at the moment. One of the most fundamental distinctions between the schemes is which UK nation you're applying to for funding.

The version of student finance which is applicable to you is determined by where you have been ordinarily resident for the three years before your course begins. You may also need to be resident in that country on the first day of your course in order to be sure of qualifying for the available financial support.

An overview of the statutory funding in each of the UK nations looks like this:

England

Full-time

Tuition Fee Loan

Maintenance Loan

Dependants' Grants (Parent's Learning Allowance, Adult Dependants' Grant, Childcare Grant)

Travel Grant (for some courses only)

Disabled Students' Allowances

Part-time

Tuition Fee Loan

Disabled Students' Allowances

Northern Ireland
Full-time

Tuition Fee Loan

Maintenance Loan

Maintenance Grant/Special Support Grant

Dependants' Grants (Parent's Learning Allowance, Adult Dependants' Grant, Childcare Grant)

Disabled Students' Allowances

Part-time

Tuition Fee Grant

Course Grant

Scotland
Full-time

Tuition Fee Grant (if you're ordinarily resident in Scotland and studying in Scotland)

Tuition Fee Loan (if you're ordinarily resident in Scotland and studying elsewhere in the UK)

Young Student's/Independent Student's Bursary

Maintenance Loan

Lone Parent's Grant

Dependants' Grant

Care Leaver's Vacation Grant

Disabled Students' Allowances

Part-time

Tuition Fee Grant

Disabled Students' Allowances

Wales
Full-time

Tuition Fee Loan

Tuition Fee Grant

Maintenance Loan

Welsh Government Learning Grant/Special Support Grant

Dependants' Grants (Parent's Learning Allowance, Adult Dependants' Grant, Childcare Grant)

Travel Grant (for some courses only)

Disabled Students' Allowances

Part-time

Tuition Fee Loan

Course Grant

Dependants' Grants (Parent's Learning Allowance, Adult Dependants' Grant, Childcare Grant)

Disabled Students' Allowances

Cash for specific professions
The government makes a priority of some subject areas which lead directly to professions seen as a priority for the UK.

If you study a course in the following subject areas, you may be able to access bespoke funding for that course which may differ from the usual statutory financial support package:

- ✔ NHS courses
- ✔ Social Work courses
- ✔ Initial Teacher Education courses

If you study any of the above professions, or the additional ones listed below, you can access further Maintenance Loan support even if you already hold an equivalent or higher level qualification.

- ✔ Veterinary Science
- ✔ Architecture

Chapters 7, 8 and 9 tell you more about profession-based grants and loans.

Other government schemes: benefits and tax credits

The general rule is that, as a full-time student, you don't qualify for welfare benefits, but there are some groups of students who do qualify for support from the welfare benefit and tax credit system during their studies.

Check out Chapter 14 for a breakdown of circumstances in which you may be able to apply for welfare benefit support.

Part-time students are able to access the welfare benefit and tax credit systems – but you should note that you may be required to adhere to the requirements of some benefits (a jobseeker's agreement for Jobseeker's Allowance, for example) even though you're registered on your course. Part-time funding is usually paid in respect of tuition fees, course-related costs or dependant-related costs and so is usually disregarded for benefit purposes.

Returning to higher education

If you're returning to higher education after studying on a previous course, you may find that your entitlement to student finance is affected as a result.

If you plan to study for a qualification which is equivalent to or lower than one you already hold, you may find that no funding is available for the course you wish to study (or the funding is severely reduced).

If you've studied previously but didn't achieve a qualification, you may find your future entitlement is reduced according to the number of years you spent on the previous course. For student finance purposes, one day spent registered on a course can count as one academic year when working out future entitlement to funding.

If you left your original course due to some personal circumstances (such as your health, a bereavement, pregnancy, and so on) you may be able to apply for 'compelling personal reasons', which could help you restore some or all of your funding entitlement for your new course.

Tapping into Other Sources of Funds

The statutory student finance system is not the only source of financial support available to you during your studies. I strongly recommend that you take the time to research additional sources of funding in order to maximise the financial support available to you whilst you study. There are a variety of sources of additional funding, ranging from your course provider, through educational trusts and charities to professional bodies.

Talking to the university

Your course provider can be an effective and convenient option for identifying additional financial support. Course providers have an interest in the retention of their students, so if you're finding it difficult to continue your studies due to financial reasons, you can expect your course provider to make services available to you that seek to assist with your financial difficulties, sometimes going so far as to provide additional financial assistance.

Additional financial support from a course provider may be available in a number of ways. There may be bursary or scholarship schemes in place which are designed to be paid alongside the statutory financial support package. Checking for the availability and eligibility criteria of such schemes helps you to maximise your entitlement to financial support.

Course providers can often make discretionary funds available to support you if you're in a priority group (such as those with children, care leavers or disabled students) or if you're experiencing financial hardship. The availability of discretionary funds is usually determined by making a detailed application which describes your current circumstances. Whilst the process can be time-consuming, the support that is available can be substantial, so it's usually time well spent. If you're in doubt as to the effectiveness of the application you make, or the reasons behind your application, you can usually speak to an adviser from your course provider or student union who can offer you further information about your available options.

Trusts and charities

There are hundreds if not thousands of small educational trusts and charities across the UK. Many operate to their own eligibility criteria and timescales for application deadlines, so if you wish to access these sources, you need to research and make notes of what is required and when, for each trust or charity you identify as being of use to you.

Whilst the typical amounts of financial support from an individual trust or charity may be relatively small, they can nevertheless be an important resource for you – particularly as the money they make available seldom has to be repaid.

Contacting your advice service at your course provider is usually a good way to begin searching for trusts or charities which may be applicable to your area of study. Advisers may already be familiar with possible trusts/charities that students on courses similar to your own have used in the past. Also flick through to Chapter 12 for more details about funding from charities and trusts.

Paying it Back

The bad news is that loans need to be paid back. Sorry! If you receive a mixture of grant and loan support, you usually only need to pay back the elements of financial support paid to you as a loan. You don't usually need to make any repayments of a student loan until you have finished your time in higher education and your earnings are over the applicable threshold.

You usually have no repayments to make on your student loans until the April after you leave/complete your course at the earliest. This is because loan repayments are managed via the UK tax system, and your repayments begin at the start of the next tax year (if you're in employment and your income is above the earnings threshold applicable to your student loans). Any repayments you're required to make are calculated and deducted from your income by your employer – so you don't usually need to make arrangements to repay the loan yourself. However, if you find your career takes you abroad, you need to make repayment arrangements directly with the Student Loans Company (not doing so can leave you with a very expensive loan if you incur penalty charges and penalty interest as a result of the Student Loans Company not being able to get in touch with you).

Some exceptions to the general rule for repayments may be triggered, however, and these arise if you leave your course early (if you withdraw, or for some other reason). If this happens, you may find yourself incurring an overpayment of student loan and/or grant which can lead to you being asked to pay money back.

Grant overpayments are usually immediately recoverable, so you should bear this in mind if you're thinking of leaving your course, and try to leave the money alone in your bank account so that it can be returned (for any amounts relating to the period when you are no longer attending your course).

The usual practice for recovering an overpayment of Maintenance Loan is to deduct it from the next instalment payable. If, however, you haven't taken appropriate action to keep the Student Loans Company, one of its agencies or your course provider informed of your situation, you may find that the overpayment becomes immediately recoverable and as a lump sum.

There have been instances reported where immediate recovery of Maintenance Loans or Grants has been sought, even where students have taken reasonable action to keep their course provider and/or their funding bodies informed. If you find yourself in this situation, make sure that you contact the advice service at the institution where you studied, and they will seek to assist you in exploring whether recovery of the overpayment can be challenged, or assist you in negotiating repayment in instalments if you can show making a lump sum repayment would leave you in financial hardship.

To find out more about repaying your student loans, read Chapter 5.

Looking after Your Money

Applying for your statutory student finance and researching additional sources of financial assistance can amount to a time-consuming process. Once you have secured the funds available to support your studies, you need to put the money to its best possible purpose in supporting you through your studies.

In short, you may wish to do your utmost to introduce measures to safeguard your finances and ensure that your money doesn't go astray. Investing a little more time in identifying strategies that help you to manage your money effectively is an extremely worthwhile undertaking.

The importance of budgeting

Planning ahead is the best strategy for staying in control of your finances. It gives you a realistic appreciation of how much money you have, and helps you understand your spending patterns.

The first step towards successfully managing the money available to you during your studies is to gain a thorough understanding of how much you have available to you, and the best way of doing this is by setting yourself a budget.

For more advice on successful budgeting, skip through to Chapter 15.

If you have a *surplus* (income left over), or your budget balances, you have created a successful budget that should allow you to use your money effectively. If you find that you have a *deficit* (expenditure is more than your income), you may need to spend some time re-examining your budget to see if there are any additional savings you can make, or any other possible sources of income you can make use of.

Making money and using credit wisely during study

Earning additional money through part-time work (or full-time work during vacation periods) can be an extremely valuable source of financial support in addition to your statutory student finance.

Getting a job alongside your studies is a good idea for the following reasons:

- ✔ Working provides a regular income which is really easy to budget with (weekly or monthly).

- ✔ Additional income from work means you're less likely to require a bank overdraft or other forms of credit.

- ✔ Employment opportunities can help you add experience to your CV and increase your employability as a graduate.

- ✔ Your income from work doesn't affect your student finance entitlement – so try to take advantage of employment opportunities as often as you can.

Finding work alongside study can have its challenges, especially in situations where the economy takes a downward turn. However, you can reasonably expect your course provider's careers service to have some information about local vacancies which are suitably flexible to fit around your studies. The careers staff are usually ready to help you in making an effective job application and advise on how you can best present the experience you gain in your CV.

Remember your priorities when working alongside study. Don't lose sight of your studies even if the prospect of earning more money seems attractive. The reason you have that part-time position is in order to support your studies – make sure your studies maintain priority status (otherwise you could be working full-time and earning more in any case!).

Undertaking employment opportunities reduces the likelihood of you having to explore taking on credit during your studies.

First and foremost you must distinguish between student loans from the Student Loans Company and all other forms of credit. Student loans are significantly subsidised by the government and are markedly cheaper to you as a borrower as a result.

Any other form of credit is going to cost you more money by definition. The only exception to this is likely to be an interest-free overdraft attached to your student bank account (but if you end up using a facility such as this, make sure you set it up correctly so you do not incur any charges).

If you can avoid using credit you should do so. If you must use credit, make sure you only choose credit you can afford to service, ideally over a short period of time. Try to avoid expensive short-term loans – the pay day lending sector has had a very high profile in recent years, both in terms of its marketing and in terms of the regulations that have been introduced to ensure responsible lending. As pay day loans usually assume a monthly income, and most students are paid termly, you can easily appreciate that pay day loans are largely incompatible with most students' financial situations and are best avoided as a result.

If you think you need to take on credit, always speak to an adviser at your course provider first, who can advise you of all the options available to you before you sign up to a loan or other type of credit agreement. To find out more about credit and looking after your finances, read Chapter 18.

Class dismissed!

Chapter 2

Putting the Pounds in Place: Planning

*G*et your student finance in great shape for the duration of your course by planning your financial strategy from the outset.

As well as making your student finance application as early as you can, you should consider other ways to support your finances and make them work for you during your studies.

In this chapter, I provide information on preparing the way for your student finance application, give suggestions for other strategies you may adopt both before and during your studies, and provide an overview of the application process, describing the key stages.

Planning Before You Start

As soon as you begin thinking about study in higher education, that is the time when you should start planning financially as well.

Use the time available to you before the start of your course to your advantage, if you can. You may consider the following:

- ✔ Check the opening and closing dates for any statutory funding for which you're applying (for example, from Student Finance England or the equivalents in Wales, Scotland and Northern Ireland).

- ✔ Check for the availability of any additional funding such as from educational trusts or charities.

- ✔ Take any opportunity you can to save up some money as a 'nest egg' for your studies.

This last point is one to take note of. You don't receive any student finance until you've registered on your course, but you may find there are some costs that need to be met before then. For example, you may need to pay for a deposit for the accommodation you stay in, or there may be fees to pay for membership of an association if your course leads to a professional career. So, any money that you can get in place in addition to your student finance usually comes in really useful for you. That's the case even if you don't have any up-front costs to meet.

If you've the opportunity to make some forward planning in terms of the vacation periods on your course, that can be extremely helpful as well. Some employers may hold job opportunities open for you, or allow you to switch employment from town to town (this is often the case with supermarkets), so if you can explore any options of this kind, they can be really useful in helping you plan your finances throughout the year (you may not be so concerned about having to use your student bank account's overdraft if you know you've a job lined up in the summer that allows you to pay it off).

The foundations of funding

You can get the most out of your student finance by familiarising yourself with some key facts. Here are some of the principles which underpin the current student finance system, and which can help you use it to your advantage.

No up-front costs

When the higher rate of tuition fees was introduced in 2012, the government was careful to stress that the increase was entirely affordable for students as there remained no 'up-front' cost to higher education.

This principle remains in place today – as long as you are eligible for a Tuition Fee Loan in order to pay for your studies, there is no requirement to pay any tuition fees up front (the loan meets these costs for you and you do not usually need to pay it back until you've finished your studies and you're earning over £21,000 per year).

By using a Tuition Fee Loan to pay for your fees, you can take advantage of the repayment system, which often results in students paying less back than is due under the terms and conditions of the loan.

For example, let's imagine you study a three-year degree. Interest is added to your loan during your studies and for 30 years afterwards. But, if your graduate earnings start at less than £38,000, you probably won't have to make full repayment of your loans (tuition fee and maintenance) and the interest they accrue. This is because repayments are always based on what you earn rather than what you owe, and the repayments you are required to make (based on 9% of your taxable income over £21,000) may not be sufficient to repay your loan (and interest) over the 30-year lifetime of the loan. Some graduate careers have starting salaries at much lower thresholds, meaning it's even less likely you have to repay all the money over the lifetime of the loan.

Apply early

Never forget the old countryside saying, 'The early bird secures the funding!'

Always, always, always remember to apply for your student finance as early as you can:

- ✔ Set reminders for yourself on your mobile devices to alert you to the times you should be applying.

- ✔ Bookmark the website you're applying through (different sites exist for students who usually live in England, Wales, Scotland and Northern Ireland).

> ✔ Once you've applied, set a reminder for 8 weeks after the date your completed application is submitted, so that you can check on progress through your online account.
>
> ✔ Always follow up on your application if you've not heard anything after 8 weeks.

Income assessment

If you make an income-assessed application for student finance, you can be sure you're maximising the amount of financial support available to you.

If your household income (any unearned income you have, plus the taxable income of your parent(s) or partner) is less than around £62,000 (£67,000 if you study in London), then you probably qualify for some form of additional financial support, based on an assessment of that income.

If you're in this situation, make sure that you check to see who should be supporting your application and provide their details when you apply online (see Chapter 4 for more detail). Once you've provided the details, the relevant members of your household can log in to their own student finance accounts and provide the financial details necessary to support your application.

If you've children, or an adult living with you who depends on you financially, income assessment may mean you can access grants as well as loans. If you have a disability, you should always check to see what help may be available to you from the Disabled Students' Allowance – this is not income-assessed but always paid according to need, whatever your household income circumstances.

Getting the best out of student finance

Making sure you have all the money that you're entitled to during your studies is an important part of ensuring your student experience is a success. Taking the time to familiarise yourself with the student finance system is a worthwhile first step when you're making preparations to enter higher education.

Finding out about the student finance available to you makes you better prepared when you start your course – and more aware of whether you're receiving all the financial support you should have.

Get proactive

When you apply for student finance, don't be complacent about it. If you don't understand something, or something seems to be wrong or not what you expected, ask someone.

You can contact the advice lines for student finance (although they prefer you to check online information before ringing), or you can contact the advisers at your course provider. I would recommend the latter, as they're more familiar with seeing student finance from the student angle, so they're more likely to be familiar with the quirks of the system.

Student finance online systems are created with the most typical student in mind. Functionality for students in more complex situations is 'bolted on'. This can mean the systems become more complex if your circumstances are not straight-forward.

Whilst the agencies delivering student finance are committed to improvement, they are not yet perfect – so make sure you ask if either you don't understand something or you think something is not right. The following pointers can help you to keep on top of things:

- ✔ Make sure you apply as early as you can!
- ✔ Make a note of deadlines.
- ✔ Make a note of when your application should be processed.

Make enquiries if you've not heard anything 8 weeks after sending information supporting your application. Check your online account first and if there is no news, start to contact your course provider and/or student finance direct.

You really cannot afford to make the assumption that every-thing will be alright with your student finance application once you've clicked submit. In the past, there have been years where thousands of students have been affected by systematic failures which have disrupted payments of student finance to students nationally. Whilst this situation has improved in recent years, the fact that the government makes regular changes to student finance means such scenarios cannot be ruled out in future. Plus, regular updating and improvement of software and hardware in the delivery of student finance means further risks can arise.

Always make regular checks of your student finance online account to check on progress and to see if there are any messages about further information being required to support your application.

If your parent(s) or partner provide additional financial information to support your application for income-assessed student finance, check with them to ensure they have completed the details they need to send. Any delay with that information can lead to delays in you receiving your full entitlement to financial support.

Going the distance: studying for three years or more

You need to apply for your student finance one year at a time. Applications are managed this way so that they can be flexible in taking into account circumstances which can occur during the time you're studying. Various family events can have an effect on student finance entitlement. For example, the loss of a parent or partner would usually mean a substantial decrease in household income. If your student finance were worked out at year one for the entire duration of your studies, such changes could not be taken into account, and you may be worse off as a result.

Following a Timeline

The student finance application cycle starts in the new year (January – we're talking calendar years rather than academic years for a change), but if at all possible, your planning for your student finance should start earlier.

15 months before your course starts:

- ✔ Consider setting money aside from part-time/summer work.
- ✔ Research alternative sources of funding (for example, educational trusts/charities).

12 months before your course starts:

- ✔ Bookmark the website you're using to apply for your student finance.
- ✔ Set a reminder so that you can apply early.
- ✔ Research the student finance system so that you know what money you should receive from it.
- ✔ Make some simple budget planning.

9 months before your course starts:

- ✔ Register your student finance account.
- ✔ Start your online application.
- ✔ Make sure that you provide all the information required to support your application (online and by sending any additional documents required by Student Finance).
- ✔ Ensure that you ask anyone who is supporting your application to send the information they need to (and check they have done so).
- ✔ Remember to send your declaration form and any other paperwork to complete your application.
- ✔ Make a note of the standard processing period of 6–8 weeks and check your online account at that time to see if there is any news.

4 months before your course starts:

- ✔ Observe the processing deadline date and ensure that you've submitted your completed application before it expires.
- ✔ Check your application is complete by logging in to your student finance online account – check to see if there are any messages requesting more information.
- ✔ If necessary, contact Student Finance to ensure that they've received the information they require from you.

At the start of your course:

- ✔ Payment of your student finance depends on the registration processes at your course provider.

- ✔ If you register in advance you may receive payment on the very first day of your course.

- ✔ If you register on the first day of your course, your student finance may be delayed by 3–4 days (the time it takes to be activated and reach your bank account).

- ✔ If your student funding delays will cause you financial hardship, ask your course provider if there is any emergency assistance available.

- ✔ If you've not received any of your student finance, or only some of it, enquire with the advice service at your course provider – they should be able to help you identify what the issue is. Your advice service is usually able to use its hotline to Student Finance so you don't have to wait in a long queue to get your enquiry answered.

Flowchart of the application process

Your student finance application itself follows the basic process shown in Figure 2-1. It is important to note that student finance applications are completely independent of your application for your course – one is in no way dependent on the other.

Don't hold off applying for student finance until you've had a definite offer of a place on a course. Apply as early as you can using your desired course provider and programme of study. You can always change those details if the need arises.

For 2016/17 entry:

- ✔ Applications open at the start of February 2016.

- ✔ The relevant tax year is 2014/2015 (not 2015/2016, as the tax year is not complete until the end of March 2016).

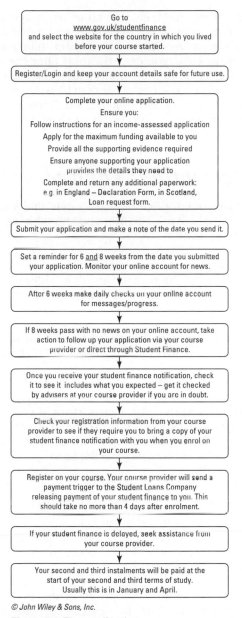

© John Wiley & Sons, Inc.

Figure 2-1: The application process.

Figure 2-1 represents the ideal timetable for applying. Sometimes, going to university is a last-minute decision, in which case you may be applying much later than is set out here. If this is the case, you can still apply after the start of the course (usually up to nine months after the start) but, obviously, the sooner the better. It may be wise to contact course providers if you know that you won't have your funding in place by the start of the course to check that they will still allow you to register on the course.

Key information required

When you make your application for student finance, there are some key pieces of information you should have at hand to make your application easier.

The online form suggests that it takes around 30 minutes to complete. This may be true for a very straightforward application, but please be aware the process could take you up to an hour.

You can save sections of your application and return to it later if you don't have time to complete the application at one sitting.

Take time to gather the following information:

- ✔ Your valid (unexpired) UK passport (or, if you do not have a UK passport, your original birth/adoption certificate, and non-UK passport if you need to provide evidence of Indefinite Leave to Remain)
- ✔ Your National Insurance number
- ✔ Your bank details
- ✔ If you've already applied through UCAS, your UCAS application details (these are optional and can be used to import information about your course/university to your student finance application)

If you need to submit a birth/adoption certificate, please note you need to fill in a birth/adoption certificate evidence form, which is available from the www.gov.uk/studentfinance website. This form needs to be countersigned by a person in a position of responsibility and needs to accompany your birth/adoption certificate when you send it.

If you've changed your name since you were born, then you need to provide your original birth certificate together with originals of any additional documentation regarding your change of name, such as deed poll documentation or your marriage certificate.

Anyone supporting your application with financial information (parent(s)/partner) requires their National Insurance number to hand. The income assessment is done using information for the last complete tax year before the application cycle began.

If your studies begin in 2016/17, the student finance cycle will have opened around February 2016. The last complete tax year at this point would be 2014/15, so this is the relevant tax year for 2016/17 applications.

Online resources

There are numerous online resources which can help you to better understand student finance. As well as the government's www.gov.uk/studentfinance site, further information is available from the agencies for each of the four nations of the UK. These sites can be found at:

Wales: www.studentfinancewales.co.uk

Northern Ireland: www.studentfinanceni.co.uk

Scotland: www.saas.gov.uk

Information for students resident in England can be found hosted by the Student Room website, and a link is available from: http://www.sfengland.slc.co.uk/

In addition, there are a number of independent sites providing information with a student audience in mind. For example:

National Union of Students: www.nus.org.uk/en/advice/money-and-funding/

Brightside Student Calculator: studentcalculator.org/

Money Saving Expert: www.moneysavingexpert.com/students/student-loans-tuition-fees-changes

Key resources

Your student finance can be quite complex, particularly if you're new to it or you've additional circumstances such as a disability or a family financially dependent upon you.

Fortunately, there are a number of places to turn to for additional assistance and information.

Sources of guidance

If you don't have Internet access (so can't check out the resources shown in the nearby sidebar, 'Online resources'), or something you've read is not clear, remember you can make enquiries direct to the advice service at your course provider – there is usually a team giving confidential, impartial and independent advice who can give you bespoke information about the student finance available to you, and how to apply for it.

You can also contact your student finance agency by telephone, but be aware that you may need to wait in a queue. I recommend that you get a second opinion on the information you get from Student Finance, as at peak periods they use temporary staff on their phone lines to deal with demand – this can lead to issues with the quality of advice available, so your course provider's advice service can verify the accuracy of what you've been told.

In-depth resources

There is a very high level of detail available online regarding your student finance. The www.gov.uk/studentfinance site, and even the student-facing sites for England, Wales and Northern Ireland have a basic level of information available. Scotland probably fares best in the level of information available.

If you wish to delve deeper into understanding your student finance, higher level resources are available in the public domain. However, you probably only want to explore this level of information if you're experiencing some kind of issue or difficulty – this is not material intended for student consumption so isn't particularly accessible or, in any sense, a 'light read'.

Firstly, there are the Guidance Chapters which interpret the legislation underpinning student finance. Scotland and Northern Ireland rely on direct reference to their Regulations, so Guidance Chapters are only available in Wales and England. An Internet search for Student Finance England/Wales brings up either site. From there you can access the Guidance Chapters in the Policy Information section of the site. The key documents are those for Assessing Eligibility and Assessing Financial Entitlement, but other areas are covered as well. The Guidance Chapters are particularly useful for detailed information relating to residency and previous study.

Student Support Information Notices are available from the Practitioners' sites – these can provide early updates of developments in student finance legislation.

If you've been unable to find an answer from any other source, you may wish to go straight to the legislation governing student finance. Be aware that this is probably the least accessible information source because the documents use legal terminology.

An Internet search for the Education (Student Support) Regulations for each nation of the UK takes you to the relevant documents on the government's `legislation.gov.uk` website, but you also need to be aware the main regulations are updated by Amendment Regulations – so you need to check for those as well to be sure that you're looking at the correct version.

If you're in any doubt about using the Regulations or would rather not (perfectly understandable), contact the advice service at your course provider. They should have a good working knowledge of the Regulations and related guidance.

Looking Ahead to University Days

The moment you reach the decision you're going to study in higher education is the ideal time to begin planning your finances. Being a student usually necessitates going through a period of low income, so anything you can set in store to help you through your period of study is going to help.

Financial preparations

If you've a part-time or summer job, setting aside some savings to contribute towards your studies is something to consider. Setting aside your own personal investment in your future can be a very powerful way of establishing good financial habits to help you use your money wisely once you're a student. You know how hard you worked for those savings, so you won't wish to spend that money lightly.

This is also a good time to research the student finance system as well as other non-statutory sources of financial support such as educational trusts and grants. These sources don't stick to the same deadlines and timeline as the statutory student finance system. Identifying alternative sources of funding as early as you can means you're far less likely to miss out. Not only that, but by identifying those sources which can assist before, during and towards the end of your studies, you can begin to map out when you need to take action during your studies. You could even set yourself reminders years in advance of when you need to take action to apply.

The autumn term of the academic year before your course begins is the ideal time to familiarise yourself with the website hosting your online application – bookmark the site and set a reminder for yourself to ensure that you start your application at the earliest opportunity once the application cycle opens (usually in February).

If you've not already done so, the autumn is also the ideal time to research the student finance system itself, so you can begin to plan for how much money you're likely to have available to you during your studies.

Good habits

Using your student finance effectively is usually a challenge, because it's a limited income which may not even meet all of your basic living costs. This is particularly true if you don't receive the maximum funding available, and especially true if you only have the basic non income-assessed Maintenance Loan available to you.

This being the case, you should consider strategies to help ensure your student finance is used to target the most important costs you face, and a big part of doing that is undertaking some budgeting exercises to work out how much of your income needs to be set against essential costs such as accommodation, food, bills and course-related expenditure.

You may also consider setting some basic rules for yourself to follow – budgeting for a set number of nights out a week, or a set amount to spend each week on socialising/entertainment. Once you've done this, you can get a better understanding of when your spending may become problematic – and you know something needs to change as a result. For example, you may consider part-time work.

Looking out for number one

Your university studies may be the first time you're responsible for managing your own financial situation. You need to take that responsibility on and be careful to ensure your finances are not vulnerable to abuse.

Here are some simple precautions you may consider:

- Shop with friends rather than on your own – that way you can all cut down on duplicating purchases like cleaning products and detergents.

- Cook with friends – cooking for more than one can work out cheaper. It's fun and a great way to form friendships.

- Limit expenditure on take-away food – it's usually always more expensive than preparing a packed lunch or cooking a meal yourself from fresh ingredients.

- Do not take sole responsibility for household bills if you're in shared accommodation – try and encourage everyone's name to be on the account.

- Don't offer to pay for large rounds if you're out with friends. Break the group down into smaller groups so that no one gets left with a really large bill to pay.

Any saving you make is worth it. Always ask yourself whether you really need to make a purchase, and whether you can really afford it. The more times you make a saving, the greater the overall savings you make over the length of your studies.

Part II

Applying for Government (Statutory) Funds

Top 5 Ways to Make Your Student Finance Application More Effective

- **Prepare** for your student finance application by getting to know the key rules governing it.

- Check the types of student finance available to you according to **where you live** and **where you study.**

- Get to know the **application process** inside out – when you should apply and how often.

- Explore **student loans and grants** in detail – how much you can get and how much you need to repay.

- Learn about student loan **repayments** and whether you will need to repay all that you borrow.

Income assessment maximises the student finance available to you. Get an idea of how much extra student finance you can get with the illustrative tables available at www. dummies.com/extras/studentfinanceuk.

In this part . . .

✔ Get to know what is involved in making your student finance application.

✔ Find out how to check your entitlement and recognise when you need to take further action.

✔ Explore the different kinds of loans available, and how much you can get.

✔ Gain an understanding of grants, when they are payable to you and how much support they provide.

Chapter 3

Taking the First Steps

. . . .

In This Chapter

▶ Figuring out your eligibility for student finance

▶ Knowing the variations among UK nations for tuition fee and maintenance (living cost) support

. . . .

*Y*ou have to check that you're eligible to receive student
finance. Doing so is all the more important if you've studied previously in higher education, or if you've been living
outside the UK or Europe before the start of your course.

Whilst there are some common themes for student finance
throughout the UK, you need to be aware of the differences.

In this chapter, I provide detailed information on the student
finance available in each of the nations of the UK. This chapter is a key resource for students from Wales, Scotland and
Northern Ireland when referring to other chapters, which use
England as the default system of student finance in the main.

Determining Your Eligibility

You first need to check that you're eligible to receive student
finance by comparing your circumstances against the
requirements of the student finance system.

Being a UK citizen does not necessarily guarantee access to
funding to study a higher education course in the UK, as other
factors are taken into account.

As well as your nationality, other considerations include where you live, your place of study and the course that you're intending to study. If you have studied previously in higher education, this will also need to be taken into account.

Some circumstances usually rule out your eligibility for student finance automatically, such as:

- ✔ If you should have made repayment on a student loan you previously applied for, but did not

- ✔ If your conduct has meant that you're deemed 'unfit' for financial support (for example, if you've been found guilty of fraud)

 If you spend any time in prison during the academic year you're not usually eligible to receive financial support for your living costs (though you may still be able to get living cost support in some exceptional circumstances). Tuition fee support is available to prisoners.

Where you live

Two factors are important in determining your eligibility for student finance relating to where you live. The first is whether you have 'settled status', and the second is your 'ordinary residence'.

Settled status

You must have no restrictions on your stay in the UK. If you're not a UK passport holder, and you have a time-limited visa of any kind in your passport, then you're unlikely to qualify for student finance, with the one exception of persons granted 'humanitarian protection'.

 If you have a valid UK passport, you automatically fulfil the settled status requirement. If you're a UK national but don't hold a valid passport, you need to provide other evidence – usually your birth certificate. Whilst your passport details can be checked electronically, if you need to use your birth certificate, you need to send your original together with a Birth or Adoption

Certificate Form (available from www.gov.uk/student finance). Your National Insurance number is also required.

You can obtain settled status with a non-UK passport if any of the following apply to you:

- ✔ You have 'indefinite leave to remain'

- ✔ You have refugee status

- ✔ You are a British citizen by descent

- ✔ You have a right of permanent residence (EEA and Swiss nationals)

- ✔ You are from a British Overseas Territory

- ✔ You have 'EEA migrant worker', 'EEA self-employed person' or 'Swiss employed person' status

If any of the above categories apply to you, you may wish to contact the advice service at your course provider to check that you meet the requirements for student finance.

If you have been granted 'humanitarian protection', you can still be eligible for student finance even though your status is time limited. Once you have had humanitarian protection for 5 years, you may apply for indefinite leave to remain, but if you're applying for student finance during the 5-year period, you need to provide evidence of your status each year that you apply.

If you acquire humanitarian protection during the academic year, you're eligible for student finance from that date.

Ordinary residence

In addition to the 'settled status' requirement, you must also satisfy the ordinary residency requirement. This requirement relates to the full three-year period prior to the start of your course (usually 1 September in England, Wales and Northern Ireland, or 1 August in Scotland).

UK citizens who have lived in the UK during the three years prior to the start of their course automatically satisfy this condition. However, being a UK citizen does not guarantee you satisfying the 'ordinary residence' requirement if you have left the UK/EEA.

The legal interpretation of the term 'ordinary residence' is that it describes 'habitual and normal residence from choice and for a settled purpose throughout the prescribed period, apart from temporary or occasional absences'. So, as long as your reasons for being in the UK are those usually associated with living somewhere, occasional absences such as holidays are tolerated under the definition.

In order to be ordinarily resident, you must be in the UK lawfully.

Being in the UK wholly, or mainly, for the purposes of receiving full-time education isn't usually interpreted as 'ordinary' residence. However, you may be accessing full-time education and still be deemed ordinarily resident if your education is not the 'whole' or 'main' reason for your being in the UK. For example, your parents may be temporarily employed abroad and you're staying with relatives in order to continue attendance at your school.

Being employed abroad can mean that you're not deemed ordinarily resident in the UK. However, if you can show that your employment is temporary, and that you fully intend to return to the UK at the end of the contract, you may still qualify.

In addition to your contract of employment, you should provide a 'body of evidence' to show your intention to return, such as registration with a GP/dentist, your UK bank account or any UK address which you have maintained during your absence. If you or your partner/parent(s)) take up employment within the European Economic Area (EEA), you may qualify as remaining ordinarily resident if you can show that you're 'exercising your right to reside' within the EU.

If you or your family has emigrated from the EU/EEA, you're unlikely to qualify for student finance if you've been out of the UK during the relevant three-year period, because it would be difficult to show the required level of residency within the UK when permanent residency has been taken up elsewhere.

Your age

Whilst there is no age limit on the majority of the student finance packages available to you, there are some considerations that you need to be aware of.

Firstly, in Wales and Northern Ireland, you must be under the age of 60 (50 in Scotland) on the first day of the first academic year of your course in order to qualify for a Maintenance Loan for any course that started before September 2016. The revised student finance package for England from 2016 onwards makes Maintenance Loans available to new students with no age limit.

If you live with a partner but aren't married, you need to be aware that if you're under 25, the student finance system doesn't recognise your partner.

If you've not lived independently of your parents for the full three-year period before the start of your course, their income is used in any income assessment rather than your partner's. This remains the case until you're married/enter a civil partnership, or you turn 25 before the start of an academic year.

If you live with a partner and you or your partner has a child who lives with you, you can apply for student finance as a parent. Your partner's income is taken into account when determining who has financial responsibility for the child, even if you're under 25.

Where you study

If you study on a 'designated course' at a publicly funded higher education establishment, you satisfy one of the criteria for student finance. Most long-established UK universities fall under this category, but more recently the government has enabled private providers to enter the UK higher education market.

If you intend to study at a private institution, you need to check that your course has been specifically designated for the purposes of student finance. If it hasn't, you can't obtain the funding for your course via the student finance system.

So, if your prospective course provider is a private provider, make sure that you ask if your course has been designated for student finance.

The four nations of the UK have slightly different versions of the student finance system. However, where you live ordinarily determines which nation assesses you for your student finance. For example, if you usually live in Scotland but are going to study in England, you need to apply to the Student Awards Agency for Scotland for your student finance.

What you study

Your course usually qualifies for student finance if it is run by a publicly funded educational establishment (or by a private provider who has taken steps to designate your course) defined within the list of 'designated courses' within the Education (Student Support) Regulations, as follows:

✔ A course for a first degree (BA, BA (Hons), BSc, BSc (Hons) or B Ed)

✔ A course for a Certificate of Higher Education (CertHE)

✔ A course for a Diploma of Higher Education (DipHE)

✔ A course for a Foundation degree (FdA or FdSc)

✔ A course for the Higher National Certificate (HNC) or Higher National Diploma (HND) that is validated by either the Business & Technician Education Council (BTEC) or the Scottish Qualifications Authority (SQA)

✔ A course for the initial training of teachers (for example, PGCE, PGDE)

✔ A course for the further training of youth and community workers

✔ A course in preparation for a professional examination of a standard higher than that of either:

 • Advanced level for the General Certificate of Education or the examination at higher level for the Scottish Certificate of Education.

- The National Certificate or the National Diploma validated by either BTEC or the SQA not being a course for entry to which a first degree (or equivalent qualification) is normally required.

✔ A course providing education (whether or not in preparation for an examination), the standard of which is higher than that of courses providing education in preparation for any of the examinations mentioned in the previous bullet points, but not higher than that of a first degree course; and for entry to which a first degree (or equivalent qualification) is not normally required.

As is always the case, there are exceptions to the rule. If you are studying an NHS course, you have a reduced entitlement to elements of funding available under the student finance system – alternative funding is available by applying to the NHS Business Services Authority (http://www.nhsbsa.nhs.uk).

If you have studied in higher education before

Any previous study you have undertaken in higher education is taken into account in order to work out your future entitlement to student finance.

Previous study usually reduces your entitlement for future study but how much effect it has depends on the extent of the study you have already undertaken.

If you studied a higher education course in the past and you achieved a qualification, this usually means that you can only apply for funding for a course at a higher level than the qualification you have obtained. The government doesn't usually fund a course which is at an equivalent or lower level to a qualification you already hold (this is known as the Equivalent or Lower Qualification (ELQ) rule). There are some exceptions to this rule, as outlined in Chapter 10.

For example, if you've already achieved a Higher National Diploma or a Foundation Degree, the government allows you funding to further your study for a first degree because a

BA/BSc (Hons) is a higher level qualification. However, the years of study you undertook on your original course (or courses) would be taken into account.

This usually means that you would only be in a position to receive funding for the last year of a degree course in order to 'top up' your qualification, rather than receive funding for the degree in its entirety from year one. A similar principle applies if you finish your degree studies and achieve an 'ordinary' degree – if you wish to 'top up' to an Honours degree, you are able to obtain funding to do so.

If you studied on a previous course and did not achieve a qualification, the years of study you undertook could count towards your next course and reduce the funding available.

This would be the case if you previously studied full-time and you plan to study full-time on your new course. If, however, you studied part-time (but did not achieve a qualification) and now wish to study full-time, the years of study on the previous course would be disregarded. (Similarly, if you previously studied full-time but did not achieve a qualification, and now wish to study part-time, the previous years of study would not count).

Previous study usually affects some aspects of the student finance available to you more than others. Usually it's your Tuition Fee Loan and any Maintenance Grant/Special Support Grant entitlement which is affected.

You can usually obtain a Maintenance Loan if you're not studying for a qualification which is lower or equivalent to one which you already hold. If you didn't achieve a qualification from your previous study in higher education, the Maintenance Loan should be available to you for your new course.

The student finance system in all nations of the UK is able to offer you one year of additional funding, should you require it. Once you have received funding for the ordinary duration of your course (plus one year if required) or you achieve a first degree qualification, your entitlement will be used up. Although this principle operates slightly differently in Wales and Scotland, the outcome is the same.

You can usually expect to receive funding for the duration of your course plus one year. This gives you the flexibility to change courses if you feel you have chosen the wrong one for you, or allows you a year to fall back on if you've struggled academically and you need to retake a year.

If you find your studies disrupted by ill health, a caring responsibility or some other personal reasons, you can apply for 'compelling personal reasons'. It's important to do this because any year in which compelling personal reasons are found to have arisen is removed from any calculation for future funding.

If you had to leave your previous course because you were ill, make sure you submit evidence of the compelling personal reasons, because that could mean an additional year's funding for your new course.

Financing Your Tuition Fees

The usual assistance for tuition fee funding comes in the form of the Tuition Fee Loan. This is the case in all nations of the UK with the exception of Scotland, where Scottish students studying in Scotland can obtain non-repayable assistance with their tuition fees from the Scottish government. Specific details for each nation are in the following sections.

England

The following student finance arrangements are available if you're ordinarily resident in England for the three years prior to the start of your course, and are starting your course in 2016/17.

Full-time

If you're an eligible full-time student you can apply for a non income-assessed Tuition Fee Loan. You need to make an application for a Tuition Fee Loan for each year of your course.

The Tuition Fee Loan is available for any amount up to the tuition fee cap of £9,000 per year. Any fees over £6,000 must be accompanied by an Access Agreement approved by the Office for Fair Access (OFFA), otherwise the maximum tuition fee loan available is £6,000. From 2017/18 the government is considering allowing higher fees for course providers offering 'high teaching quality', but this is yet to be confirmed.

The European Community Action Scheme for the Mobility of University Students (ERASMUS) and non-ERASMUS study and work placement years have their Tuition Fee Loans capped at 15% of the relevant fee cap (depending on whether an OFFA-approved Access Agreement is in place). Sandwich degree work placement years have their Tuition Fee Loans capped at 20% of the relevant fee cap (depending on whether an OFFA-approved Access Agreement is in place).

Whilst you apply for the loan, and are liable for paying it back, the loan itself is paid directly to your course provider, not to you. If your fees are less than £9,000, the Tuition Fee Loan is available at an amount which matches the cost of your course.

Specifically designated courses at private institutions have full-time Tuition Fee Loans capped at £6,000. This also affects the amount of Tuition Fee Loan available for ERASMUS/non-ERASMUS study and work placement years, and sandwich degree work placement fees, as described earlier.

Part-time

If you're an eligible part-time student you can apply for a non income-assessed Tuition Fee Loan. You need to make an application for a Tuition Fee Loan for each year of your course.

Intensity of study

Intensity of study refers to the proportion of a full-time course you study in one year as a part-time student. A full-time year is typically made up of 120 credits. If you study 60 credits, you are studying at 50% intensity. If you study 90 credits, you are studying at 75% intensity.

The Tuition Fee Loan is available to assist with part-time tuition fees equivalent to a minimum intensity of study of 25% of a full-time course, up to a maximum intensity of 75% of a full-time course. This means the maximum Tuition Fee Loan available to a part-time student is £6,750 per year.

As for full-time students, the loan itself is paid directly to your course provider, even though you apply for the loan and are liable for paying it back. If your fees are less than £6,750, the Tuition Fee Loan will be available at an amount which matches the cost of your course.

Specifically designated part-time courses at private institutions have Tuition Fee Loans capped at £4,500.

Distance learning

If you're an eligible full-time student you can apply for a non income-assessed Tuition Fee Loan. You need to make an application for a Tuition Fee Loan each year of your course.

The Tuition Fee Loan is available for any amount up to the tuition fee cap of £9,000 per year. Any fees over £6,000 must be accompanied by an Access Agreement approved by the Office for Fair Access (OFFA), otherwise the maximum tuition fee loan available will be £6,000.

Again, the loan is paid directly to your course provider, not to you, but you are liable for paying it back. If your fees are less than £9,000, the Tuition Fee Loan will be available at an amount which matches the cost of your course.

Specifically designated courses at private institutions will have full-time Tuition Fee Loans capped at £6,000.

Wales

The following student finance arrangements are available for students who are ordinarily resident in Wales for the three years prior to the start of their course.

Full-time

If you're an eligible full-time student you can apply for a non income-assessed Tuition Fee Loan and/or a Tuition Fee Grant.

You need to make an application for tuition fee support each year of your course.

The Tuition Fee Loan is available for the first £3,810 of your tuition fees per year. You can also apply for a Tuition Fee Grant to cover the remaining £5,190.

If you wish, you can apply for the Tuition Fee Grant on its own but you need to make arrangements to pay the remaining amount of tuition fees with your course provider. This usually means the tuition fees become due within the academic year and you aren't able to defer payment of your tuition fees in the way you can by taking out a Tuition Fee Loan.

ERASMUS and non-ERASMUS study and work placement years have their tuition fees capped at 15% of the maximum tuition fee. A Tuition Fee Loan is available to pay half of your tuition fees, with a Tuition Fee Grant available to cover the other half.

Sandwich degree work placement years will have their tuition fees capped at 20% of the maximum tuition fee. A Tuition Fee Loan is available to pay half of your tuition fees, with a Tuition Fee Grant available to cover the other half.

The loan itself is paid directly to your course provider but you remain liable for paying it back. If your fees are less than £9,000, the Tuition Fee Loan is available at an amount which matches the cost of your course.

Specifically designated courses at private institutions have full-time Tuition Fee Loans capped at £6,000. No Tuition Fee Grant is available to you for study at a private provider.

Part-time

If you're an eligible part-time student you can apply for a non income-assessed Tuition Fee Loan. You need to make an application for a Tuition Fee Loan each year of your course.

The Tuition Fee Loan is available to assist with part-time tuition fees equivalent to a minimum intensity of study of 25% of a full-time course, up to a maximum intensity of 75% of a full-time course. This means the maximum Tuition Fee Loan available to a part-time student is £6,750 per year.

If you study at a Welsh university, you can access a Tuition Fee Loan of up to £2,625 per year. If you study at a university elsewhere in the UK, you can access a Tuition Fee Loan of up to £6,750 per year. If you study at a private institution, you can access a Tuition Fee Loan of up to £4,500 per year.

Whilst you apply for the loan and are liable to pay it back, the loan itself is paid directly to your course provider, not to you. If your fees are less than £6,750, the Tuition Fee Loan will be available at an amount which matches the cost of your course.

No fee grants are available for part-time study.

Distance learning

If you're an eligible full-time or part-time student you can apply for tuition fee support. You need to make an application for tuition fee support each year of your course.

The arrangements for distance learning students from Wales mirror those described above for full-time and part-time students.

Northern Ireland

The following student finance arrangements are available for students who are ordinarily resident in Northern Ireland for the three years prior to the start of their course.

Full-time

If you're an eligible full-time student you can apply for a non income-assessed Tuition Fee Loan. You need to make an application for a Tuition Fee Loan each year of your course.

If you study at a university in Northern Ireland, the maximum tuition fee you can be charged will be £3,805 (2015/16 figure) and an equivalent Tuition Fee Loan is available.

If you study elsewhere in the UK, you can be charged up to a maximum of £9,000 for your tuition fees and an equivalent Tuition Fee Loan is available.

If you study in the Republic of Ireland, you can receive a Student Contribution Loan equivalent to the contribution charge.

Whilst you apply for the loan and are liable to pay it back, the loan itself is paid directly to your course provider, not to you. If your fees are less than £9,000, the Tuition Fee Loan is available at an amount which matches the cost of your course.

Only specifically designated courses at private institutions qualify for Tuition Fee Loan support.

Part-time

If you're an eligible student studying at least 50% intensity of a full-time course, you can apply for an income-assessed Tuition Fee Grant to assist with your course costs. You need to make an application for tuition fee support each year of your course.

How much Tuition Fee Grant you receive depends on the intensity of your study and your household income, as shown in Table 3-1 (2015/16 figures).

Table 3-1	Northern Ireland Tuition Fee Grants
Study Intensity	*Tuition Fee Grant Available*
50–59%	£820
60–74%	£985
75% or more	£1,230
Household Income	*Tuition Fee Grant Payable*
£0–£16,842	Maximum Fee Grant available
£16,843–£25,420	Partial Fee Grant
£25,421 and above	No Fee Grant

If you have a partner, the household income threshold is increased by £2,000. A further £2,000 is added for your first child, and £1,000 for each additional child. So, if you're part of a couple with two children, you can receive a maximum fee grant on a household income up to £21,842.

The fee grant is paid directly to your course provider.

Distance learning

If you're an eligible part-time distance learning student, you can apply for tuition fee support. You need to make an application for tuition fee support each year of your course.

The arrangements for part-time distance learning students from Northern Ireland mirror those described above for part-time students.

No funding provision exists if you're a full-time distance learning student from Northern Ireland.

Scotland

The following student finance arrangements are available for students who are ordinarily resident in Scotland for the three years prior to the start of their course.

Full-time

If you're an eligible full-time student you can apply for non income-assessed tuition fee support. You need to apply for tuition fee support each academic year.

If you study in Scotland, your tuition fees are paid direct to your course provider. Different fee levels apply to different types of courses. In 2015/16, the amount of tuition fee support available is shown in Table 3-2.

Table 3-2	Scotland Tuition Fee Grants
Type of Course	*Tuition Fee Support*
HNC/HND or other course at sub-degree level	£1,285
BA/BSc (Hons) or PGDE	£1,820
Medicine degrees (starting prior to 1 August 2011)	£2,895
Courses at private institutions	£1,205

If you choose to study elsewhere in the UK, you will be able to apply for a Tuition Fee Loan of up to £9,000.

 The Scottish government has also introduced an EU Portability pilot scheme allowing Scottish students to study at a selection of universities in the EU. More information is available at: www.saas.gov.uk/_forms/eu_portability.pdf.

Part-time

If you're an eligible part-time student you can apply for non income-assessed tuition fee support. You need to apply for tuition fee support each academic year.

You can apply for a part-time undergraduate Tuition Fee Grant. How much grant is available depends on your intensity of study and the kind of qualification you're aiming to achieve, as Table 3-3 shows.

Table 3-3 Scotland Part-time Tuition Fees	
Qualification	*Tuition Fee Grant*
Publicly funded BA/BSc (Hons)	£1,805
120-credit degree-level course at	
non-campus-based universities	£1,820
Publicly funded HNC/HND	£1,274
Courses at private institutions	£1,195

Note that the amount of fee grant you receive may not be equivalent to the amount your course provider is charging for fees. For example, you might study 90 credits at degree level and be charged £1,600. Your fee grant would be worked out as follows:

90 credits = 75% of 120 credits

75% of £1,820 = £1,365

Tuition Fee Grant = £1,365

You would need to pay the additional £235

If you're studying at postgraduate level on a part-time basis, you can apply for a part-time Tuition Fee Loan of up to £1,700.

If you withdraw from your part-time course (undergraduate or postgraduate), you may no longer qualify for tuition fee support – you could be required to pay the fees to your course provider yourself.

Distance learning

There is no statutory funding for distance learning courses in Scotland. If you're studying a distance learning course, you may wish to apply for a Professional and Career Development Loan – more information is available at: `www.gov.uk/career-development-loans/overview`

Channel Islands and Isle of Man

If you're from the Channel Islands or the Isle of Man, you need to make enquiries through your local government administration about the tuition fee support available for your studies.

Each of the governments in Jersey, Guernsey and the Isle of Man publishes information about its student finance schemes on its website:

- Guernsey: `www.education.gg/article/2127/Funding-for-University`
- Jersey: `http://www.gov.je/Working/Careers/16To19YearOlds/EnteringHigherEducation/FinancingHigherEducationCourses/Pages/index.aspx`
- Isle of Man: `https://www.gov.im/categories/education training and careers/student grants/`

Financing Your Living Costs (Maintenance)

The usual assistance for living costs, or maintenance funding, comes in the form of the Maintenance Loan. This is the case in all nations of the UK, but additional grants exist in various forms in each of the nations. Specific details for each nation are in the following paragraphs.

England

From 1 September 2016, if you're starting your course as a new full-time student, the main source of student finance for your living costs is the Maintenance Loan. There are several rates of loan payable according to where you live whilst you study. The loan has a basic non income-assessed component, but you can apply for an additional income-assessed component based on household income.

Table 3-4 describes the maximum rates of loan available if you don't have an underlying entitlement to welfare benefits (most students fall into this category).

Table 3-4	England Maximum Loans Available without Welfare Benefits		
Continuing Year Students	*Total Loan Assessed*	*Non-Income Assessed*	*Income*
Parental Home	£6,904	£3,039	£3,865
London	£10,702	£5,330	£5,372
Elsewhere	£8,200	£3,821	£4,379
Overseas	£9,391	£4,540	£4,851
Final Year Students			
Parental Home	£6,496	£2,792	£3,704
London	£9,914	£4,855	£5,059
Elsewhere	£7,756	£3,553	£4,203
Overseas	£8,406	£3,945	£4,461

Table 3-5 describes maximum rates of loan available if you've an underlying entitlement to welfare benefits during study (this tends to be lone parents, student couples with children and some disabled students entitled to disability/sickness benefits).

A reduced non income-assessed rate, shown in Table 3-6, of student loan is available if you:

- ✔ Are studying a full-year sandwich course paid placement (where periods of study are less than 10 weeks in aggregate over the year)

> ✔ Are eligible to apply for an NHS bursary or Scottish
> Health Care allowance.

Table 3-5 England Maximum Loans Available with Welfare Benefits

Continuing Year Students	Total Loan Assessed	Non-Income Assessed	Income
Parental Home	£8,144	£3,039	£5,105
London	£11,671	£5,330	£6,341
Elsewhere	£9,347	£3,821	£5,526
Overseas	£10,453	£4,540	£5,913
Final Year Students			
Parental Home	£7,765	£2,792	£4,973
London	£10,938	£4,855	£6,083
Elsewhere	£8,935	£3,553	£5,382
Overseas	£9,538	£3,945	£5,593

Table 3-6 England Reduced Non Income-assessed Rates

Reduced Rate Continuing Year	Reduced Loan (Sandwich Year)	Reduced Loan (NHS Bursary Year)
Parental Home	£1,863	£1,744
London	£3,487	£3,263
Elsewhere	£2,483	£2,324
Overseas	£2,970	£2,324
Reduced Rate Final Year		
Parental Home	£1,414	£1,324
London	£2,669	£2,498
Elsewhere	£1,936	£1,811
Overseas	£2,170	£1,811

From 1 September 2016, if you're over 60 at the start of your course you may qualify for an income-assessed Maintenance Loan.

A maximum loan is available if you're 60 or over with a household income of £25,000 or less, and a partial loan is available on household incomes up to £43,668 (the minimum loan is £50 for the year). Once the £43,668 is exceeded, no maintenance loan is available.

Additional income-assessed amounts of Long Courses Loan are available if your academic year exceeds 30 weeks and 3 days. The Long Courses Loan is not applicable to Reduced Rate Loans.

 In addition to the Maintenance Loan, you may apply for the following non-repayable income-assessed grants if your circumstances make you eligible:

Parent's Learning Allowance:	up to £1,573
Adult Dependants' Grant:	up to £2,757
Childcare Grant:	up to £155.24 per wk (1 child)
Travel Grant (for some study abroad or medical/dental clinical placements in the UK):	up to £266.15 per wk (2 or more children)

If you have a long-term disability, mental health or specific learning difference, you may be eligible to receive a Disabled Students' Allowance (DSA) for additional course costs arising out of your condition. The DSA is paid according to need and is not conditional upon any income assessment.

No maintenance support is available to part-time students in England. The Disabled Students' Allowance is available if you study part-time and at least 25% of the intensity of a full-time course.

Wales

From 1 September 2016, if you're starting your course as a new student, the main source of student finance for your living costs will be the Maintenance Loan.

How much loan you can get depends on where you live during term-time as well as your household income. Table 3-7 describes the support available (2015/16 figures).

Table 3-7	Wales Maintenance Loans
Where You Live	*Maximum Maintenance Loan Available*
Parental Home	£4,162
London	£7,532
Elsewhere	£5,376
Overseas	£6,410

Additional income-assessed amounts of Long Courses Loan are available if your academic year exceeds 30 weeks and 3 days.

The Welsh government cancels up to £1,500 from your Maintenance Loan balance once you make your first repayment of student loan (once you've finished your time on your course and you're earning enough to make repayments).

The partial cancellation does not apply if you have any outstanding charges or penalties in relation to your loan, or if you are in breach of the terms and conditions of your student loan agreement. At the time of writing, it is not clear whether the partial cancellation will continue to operate for new students from 2016/17 onwards.

In addition to the Maintenance Loan, you may apply for the following non-repayable income-assessed grants if your circumstances make you eligible.

The Welsh Government Learning Grant is the main item of grant funding you may be eligible to receive. The Learning Grant is income-assessed and Table 3-8 indicates how much you can receive (2015/16 rates).

Table 3-8	Welsh Government Learning Grants
Household Income	*Amount of Maintenance Grant*
£0–£18,370	£5,161
£18,371–£50,752	Partial Grant
£50,753 or more	No Grant

If you're a lone parent, one of a student couple with responsibility for a child or a disabled student (with an entitlement to the disability premium for welfare benefits), you can apply for an alternative grant called the Special Support Grant (SSG). The SSG is of identical value to the Maintenance Grant but is wholly disregarded for benefit purposes, and also passports you to the maximum rate of student loan available according to where you live.

In addition to the Maintenance/Special Support Grant, the following income-assessed grants are available if you have specific circumstances making you eligible to receive them (2015/16 figures):

Parent's Learning Allowance:	up to £1,557
Adult Dependants' Grant:	up to £2,732
Childcare Grant:	up to £161.50 per wk (1 child)
Travel Grant (for some study abroad or medical/dental clinical placements in the UK):	up to £274.55 per wk (2 or more children)

If you have a long-term disability, mental health or specific learning difference, you may be eligible to receive a Disabled Students' Allowance (DSA) for additional course costs arising out of your condition. The DSA is paid according to need and is not conditional upon any income assessment.

If you're a part-time student in Wales, you may be able to receive an income-assessed Course Grant of up to £1,155 (2015/16 rate). The full grant is available to students with household incomes up to £26,095, with a partial grant available on higher incomes up to £28,180.

If your circumstances match the relevant criteria, you can also apply for part-time versions of the Parent's Learning Allowance, Adult Dependants' Grant and Childcare Grant. How much you receive depends on your household income, and the intensity of your studies in relation to a full-time equivalent course. More information is available at www.student financewales.co.uk.

The Disabled Students' Allowance is available if you study part-time and at least 25% of the intensity of a full-time course.

Northern Ireland

From 1 September 2016, if you're starting your course as a new full-time student, the main source of student finance for your living costs is the Maintenance Loan. There are several rates of loan payable according to where you will live whilst you study. The loan has a basic non income-assessed component, but you can apply for an additional income-assessed component based on household income.

How much loan you can get depends on where you live during term-time as well as your household income. Table 3-9 describes the support available (2015/16 figures).

Table 3-9	Northern Ireland Maintenance Loans
Where You Live	*Maximum Maintenance Loan Available*
Parental Home	£3,750
London	£6,780
Elsewhere	£4,840
Overseas	£5,770

Additional income-assessed amounts of Long Courses Loan are available if your academic year exceeds 30 weeks and 3 days.

If you're an eligible Northern Ireland student, you may also be able to apply for the following non-repayable income-assessed grants if your circumstances make you eligible (the following are 2015/16 rates which are expected to be frozen for 2016/17).

The Maintenance Grant is the main item of grant funding you may be eligible to receive. Amounts available are as shown in Table 3-10 (2015/16 figures).

Table 3-10	Northern Ireland Maintenance Grants
Household Income	**Amount of Maintenance Grant**
£0 – £19,203	£3,475
£19,204 – £41,605	Partial Grant
£41,606 or more	No Grant

If you're a lone parent, one of a student couple with responsibility for a child or if you have a disability (with an entitlement to the disability premium for welfare benefits), you can apply for an alternative grant called the Special Support Grant (SSG). The SSG is of identical value to the Maintenance Grant but is wholly disregarded for benefit purposes, and also passports you to the maximum rate of student loan available according to where you live.

In addition to the Maintenance/Special Support Grant, the following income-assessed grants are available if you have specific circumstances making you eligible to receive them (2015/16 figures):

Parent's Learning Allowance:	up to £1,538
Adult Dependants' Grant:	up to £2,695
Childcare Grant:	up to £148.75 per wk (1 child) up to £255 per wk (2 or more children)

If you have a long-term disability, mental health or specific learning difference, you may be eligible to receive a Disabled Students' Allowance (DSA) for additional course costs arising out of your condition. The DSA is paid according to need and is not conditional upon any income assessment. If you're a part-time student studying at least the equivalent of 50% intensity of a full-time course in Northern Ireland, or elsewhere in the UK, you can apply for an income-assessed Course Grant of up to £265, intended to assist with costs arising from books and materials.

Scotland

Student finance in Scotland is paid in monthly instalments except for the first one – the first instalment is of double value.

From 1 September 2016, if you're starting your course as a new full-time student, the main source of student finance for your living costs is the Maintenance Loan. In Scotland, you can apply for the non income-assessed rate of loan up to £4,750 (15/16 rate).

If your household income is £33,999 or less, and you qualify for the Young Person's Bursary, you can apply for an income-assessed rate of loan of up to £5,750 (2015/16 rate).

If your household income is £23,999 or less and you qualify for the Independent Person's Bursary, you can apply for an income-assessed rate of loan of up to £6,750 (£6,250 if your income is between £24,000 and £33,999) (2015/16 rates).

You need to decide how much of the income-assessed or non income-assessed loan you wish to apply for.

Non-repayable bursaries are available if you're an eligible student in Scotland. Which bursary is applicable to you is determined by your circumstances.

If you're a college leaver, you may qualify for the Young Student's Bursary and if you're over 25, married, living with a partner or have responsibility for a child who lives with you, you can apply for the Independent Student's Bursary.

The bursary rates are shown in Table 3-11.

Table 3-11	Scotland Bursary Rates	
Household Income	*Young Student's Bursary*	*Independent Student's Bursary*
£0 – £16,999	£1,750	£750
£17,000 – £23,999	£1,000	nil
£24,000 – £33,999	£500	nil
£34,000 or more	nil	nil

In addition to the Young/Independent Student's Bursary, the following income-assessed grants are available if you've specific circumstances making you eligible to receive them (15/16 figures):

Lone Parent's Grant:	up to £1,305
Dependants' Grant:	up to £2,640
Vacation Grant for Care Leavers:	up to £105

There is no statutory Childcare Grant in Scotland, but all higher education course providers have a Childcare Fund that you can apply to for help towards the cost of registered or formal childcare. Eligibility for the Childcare Fund requires that you must take out the maximum student loan available to you and you must be eligible to have your fees paid by your funding body.

If you have a long-term disability, mental health or specific learning difference, you may be eligible to receive a Disabled Students' Allowance (DSA) for additional course costs arising out of your condition. The DSA is paid according to need and is not conditional upon any income assessment.

If you're a part-time student studying in Scotland, no statutory maintenance support is available. If you have a long-term disability, mental health or specific learning difference, and you are studying at least 50% of the intensity of an equivalent full-time course, then you can apply for a Disabled Students' Allowance.

Channel Islands and Isle of Man

If you're from the Channel Islands or the Isle of Man, you need to make enquiries through your local government administration about the maintenance support available to assist with your living costs during your studies.

Each of the governments in Jersey, Guernsey and the Isle of Man publishes information about its student finance schemes on its website:

- ✔ Guernsey: `www.education.gg/article/2127/Funding-for-University`

- ✔ Jersey: `http://www.gov.je/Working/Careers/16To19YearOlds/EnteringHigherEducation/FinancingHigherEducationCourses/Pages/index.aspx`

- ✔ Isle of Man: `https://www.gov.im/categories/education-training-and-careers/student-grants/`

Chapter 4

Filling it in:
The Application in Detail

*S*ecuring your student finance is far more straightforward if you can make an effective application right from the start of the process.

Make sure that you've the necessary information ready and accessible when you're making your application.

When you've made your application, there follows a lengthy period where you need to wait for your application to be assessed. Monitor this period and don't just assume that everything is alright and that you'll hear in due course. Make a note in your diary from 6 to 8 weeks from the date you applied – check your online account to see if there has been any progress. If you haven't heard anything about your application by the time an 8-week period has elapsed, you need to follow up and find out why.

In this chapter, I provide information on making an effective application. I've based it on materials for applying in 2015/16, as these are the most up-to-date resources available at the time of writing – no major changes to the application are expected for 2016/17. The chapter follows the application for

England. Where necessary, differences are noted for Wales, Scotland and Northern Ireland.

Making an Application

In order to receive your statutory student finance for study in higher education, you need to apply each year of your course. The initial application is usually the most time consuming because it has some additional requirements such as personal identification and university/course details which may not be required in your applications for later years of study (unless, of course, these details change and you need to update them).

You need to choose whether you wish to make an income-assessed or non income-assessed application. An income-assessed application gives you access to the full range of support available, but how much you get is determined by your individual circumstances.

If your application does not run smoothly, or you have any general concerns about how it is progressing, always check your online account in the first instance to see if there are any messages about what you need to do next. If you can't see any instructions online, follow up by contacting your student finance agency directly using the following details:

Student Finance England

PO Box 210

Darlington

DL1 9HJ

Telephone: 0300 100 0607

Monday to Friday: 8am to 8pm

Saturday and Sunday: 9am to 4pm

Textphone: 0300 100 0622

Monday to Friday: 8am to 4pm

Student Finance Northern Ireland

Telephone: 0300 100 0077

Minicom: 0300 100 0625

Monday to Friday: 8am to 8pm

Saturday and Sunday: 9am to 4pm

If you require the address of your Education and Library Board, use the online address finder at: http:// www.studentfinanceni.co.uk/portal/page?_ pageid=54,1267852&_dad=portal&_schema=PORTAL

Student Awards Agency Scotland

Saughton House

Broomhouse Drive

Edinburgh

EH11 3UT

Telephone: 0300 555 0505

Monday to Thursday: 8.30am to 5pm

Friday: 8.30am to 4.30pm

Saturday and Sunday: Closed

Student Finance Wales

PO Box 211

Llandudno Junction

LL30 9FU

Telephone: 0300 200 4050

Minicom: 0300 100 1693

Monday to Friday: 8am to 8pm

Saturday: 9am to 4pm

Sunday: Closed

Student Finance Services Non-UK Team

Student Finance England

PO Box 89

Darlington DL1 9AZ

Telephone: 0141 243 3570

From outside the UK: +44 (0)141 243 3570

Monday to Friday, 9am to 5.30pm

European Economic Area (EEA) Migrant Worker Applications

Student Finance England

PO Box 89

Darlington DL1 9AZ

When to apply

The deadlines for student finance are generous. In England, Wales and Northern Ireland you can usually apply at any time up until the end of May after your course has started (a period of nine months from your course start date). In Scotland, the deadline is the March after your course has started. Why anyone would decide to leave it so late to apply is a question that I can't answer – don't leave it that late, apply as early as you can.

The earliest you can apply is usually the January/February before your academic year begins. This gives you up to a 17-month window in which to apply!

The general rule is that the earlier you apply, the more chance your student finance has of being processed successfully and available to you when your academic year starts – and that is usually when you want it in place by.

Bookmark the website where you make your application so that it is ready and waiting when you need to apply.

In practice, this gives you up to an 8-month window in which to make your application if you want it in place when your course starts.

Don't wait until you hear whether you've a place on your course before applying for student finance – apply as early as you can.

In order to help you make a timely application, the following dates are published by the four nations of the UK by way of processing deadlines. The deadlines are not absolute – they just give an indication that if you apply by the given date, you can expect your student finance to be ready at the start of the academic year:

- England and Wales:
    - New students: May
    - Continuing students: June
- Scotland:
    - New students: June
    - Continuing students: June
- Northern Ireland:
    - New students: April
    - Continuing students: April

The above deadlines apply to your application for 'core' student finance. Depending on your circumstances, your normal country of residence and household income, your core funding can include:

- Tuition Fee Loan
- Tuition Fee Grant (Wales, Scotland)
- Maintenance Loan (both income-assessed and non income-assessed)
- Maintenance Grant/Special Support Grant (in England, full-time students whose course began before 1 September 2016 only)
- Living Costs Bursary/Grant (Scotland)

Additional deadlines are in place for other items of student finance, as detailed in the following sections.

Disabled Students' Allowance (DSA)

If you're applying for core funding, do that first and then apply for your DSA using the DSA (Slim) form, which you can download from www.gov.uk/disabled-students-allowances-dsas/overview. This is a simplified version of the form which avoids repeating information given for your core funding application. If you're only applying for a DSA and no other funding, use the longer DSA1 form.

Apply as soon as you can once your core application has been submitted (you can download the form to apply). You must have applied for your DSA before the 9-month deadline after the start of the academic year, but the longer you leave it may mean you get less support (particularly in your final year of study).

Childcare Grant (CCG)

Once you've applied for your core funding, if you're going to use registered childcare during your studies, you can apply for the Childcare Grant. The application is initially made on a CCG1 form (you can download this from www.gov.uk/student-finance-forms) and requires you to provide details of your childcare provider, and to estimate how many hours of childcare you're going to use. Try and make as accurate an estimate as you can because any money you receive for childcare that you don't use needs to be paid back. Later in the year, you are asked to verify your actual childcare hours using the CCG2 form (and checks are made with your childcare provider).

Where to apply

All applications for student finance in the UK start from the http://www.gov.uk/studentfinancesteps website. Since 2009, the administration responsible for the processing of student finance applications has been geared up to receive online applications, and you're best advised to make an online application if you're in a position to. Paper alternatives still exist, but using a paper form for your core funding application invariably takes longer than applying online.

In order to make your first application, you need to visit the www.gov.uk/studentfinance webpage. You'll find a range of information about various items of funding, but if you wish to get your application started, follow the 'student finance login' link in order to register and create your account.

Make sure you keep your login details safe and secure for future use. You need to access your account several times during the year, and you need to use your account to apply for funding before the start of each academic year.

Links are available from www.gov.uk/studentfinance if you need to apply for your student finance via Student Finance Wales, Student Finance Northern Ireland or the Student Awards Agency for Scotland. The respective websites are:

- ✔ www.studentfinancewales.co.uk
- ✔ www.studentfinanceni.co.uk
- ✔ www.saas.gov.uk

Regardless of location, you must make an online application in the first instance, but you need to be careful to look out for additional documents required to support the application (for example, in Scotland you need to download an additional form to apply for a student loan).

The information you need to complete an application

The application breaks down into four main parts:

- ✔ Personal identification
- ✔ Information about your course and course provider
- ✔ Financial information
- ✔ Are you financially responsible for anyone else?

Before starting your application, you should make some initial preparations by having the following available:

- ✔ Proof of identity: A passport or birth/adoption certificate (original)
- ✔ National Insurance number
- ✔ Bank details
- ✔ UCAS details

Personal identification

Your identity is checked in the very first stages of processing your student finance application. Checking the evidence requirements is very important. For example, in England, you can use your UK passport number to complete the evidence requirements on the online form, but if you don't have a current passport, you need to send your original birth/adoption certificate together with a birth/adoption certificate form which must be countersigned by a person in a position of responsibility.

Your National Insurance number is required so that it can be established, right from the outset, that you're registered with the UK tax system, as this is the mechanism for all repayments of student loans you may take out whilst you study. No student finance is paid to you until your National Insurance number has been verified with HM Revenue and Customs – so this is a vital part of your application.

Confirmation of course/university

If you've already made an application for your course via UCAS by the time you apply for your student finance, you can take advantage of a handy import facility which fetches the details of your UCAS application so you do not need to enter all the information (and is less prone to error as a result). Note that you don't have to have applied to UCAS before making a student finance application – the two processes are entirely separate and don't depend upon one another.

You are also required to provide details of any previous courses you've studied at higher education level, as any study you've undertaken could have an impact on the amount of funding available to you in future years.

Financial information

You are also required to provide bank details as part of your application, but don't worry if you're not yet using the account you intend to use when you're studying, as you can change your bank details once your student finance account is up and running. It's always worthwhile checking that student accounts are available to you from your bank, as you may be able to take advantage of interest-free overdrafts and other offers exclusive to students.

Your bank details are necessary because any payments of student finance for living costs (maintenance) and your dependants are made direct to your account. In addition to your account details, you are also required to declare your income if you wish to make an income-assessed application.

 Full-time students have the choice of making an income-assessed or non income-assessed application. At the time of writing, income-assessed support is available to students in England with household incomes of around £60,000 per annum (gross) or less (in London the figure is nearer £67,000 and for students living with their parents, slightly lower at around £58,000).

Part-time students are only required to make a non income-assessed application if their course started after 1 September 2012, as they can only apply for the Tuition Fee Loan, which is entirely non income-assessed.

As a full-time student, any money you get from employment is disregarded in full for the period of the academic year. This is a deliberate incentive to encourage students to seek employment and support themselves during study. The only income you have which can be counted in the assessment of your application is any 'unearned taxable income' available to you during the academic year. Unearned income of this kind may include:

- ✔ Rent you receive for any property you own
- ✔ Payments from a pension
- ✔ Dividends or other payments from trust funds or shares
- ✔ Interest on savings

If you work and an employer releases you to attend your studies (this may often be the case for students on foundation degree courses), then you must declare the income you receive from your employer for the days you attend your course. Note that you're not required to declare your entire income, only the portion which relates to the hours you attend your course.

Being financially responsible for someone else

If you have a child, or a partner (or other member of your household) for whom you have a financial responsibility, this will be taken into account through your application.

In the case of financial responsibility for a child, if you have a partner, the first thing which will need to be established is whether it is your partner or you who is financially responsible. This usually involves a comparison of your income with that of your partner. Note that even if you are under 25 and co-habiting, in which case your partner is not formally recognised by the student finance system, their income will still be considered to establish who has financial responsibility.

Determining financial responsibility for your partner will be done in a similar way, by comparing their income with yours.

Getting Additional Evidence for Your Application

If you're under 25, or you're married, or in a civil partnership or you're co-habiting with a partner and you're aged over 25, then you may need to ask other members of your household to provide information in support of your student finance application if you're making an income-assessed application.

The agency which assesses your student finance application makes some default assumptions which you need to be aware of. If you're aged under 25, the agency assumes that you're a 'dependent student' who has:

✔ Spent the last three years living with your parents

✔ Has two parents in your household

✔ Does not have a partner (unless you're married)

If you've been living with one parent only, then evidence of their single status needs to be sent to the agency assessing your student finance. This evidence can be paperwork relating to a divorce, separation, bereavement or a letter from a person in a position of responsibility such as a GP, which confirms the parent's single status. Supporting evidence of a council tax bill with single person's discount, or Child Tax Credit letters can also be sent. If you don't have parents, or haven't lived with them for a lengthy period, see the sidebar, 'Independent students and students with no parents'.

If you're under 25 and live with a partner and you're unmarried, you are treated as single for student finance purposes and the above assumptions apply unless you're able to show you've been living independently of your parents for a 36-month period before your course begins.

Household income calculations

When applying for income-assessed student finance, your application is subject to a household income calculation. Whose income is taken into account depends on your circumstances.

Independent students and students with no parents

Independent student status is automatically granted to students aged over 25, and those who are or have been married, or are in a civil partnership irrespective of age.

If you're under 25 and you've not lived with your parents for 36 months before your course begins, you need to provide evidence. If you're successful in showing you've supported yourself for the entire period, then you can be assessed as an 'independent student'. The following paragraphs describe how you may evidence your situation.

If you've previously been in care, you can apply for independent status by providing a letter from social services, or your leaving care service letter. This evidence should be sufficient on its own but may need to be presented each year when you re-apply for student finance. If your circumstances mean there is never any chance of you being reconciled with your parents, you should try and obtain evidence of this.

If your parents are deceased, you need to provide evidence. You can provide copies of death certificates,

(continued)

(continued)

or you can also provide a letter from a person in responsibility who is aware of the family circumstances. Once you've provided evidence that you've no living parents, you should be given independent status for the duration of your course.

If you no longer have contact with your parents, you need to show that the relationship has broken down irreconcilably. You need to provide third party evidence to show that you've become estranged from your parents, which can sometimes be difficult to obtain, but a letter from a GP or teacher/lecturer from your school/college who is aware of the situation is usually enough. What you must be aware of is that any contact with your parents themselves means that you're unlikely to be recognised as estranged, as contact is still ongoing. The student finance agencies usually expect a reasonable amount of time to have passed to establish a period of estrangement, but they do have discretion to consider periods of less than one year. If you're in a situation where relations have broken down irretrievably between you and your parents, you should seek to try and provide evidence of this if you can.

You may be asked to provide evidence when you re-apply for student funding in later years, so maintain contact with the people who can verify your circumstances (such as your GP and/or teaching staff from your college) and keep them up to date with the relevant information about your estrangement.

You may be under 25 and still have contact with your parents, but nevertheless have been living independently of them for a full 36-month period before your course begins. This may be because you've been working full-time, or living in a home of your own. If this is the case, you need to build up a body of evidence showing your income for the full period, as well as key documents showing that you've supported yourself financially. These could be pay slips, P60s, rent agreements, utility bills, council tax bills, any welfare benefits you may have claimed, bank statements showing regular weekly shopping at supermarkets, and so on. You should submit as much as you can to support your claim that you've lived independently.

The most difficult scenario to describe in order to claim independent status is where you've been living independently but you've remained in your parents' home during the 36-month period. It becomes very difficult to show that you've not benefited from some form of 'benefits in kind' from such an arrangement, such as meeting the full cost of your share of household shopping, bills, and so on. There is no rule which states you cannot be seen as independent in such circumstances, but it becomes very difficult to prove unless you can show regular contributions to the household as well as formal contributions for 'board and lodging' at a rate equivalent to the market value – unless you've drawn up formal documents with your parents.

If you're an independent student who lives alone in your household, or you're a lone parent, only your own income is taken into account. The period which is assessed is the forth-coming academic year – you're required to make an estimate of what your income from all sources is likely to be, and you should always seek to make as reliable an estimate as you can. Any earned income you may have is disregarded in full. If you've no 'unearned taxable income' then your household income is likely to be zero, and you are eligible to receive the maximum amount of student finance. Any 'unearned taxable income' you have does not reduce your student finance enti-tlement if it is £25,000 or less.

If you're an independent student with a partner (and you're aged over 25 and you're co-habiting, or you're married, or in a civil partnership irrespective of age) your partner's income is also assessed. Their taxable income is taken into account for the last complete tax year before the student finance applica-tion cycle opened. For example, for 2016, the application cycle is due to open in January 2016. The last complete tax year is 2014/15. Your partner is required to support your online application by making their own application online – and they are required to provide their National Insurance number so that their estimated income for the tax year in question can be checked against HM Revenue & Customs' records. Therefore, your partner should seek to make as reliable an estimate as possible, probably using their P60 or ('statement of earnings' if they're self-employed) as a guide.

For example, for September 2016, the application cycle is due to open in January 2016. In this example, the partner will not be estimating their income – they need to put precisely what their income was. If they put down a rough estimate it could slow the application down and they may be asked to provide paperwork evidence to show actual figures.

If you're a dependent student, your parents need to provide their taxable income details for the last complete tax year, once again by providing their National Insurance numbers and estimating their income for the tax year in question.

The household income calculation is based on the gross total amount of all items of taxable income, with deductions allowed for payments such as pension contributions, as well as amounts disregarded for any younger siblings who may live in the household. Once these deductions have been made, you're left with the residual income figure, which is then used in the above tables to work out the amount of grant and/or loan you can receive.

Always check to make sure that you and anyone supporting your application provide financial information for the correct time period and state exactly what the income was during the relevant tax year. If you don't, there is likely to be a delay in your funding, or you may only receive non income-assessed funding.

The household income assessment differs slightly among the four nations, and results in different amounts of funding being available depending on where you live.

England

In England (student studying outside London and living away from home during term-time), Table 4-1 applies.

Table 4-1	Household Income in England
Household Income	*Support Available*
Up to and including £25,000:	Maximum grant (with reduced loan available)
£25,000 – £42,620	Loan and grant support (continuing students)
£25,000 – £62,143	Income-assessed loan support (new and continuing students)
£62,143 and above	Non income-assessed loans only

Northern Ireland

In Northern Ireland, another version of the household income assessment is in operation, shown in Table 4-2.

Table 4-2	Household Income in Northern Ireland
Household Income	*Support Available*
£0 – £19,203	Maximum grant with partial student loan
£19,204 – £41,539	Reduced grant with partial loan
£41,540	Maximum loan only
£41,541 and above	Reduced rate loan

Scotland

In Scotland, two rates of loan exist – one for dependent students, and a higher one for independent students. The full rate of loan is available on household incomes up to £34,000. A reduced rate applies over that threshold, which is the same value for both independent and dependent students, as Table 4-3 shows.

Table 4-3	Household Income in Scotland	
Household Income	**Independent**	**Dependent**
Up to £23,999	Maximum	
Up to £33,999	Maximum	Reduced
£34,000 and above	Lower rate	Lower rate

Additional household income also affects how much bursary you receive, as shown in Table 4-4.

Table 4-4	Additional Household Income in Scotland	
Household Income	**Young Student's Bursary**	**Independent Student's Bursary**
£0 – £16,999	Maximum	Maximum
£17,000 – £23,999	Middle rate	N/A
£24,000 – £33,999	Lower rate	N/A

Tuition Fee Loans are available to Scottish students who wish to study in other parts of the UK.

Wales

In Wales, your household income affects how much loan and Welsh Government Learning Grant (WGLG) is available to you, as shown in Table 4-5.

Table 4-5	Household Income in Wales
Loan:	
Household Income	*Support Available*
£0 – £50,020	Partial loan paid alongside grant
£50,021 – £50,757	Maximum
£50,758 – £57,472	Reduced loan only
WGLG:	
Household Income	*Support Available*
£0 –£18,370	Maximum
£18,371 – £50,020	Partial grant

Current year income

There is quite a significant time lag between the academic year in which you study and the tax year your parent(s) or partner provide information for. Your household circumstances may change during this period. If so, and if the household income has decreased by at least 15% of what it was, then you can apply for a 'current year income assessment'.

You must initially apply in the standard way, providing evidence of income for the last complete tax year before the application cycle opened. Once you've gone through this stage, you can obtain a form and whoever is supporting your application can provide an estimate of income for the current tax year (the tax year may be incomplete at the time you ask for the re-assessment of income). Once the tax year is complete, your parent(s) or partner are required to provide confirmation of their income for that year. The form is usually available online but only once initial assessments have been carried out: it is recommended you do an online search for 'current year income assessment form' and you should get the form you require.

For study on the first year of a three-year degree in 2016/17:

✔ Initial application made in February 2016, including details of tax year 2014/15. Household income was over £25,000.

✔ Initial assessment completed in July 2016. Household income has decreased by more than 15% since 14/15.

> Current year income assessment requested – estimate of income in tax year 2016/17 provided.
>
> ✔ April 2017 – confirmation required of taxable income for 2016/17 (relevant HMRC checks to be made, may require submission of P60s/statement of earnings).

Note that if your household income has changed by more than 15%, your assessment will have been finalised using 2016/17 information, whilst the majority of assessments for that academic year use 2014/15 information. Assuming that you're studying a three-year course, assessments for the other students on your course don't require 2016/17 information until their third year of study. This means that your current year assessment for year 1 remains applicable until your third year of study, and there is no requirement for you to submit financial details in the following years of your course (whilst everyone else's assessments 'catch up' to yours).

Deciding What to Apply For

The student finance package you apply for is made up of at least two items of funding depending on where you live and where you intend to study. For example, Scottish students get their tuition fees paid by the Scottish government if they study at a Scottish university, but need to apply for a Tuition Fee Loan if studying elsewhere in the UK. Similarly, Welsh students pay lower fees if studying in Wales, but can obtain additional funding to meet the higher cost of fees elsewhere in the UK.

Wherever you live, or wish to study, you have the basic choice of applying for non income-assessed or income-assessed funding.

 Always check the income thresholds for income-assessed funding and don't assume that you won't qualify for income-assessed support – the thresholds may be higher than you (or members of your household) assume.

If you make an income-assessed application, you're guaranteeing that you get the maximum support that is available to you in your circumstances. You're also more likely to be able to unlock further sources of funding when you start your studies, such as discretionary funds from your course provider.

Your initial application is for the 'core funding' for your tuition fees and living costs. If you're financially responsible for children, or an adult in your household, your application also covers some grant support for them. You need to make additional applications for a Disabled Students' Allowance, and any Childcare Grant you wish to apply for. Once you've applied for the core funding, you can make the applications for other items of student finance relevant to your circumstances.

If you're studying for an undergraduate course and you're unable to obtain the core-funding package because of previous study, you can still apply for 'targeted' support for your dependants, and for any disability you may have. Targeted support includes:

- ✔ Parent's Learning Allowance
- ✔ Adult Dependants' Grant
- ✔ Childcare Grant
- ✔ Disabled Students' Allowance

The Application Form

The following section uses the Student Finance England application form as a template. Any notable variations for Wales, Scotland and Northern Ireland are highlighted, but please note the application forms may not have identical questions, or may not follow the same order. Furthermore, this information is based on the 2015/16 application (the 2016/17 version is not available at the time of writing).

Let's walk through the application form in stages. . .

1. About you

This section of the form addresses various items of data regarding your personal identification and ordinary residence in the UK.

The first question asks if you're a UK national. If the answer is 'yes', you're then asked whether you can provide your passport details – there is an option to say you will provide them later if you don't have them to hand. If you have a current

UK passport, enter your passport number on the online form (don't send your passport). If you don't have a current UK passport, you need to provide your original birth/adoption certificate together with a birth/adoption certificate form, available from: www.gov.uk/student-finance-forms.

If you've changed your name and it's no longer how it appears on your birth/adoption certificate or passport, you need to provide your original birth certificate together with any later documentation relating to your name change, such as a deed poll.

You're then asked where you've lived for the three-year period leading up to the start of your course – you need to select whether you've lived in the UK, Channel Islands or Isle of Man, or not.

The residence of your parent(s) or partner is dealt with in the next question – confirming whether they have lived or worked outside of the UK (or the European Economic Area if you're an EU or Swiss national).

The next question is about your marital status. Note that if you're aged under 25 and live with your partner as though you're married, you're treated as a single person. You can only be treated as having a partner if you're married/in a civil partnership, or you're aged over 25. The next question follows on by asking whether you've ever been married (or in a civil partnership) before the start of the academic year. If you plan to get married between the time when you apply for your funding and when your course starts, you need to answer 'yes'.

You're then asked whether you're financially responsible for anyone under the age of 18. This question helps to establish whether you may need to be considered for additional targeted grant support for student parents. Make sure that you answer 'yes' if you have children, as this can mean more financial support for you (you're asked to provide the names and dates of birth of your children). Similarly, the next question enquires whether you have any adults who depend on you financially. This could be your spouse, partner or another family member who lives with you.

You also need to indicate with whom you live. Whether this is your mother or father, both parents or neither parent. If you select one parent, you are also asked to confirm their current relationship status. If you don't currently live with your parents, you need to consider whether they have supported you during the last three years – if so, select the most appropriate choice which describes your relationship with your parents. If you've had no contact with your parents, or you've supported yourself financially, select 'neither parent'.

This brings you to the end of the opening section of the application.

The online form summarises any additional evidence you may need to provide at this stage.

2. Previous study

This section of the application seeks information to check whether any studies you've already undertaken may have an effect on the amount of student finance available to you for your future studies.

The first question in this section asks if you've already studied in higher education, and specifically mentions a first degree, foundation degree, HND, HNC and postgraduate qualifications such as an MA. There are additional qualifications which count as well, such as a Certificate of Higher Education and a Diploma of Higher Education. If you're in any doubt as to the level of study you've previously undertaken, contact the advice service at your course provider, who are usually able to assist.

If you've previously studied, this does not necessarily mean that you aren't entitled to any further student finance, but it can have an effect on how much. The important thing is to make sure that you provide accurate information. For example, you may have studied an HND or foundation degree and now wish to undertake a top-up year for a degree. This is usually fully funded and the regulations governing student finance allow for this – but you must still take care to accurately represent the course(s) you've already studied.

Once you've given details of any higher education previous study you've undertaken, this section is complete. Note that you should include any course you've taken at this level – even if it was studied outside the UK.

3. Course and fees

This section of the online form begins with some introductory information about the Tuition Fee Loan and the tuition fees your course provider can charge. You can take the opportunity to familiarise yourself with this information if you don't know about it already. Of course, in Scotland, you only need to apply for a Tuition Fee Loan if you're studying elsewhere in the UK.

The first thing you're asked to confirm in this section is the name of the course provider where you expect to study.

As you may be completing the application before you have a firm offer of a place at your chosen course provider, use your best guess as to where you wish to study. These details can be changed later if the need arises.

You're then required to select the course you are going to study. Using your UCAS course code is usually the most accurate way of selecting the title of your course, but do check to ensure the title exactly matches the course you're applying to study. Course titles can vary and may be extremely similar, so make sure that you get the right one if there is a choice, as any incorrect details have the potential to cause delays in payment of your funding.

Once you've selected your course, you are asked if it leads to a healthcare profession. This may seem odd if your chosen subject is BA (Hons) English Literature, but all this question is doing is checking whether you should be applying for student finance via the NHS system, as well as through this route. Confirm whether your course is a healthcare one or not.

Next you need to indicate whether you're intending to study an undergraduate full-time, part-time or distance learning course, or a postgraduate initial teacher training course. Make the appropriate choice. Then you need to confirm which year of study you're undertaking.

The next question asks where you are studying during the year. The choices are: at your university or college, studying abroad or on a work placement. This question can lead to confusion for students on programmes like foundation degrees, where a lot of vocational learning takes place in

the workplace. Such courses don't mean you're on placement, and you should select 'university or college' if you're
on that kind of course. The placement option should only
be used for 'sandwich courses' – usually a four-year full-time
course where three years are studied at the university or college campus and one year is spent on a placement with an
employer. A reduced rate of funding is paid for placement
years, so getting this detail right is important.

Now you are asked to confirm where you will be living during
the year. The choice is either with your parents or somewhere
else. Choose the option applicable to you. This answer determines whether you get paid the lower parental home rate
or the higher 'elsewhere' rate of student loan (including the
'London' rate if you're studying in London).

The application now suggests what your course fee is going
to be for the coming year. Check the details with information
from your course provider to ensure this is correct. If not, you
have the opportunity to enter a revised figure at this point in
the application.

Now you are asked to confirm whether you wish to apply
for a Tuition Fee Loan in order to pay for your tuition fees.
Note that applying for a Tuition Fee Loan is the only way you
can defer paying your fees until after you've left your course
(and you're earning over £21,000 per year). Having confirmed
whether you wish to take out a fee loan (we shall assume
you've said 'yes'), you then need to confirm how much you
wish to borrow.

Selecting 'maximum amount' ensures that you get the maximum fee loan applicable to you. This is often the best option
for you because it ensures you get the total amount you can
even if details get adjusted (usually by your course provider).
You can indicate you're happy for your Tuition Fee Loan
amount to be amended automatically – and this is recommended so that you can be sure it matches the fee you're
being charged.

If you're getting financial assistance from somewhere else,
such as from your employer or some other kind of sponsor,
you aren't able to use the 'maximum amount' option and you
need to work out the amount of money you require after your
sponsor's contribution. This is to ensure that your course

provider is not paid more than you should be charged for your tuition fees.

The final question in this section asks whether you wish to share your data with your university or college for the purposes of the bursary scheme(s) they offer. These schemes often rely on information you provide in your student finance application.

Ideally, you have already checked to see if you qualify for a bursary or scholarship from your course provider, but if you're in any doubt, it's usually best to allow this data sharing to take place so that you get the benefit of being considered for additional financial support. Note that allowing this data sharing to occur does not guarantee payment of any additional financial support.

You're now given the opportunity to save your application before continuing to the next section.

4. Living costs

Just as with the tuition fee section, you're given some initial introductory information about the Maintenance Loan and additional support that may be available to you.

Note that in Scotland, there is an additional form to download from the www.saas.gov.uk website in order to apply for your Maintenance Loan. (Additional forms are provided for further items of funding such as the Dependants' Grant – not applicable to students from the rest of the UK).

You are presented with an estimate of how much maintenance loan is available to you (this depends on whether you make an income-assessed application or not) and you're asked whether you wish to apply for a Maintenance Loan. The next question asks how much loan you wish to apply for – the basic amount or the full amount you're entitled to (based on your household income).

Once you've indicated whether you wish to be income-assessed, you then get the opportunity to indicate how much money you actually wish to borrow. Once again, you can indicate you wish to borrow the full amount that is available, or you can specify a lower amount. Note that taking less than the maximum amount can mean that you cannot apply later for additional funding that could be available from your course provider.

You are then given a set of circumstances and you are asked if they apply to you – most of these questions are about your eligibility to receive welfare benefits. If you're in a position to be eligible for a benefit (but not necessarily actually receive payment), then this could mean that you're entitled to more loan than would otherwise be the case. You just need to indicate whether any of the listed circumstances are applicable to you.

The final question in this section asks if you wish to apply for a Disabled Students' Allowance (this is done on a separate form you can download from www.gov.uk/studentfinance).

Once again, you get the opportunity to save your application before moving on to the next section.

5. Financial information

The first question you're asked in this section is whether you are going to be employed whilst studying. The question states you should not include part-time or casual employment, but in fact, as a full-time student, your income from employment is disregarded in full. In Scotland, an additional form for household income information is available from the www.saas.gov.uk website.

The next question asks about income from sources other than employment – or what is known as 'unearned income'. These are taxable sources of income such as rents from property you own, pension income, dividends from shares or interest from capital.

Once you've provided this information, if you're an independent student with no partner, this section is complete. If, however, your parent(s) or partner are supporting your application, you now need to provide their details. This is so that their own accounts can be created online. They then need to log in and provide the income information to support your application. The application is structured in this way to ensure any personal financial information remains confidential to the person concerned.

This section is now complete and your application can be saved. Note, however, that if someone is supporting your application, they need to provide the necessary information before your application can be income-assessed.

6. Additional information

In this last section of the form, you're asked to provide your National Insurance number, your bank details and two contact details of people well known to you.

Your National Insurance number is required (and is checked) to ensure that you're registered with the UK tax system. This is to make sure that repayments of any loans you take out can take place through the UK tax system once you're earning enough to make repayments.

You need to provide bank details so that you can receive payment of your student finance. Don't worry if you don't have your student bank account at the time you apply, as these details can be changed later.

The two contacts you're required to provide are purely there so that the Student Loans Company can contact you if they lose track of you (perhaps because you change address). These contacts are not required to act as guarantors or have any kind of obligation as a result of being named within the application other than to act as reliable points of contact for you. Make sure you give the names of people who don't live at the same address.

Once you've saved this section, you're nearly at the end of your application.

7. Check and submit

As well as having the opportunity to review the information you've given before you click 'submit', this section includes the terms and conditions of the student loans you're applying for. As with all small print, you should take the time to read it, and ideally take a copy for reference (a pdf link is provided).

Once you've agreed to the terms and conditions, the next page of the application takes you to a link to print off and sign your declaration form. Whilst the majority of the application is online, it is not complete until you print off, sign and return the declaration form. You must ensure that you undertake this final step to complete your application.

You are then taken to a screen which summarises the funding you've applied for. This information may not be entirely accurate if you've applied for income-assessed funding – it gives an indication of what is available to you rather than the actual amounts. This screen also includes a note to tell you about the interest which is attached to student loans, and how repayments work.

The final screen checks your contact details just to ensure you've provided the correct information.

Troubleshooting Your Application

After you've completed your application and clicked submit, do not be complacent. Unfortunately, the process is far from proactive and the responsibility lies with you to ensure that your application progresses and reaches the end of the process.

You should hear back regarding the outcome of your application within 6 to 8 weeks. But be careful to note this time frame only applies to completed applications where all the necessary information has been provided *and* received. This is why it is crucial that any documentary information you send in support of your application is sent recorded delivery, so that it can be tracked if necessary.

Taking the Next Steps

You may wish to consider some of the following suggestions to ensure your application is processed successfully.

Make a note of the date when 8 weeks has elapsed since you submitted your completed application (this is 8 weeks from when you submitted the last piece of information in support of your application).

Make regular checks of your online account to see if there are any messages about any further information being required.

Once 8 weeks has gone by, check to see if there are any messages on your account and also check whether you've received the summary of your financial entitlement for the year ahead. If there is no information of this kind, contact the student finance agency to see if there has been a delay, and if so, why.

Make sure you keep your student finance account up to date with any changes in respect of:

- ✔ Your course

- ✔ Your course provider

- ✔ Your tuition fees

- ✔ The amount of Tuition Fee Loan you wish to borrow

- ✔ The amount of Maintenance Loan you wish to borrow

- ✔ Your bank details

- ✔ Your address

You are able to make changes to the first three of the above until 1 September (1 August in Scotland), after that date you need to contact your course provider, who makes the changes for you.

 If you need to send in documentary evidence, always ensure that you keep a copy for your own records and write your name and customer reference number on the copy that is sent.

Applying for Future Years

The student finance application cycle usually begins around February each year. You usually receive a text message reminder to apply for your student finance for the next academic year if you've provided a mobile phone number as part of your contact details.

You need to apply online using your student finance account when re-applying for your next year's financial support – make sure that you keep your account details safe for future reference, including your customer reference number, email address that you've registered with, your password and secret answer.

 Always make sure you apply for your student finance at the earliest opportunity – set a reminder for yourself. Applying early gives you the best chance of receiving your student finance on time.

Take care to check the processing deadlines guaranteeing your student finance for the start of the academic year. Remember to check your online account to see how your application is progressing. If 8 weeks have passed since you sent some information and you've heard nothing, take action to follow up and find out why.

Getting Some Money Even if it Isn't All You Should Get

You may experience a delay in your student finance being processed. This could be for a number of reasons, examples of which are:

- ✔ You made a late application (from June onwards)
- ✔ You didn't provide all the information that was required to support your application
- ✔ Someone supporting your application didn't provide the required information
- ✔ You provided information but the delay in sending it meant your student finance could not be processed on time
- ✔ A delay has occurred beyond your control

 Make regular checks on the progress of your application. Doing so can alert you to any additional evidence requirements which may arise, and can also help you to understand if your application is not being processed within the ordinary time limits – in which case you should try and find out why.

In addition, if you have children or other dependants, there are further evidence requirements to support any application you're making for targeted grant support. This means further delays can occur in the processing of your application.

If any of the above circumstances arise, you probably won't receive the full amount of student finance you're entitled to when your course starts. However, you may be able to receive some money even if it's not all that you're entitled to.

The non means-tested portion of student loan (and your Tuition Fee Loan) rely on the most basic evidence requirements: your personal ID check, your ordinary residency, your course/university information and any previous study you may have undertaken.

If you satisfy all of the above, it may be possible for you to request payment of your non income-assessed support whilst your income assessment is being processed. Doing so can allow you to receive some funding to help you meet some of your most urgent essential costs.

Checking If Your Money Is Late

If you don't receive your student finance at the start of your course, you should enquire to find out the reason why it's delayed and ask for an indication of when a payment may be expected.

If you're told that payment is delayed by more than three to four days from the start of your course, make sure you contact your course provider and notify them of your situation.

It is standard practice for short-term loans to be made available to students whose student finance is not available to them. You are usually asked to provide some evidence that you've applied for your student finance, and that you've not yet received it, as part of a short-term loan application. Once you've been able to demonstrate your circumstances, you can expect to receive a small amount of money to make sure you have enough for the most essential costs such as food and laundry.

Short-term loans are usually paid from your course provider's discretionary funds – so once you repay the money, it's then recycled to help other students in hardship.

If your funding is late, make sure you notify your landlord. If you live in a hall of residence managed by your course provider, you're likely to find that they view your situation sympathetically, as it has become commonplace to see student finance delays occur at the start of the academic year. If you're renting from a private landlord, make sure you inform them and if any difficulty arises (for example, if the landlord insists you pay them on time) ask to speak to an adviser (or accommodation officer) at your course provider – they usually attempt negotiation with the landlord on your behalf. Most student landlords have experience of this situation, but may be further reassured if your course provider contacts them to verify the situation regarding your funding.

If you do take out a short-term loan, remember that you're not being given additional money. Use the money sparingly and wisely to see you through until your student finance becomes available. The usual arrangement is that your loan lasts until your student finance is paid to you – then you're required to repay the money to your course provider (who then uses that money to assist other students in hardship). Repaying the money is important so that students who are in genuine need, even after they have received their full student finance, can be supported.

Deciding What To Do when Your Circumstances Change

Your student finance is worked out on the assumption that you're going to be a full-time (or part-time) student for the duration of the academic year in question, and your student finance payments will support you during that time.

You may, however, find that circumstances arise which mean you find that you're not able to engage in your studies for the whole academic year, or that you consider leaving the course altogether.

You must take steps to notify your course provider and Student Finance when situations like these arise. Your student finance is likely to be affected, and you need to minimise the impact upon you as much as you can.

Taking time out

You may need temporarily to take time out of your course for a reason such as illness, a caring responsibility or other personal reasons which mean that you cannot engage in your studies as you may wish.

In the first instance, discuss your situation with your lecturers/ tutors and your course provider's advice service. They are able to advise you on the options available to you to take time out from study, and you can then decide which is the most suitable for your circumstances.

The typical options are:

- ✔ Getting an extension on pieces of work where assessment deadlines may be affected by a short-term period of non-attendance.

- ✔ Taking a short-term break for a matter of weeks until the situation is resolved (if this affects assessment deadlines you may need to apply for extensions and/or apply to the board of examiners to present your extenuating circumstances).

- ✔ Taking time out for the remainder of the year and rejoining the course in the next academic year.

Note that for periods of illness, you're treated as being in attendance (for student finance purposes) for the first 60 days of illness. So, if you're ill and unable to attend, but then recover within 60 days, this may have no effect on your student finance at all. If, however, you're unable to return during that period, it's important that you notify your course provider (and provide evidence where required, such as a GP's letter) so that Student Finance can be informed of the situation (your 60-day entitlement should still be counted even if you're off for longer).

If you're unable to rejoin your course and you don't have any other source of income, you can apply to your Student Finance agency to request a discretionary payment to support you. You need to demonstrate that you're in hardship, and this usually requires you to submit a covering letter describing your circumstances in full, as well as your last 3 months' bank statements to show that you've no other means of support. You should also include evidence of the reason you're unable to attend your course.

If you have to disrupt your study due to a caring responsibility, your student finance ceases from the day you interrupt your studies. You can, however, make an application for discretionary support if you can demonstrate hardship, as described in the previous paragraph.

Note that, due to student finance being paid in instalments, the date you interrupt your studies may mean that you've been paid student finance to which you're no longer entitled. This can be recovered with immediate effect in some circumstances. You may wish to check with the advice service at your course provider to ensure that any overpayment you're asked to repay is correct, and that the situation you're in means the money is repayable. If not, the advice service may be able to assist you in negotiations with your Student Finance agency to reduce or cancel the repayment.

If you're unsuccessful in obtaining a discretionary payment for any time that you're unable to attend your course, or you're still in hardship even after the discretionary payment has been agreed, contact your course provider – they may have additional sources of funding that can assist you until you return to study.

If the reasons you've had to interrupt your studies are resolved, but you have to wait until the start of the next academic year to rejoin your course, you may be in a position to claim welfare benefits during that time. It's worth contacting your advisers at your course provider to find out more.

Repeating parts of your course

If you've had to interrupt study and your course provider requires you to repeat some elements of your course, or if you've failed an element of your course and have to do a re-sit the next academic year, these situations can affect your student finance.

If you have to repeat an element of your course due to circumstances beyond your control, such as illness or caring responsibilities, you can make an application for compelling personal reasons by writing a covering letter describing your situation, and providing accompanying evidence (relating to the time when the circumstances arose). If successful, compelling personal reasons can mean the year's funding for the period when the circumstances arose is not counted when working out your future entitlement to student finance – so you may still find yourself fully funded (and have a year's student finance to fall back on if required).

If you need to repeat a year because you need to do a re-sit, you usually need to use your additional year's student finance entitlement. You only have one additional year to use in this way, so if you find yourself in this situation, you really need to do your best to avoid having to do a re-sit year in future.

Leaving a course early

If you decide the course you're studying is not for you, you have some choices available to you. You can:

- ✔ Leave the course and stop studying in higher education altogether
- ✔ Leave the course and consider transferring to another course, either with the same course provider or elsewhere

If you decide to leave your course outright, then you need to fill out a withdrawal form for your course provider. They inform Student Finance in due course, but I recommended that you contact Student Finance yourself (preferably in writing).

The date you leave your course is crucial. If you leave right at the start of your course, you may be able to take advantage of a 'cooling-off' period (usually no more than a couple of weeks) which allows you to leave without having any tuition fees to pay. If you've received a payment of maintenance support, note that you're only entitled to the portion relating to the time you were in attendance on the course – you may be asked to repay the rest with immediate effect.

If you stay on your course beyond the cooling-off period, but you leave during the year, the time you leave determines the amount of tuition fees you have to pay (and how much maintenance support you're entitled to keep hold of).

For example, in England, the calculations are shown in Table 4-6.

Table 4-6	Tuition Fee Liability in England
Period in Attendance	*Tuition Fee Liability*
September – December	25%
September – start of April	50%
September – rest of April	100%

So if you decide to leave your course at the beginning of December, completing the withdrawal process before the start of January is crucial, otherwise you have to pay 50% of your tuition fees for the year, rather than 25%.

If you decide to transfer to another course, once again the timing can be crucial. Some course providers allow 'in-year' transfers – but this is most common at the start of the academic year. If you transfer later than this, you may find that you need to use your 'additional year' of student finance in order to fund the first year of your second course.

Chapter 5

Exploring Student Loans

● ●

In This Chapter

▶ Checking out Tuition Fee Loans

▶ Looking at Maintenance Loans

▶ Receiving the money

▶ Repaying your student loan

● ●

Student loans are the major single item of student finance, and you should realistically expect to apply for them in order to support your studies.

Student loans support tuition fee costs as well as living costs. As the cost of tuition fees was increased to £9,000 a year in 2012, you're likely to be using them to fund your studies.

In this chapter, I provide detailed information on student loans for tuition fees and for living costs, exploring the differences between England, Wales, Northern Ireland and Scotland.

Tuition Fee Loans

A Tuition Fee Loan is the principal source of funding for your course's tuition fees if you study in higher education in England, Wales or Northern Ireland. If you are a student who is ordinarily resident in Scotland, the fee loan is only applicable to you if you choose to study in one of the other nations within the UK – if you choose to study in Scotland, fee support is in the form of a grant.

The Tuition Fee Loan is the recognised mechanism for deferral of costs of your fees until after your studies are finished. If you apply for a Tuition Fee Loan you usually have no tuition fees to pay 'up front' whilst you study, and repayments only begin once you've left your course and you're earning over the applicable earnings threshold for your loans.

The word 'usually' is in the last paragraph because Tuition Fee Loan support is limited to the ordinary duration of your course plus one year. If you exceed this allowance, you need to 'self-fund' your tuition fees. This is not usually a problem for the majority of students, but if you've studied a previous course in higher education, or you've to repeat more than one year of your course due to academic failure, then you may find you can't access a Tuition Fee Loan until later years of your course. I say 'usually' because support for full-time courses is limited to the ordinary duration of your course plus one year.

The standard allowance of Tuition Fee Loan begins with the final year of your course, and then works forward. The following examples show how this principle works:

1. Student with no previous study who is studying a three-year degree course

Year 1	*Year 2*	*Year 3*	*Additional*
Standard Tuition Fee Loan (3)	Standard Tuition Fee Loan (2)	Standard Tuition Fee Loan (1)	'+1 year'

2. Student who fails one academic year of the course:

Year 1	*Year 2*	*Year 3*	*Year 4*
Standard Tuition Fee Loan (3)	Additional '+1 year' (repeat Year 1)	Standard Tuition Fee Loan (2)	Standard Tuition Fee Loan (1)

3. Student with two years' previous study on a full-time degree course, studying full-time on a new degree:

Year 1	*Year 2*	*Year 3*
Self-fund (2 years of Tuition Fee Loan used on original course)	Additional '+1 Year'	Standard Tuition Fee Loan (1) (only standard year left after original course)

In the previous examples, scenario 1 shows standard progress through your course, leaving you with an additional year's funding to fall back on, which you may never need to use. In scenario 2, you can see how it is possible to complete a three-year course with one repeat year and still receive full funding for the course.

As the student finance regulations refer to the 'ordinary duration of the course plus one year', you still get funding for a repeat year if you are doing a four-year course. In the final example, because two years' worth of Tuition Fee Loans have been used up on a previous course, and the new course is three years long, you only receive Tuition Fee Loans for the final two years of the course (meaning you would have to find the funds for year one yourself).

Calculating how much you can get

The amount of Tuition Fee Loan you can apply for depends on which funding agency (England, Wales, Scotland, Northern Ireland) you apply to, and which nation you study in.

In England, the maximum rates of Tuition Fee Loan you can access for full-time and part-time study are £9,000 and £6,750 respectively. These figures match the tuition fee cap set by government. You can only be charged these levels of tuition fee if your course provider has an Access Agreement approved by the Office for Fair Access (OFFA). If no Access Agreement is in place, tuition fees are capped at the lower rates of £6,000 for full-time courses and £4,500 for part-time courses. Similarly, if you study a full-time course at a private provider, the maximum rate of Tuition Fee Loan is £6,000, and £4,500 if you study part-time.

In Northern Ireland, Tuition Fee Loans of up to £9,000 are available if you're ordinarily resident in Northern Ireland and study a full-time course elsewhere in the UK. If you have ordinary residence in Northern Ireland and study with a course provider in Northern Ireland, the maximum full-time Tuition Fee Loan you can obtain (and fee you can be charged) is £3,805. No Tuition Fee Loans are available for part-time study – support is in the form of a Tuition Fee Grant.

In Scotland, Tuition Fee Loans of up to £9,000 are available if you're ordinarily resident in Scotland and study a full-time course elsewhere in the UK. If you have ordinary residence in Scotland and study at a Scottish course provider, no Tuition Fee Loan support is available as your fees are paid through grant funding from the Scottish government. No Tuition Fee Loans are available for part-time study – support is in the form of a Tuition Fee Grant.

In Wales, there is a blend of funding available to assist with the cost of your tuition fees. If you're ordinarily resident in Wales you can qualify for a Tuition Fee Grant alongside a Tuition Fee Loan, which reduces the amount of funding you need to repay in respect of your tuition fees. If you study full-time you can obtain a Tuition Fee Loan of up to £3,810, or up to £2,625 if you study part-time in Wales (up to £6,750 if you study part-time elsewhere in the UK). If you study a course run by a private provider, the maximum fee loan you can apply for is up to £6,000 for a full-time course, and £4,500 for a part-time course (no fee grants are available for courses run by private providers).

Comparing tuition fee liability and Tuition Fee Loans

When considering your tuition fees and how much you're charged, and how much Tuition Fee Loan you require (and ultimately owe), it's important to recognise the distinction between your tuition fee liability and the Tuition Fee Loan itself.

In essence, your *tuition fee liability* is how much your course provider is charging you to attend your course. The Tuition Fee Loan represents the amount of funding you are applying for in order to meet the cost of your course (in turn, deferring your actual payment of those costs until such time as you have finished your course and your income is over the required earnings threshold).

A similar approach is taken towards your tuition fee liability across all nations of the UK, except if you're a Scottish student who's eligible for Tuition Fee Grant support from the Scottish government.

If you're eligible to receive a Tuition Fee Loan in order to fund your studies at any point on your course, your fee liability is structured as follows:

- ✔ Autumn term: 25% of total fee liability
- ✔ Spring term: 50% of total fee liability
- ✔ Summer term: 100% of total fee liability

Your course provider should allow a 'cooling-off' period at the start of the academic year – this usually lasts a maximum of two weeks. The cooling-off period allows you to leave your course with no tuition fee liability. You need to check with your course provider to see what arrangements they have in place.

If you remain on your course after the cooling-off period has expired, you become liable for 25% of your tuition fees for the duration of the first term of your course. As soon as you enter the second term, a further 25% liability is incurred, meaning you now owe 50% of the annual tuition fee. Remaining registered on the course at the start of the third term triggers the final 50% liability, meaning 100% of the year's fees become due for payment.

If you leave or interrupt your studies mid-year, you need to recognise that doing so can have an effect on the amount of fees you're required to pay, as well as how much Tuition Fee Loan is payable to your course provider.

For Scottish students accessing Tuition Fee Grant support from the Scottish government, there is only one liability point in the academic year on 1 December. If you leave your course before that date, no fees are payable to your course provider; if you leave on or after that date, 100% of your fees are payable.

Confirming you're on the course

Once you have registered on your course, and your course provider has been able to verify your attendance on the course, an electronic confirmation of your attendance is sent directly to the Student Loans Company.

The attendance confirmation releases payment of the first portion of your Tuition Fee Loan to your course provider. This usually occurs around the middle of October. Further attendance confirmations are scheduled at the start of the second and third terms, each of which releases the next instalment of your Tuition Fee Loan to your course provider.

The instalments of your loan follow the same structure as the tuition fee liability – so 25% of your Tuition Fee Loan is paid in the first term, a further 25% in the second term and 50% in the third term.

This payment structure means that interest doesn't start to accrue on the entire Tuition Fee Loan that you've applied for in any given year from the first day of the course – you only start to accrue interest on the portions of Tuition Fee Loan once each of the liability points has been passed.

Maintenance Loans

A Maintenance Loan is likely to be your principal source of income during your studies. Even if you qualify for a Maintenance Grant, the amount of Maintenance Loan you can apply for is usually greater than the amount of Maintenance Grant available.

The Maintenance Loan is available as both a non income-assessed loan and an income-assessed loan. The non income-assessed loan forms part of the basic student finance package alongside the Tuition Fee Loan – it's available if you satisfy the basic eligibility criteria for student finance. In addition, you must be under the age of 60 (50 in Scotland) on the first day of the first academic year of your course in order to qualify for a Maintenance Loan for any course starting before September 2016.

The revised student finance package for England from 2016 onwards makes Maintenance Loans available to new students with no age limit. The age limits still apply to the rest of the UK for 2016/17 at the time of writing.

England

In England, in 2016/17, the income-assessed loan is available to you if your household income is assessed as being lower than the thresholds shown in Table 5-1.

Table 5-1	Income-assessed Loans in England
Where You Live	*Household Income Threshold for Non Income-assessed Maintenance Loan*
Parental Home	£56,818
Elsewhere	£60,684
London	£67,193
Overseas	£62,518

The standard package of Maintenance Loan is available if you're a student under 60, as shown in Table 5-2 (other than if you have an underlying entitlement to welfare benefits).

Table 5-2	Maintenance Loans in England
	Maximum Maintenance Loan Available
Parental Home	£6,904
Elsewhere	£8,200
London	£10,702
Overseas	£9,391

If you're a student aged under 60 with an underlying entitlement to welfare benefits, the rates of loan shown in Table 5-3 apply.

Table 5-3	Welfare-assessed Loans in England
Where You Live	*Maximum Maintenance Loan Available*
Parental Home	£8,144
Elsewhere	£9,347
London	£11,671
Overseas	£10,453

If you're a student aged 60 or over at the start of your course, you can receive a Maintenance Loan of £3,469 if your household income is £25,000 or below. A partial loan is available for incomes between £25,001 and £43,668.

A final year rate of loan is payable once you reach the last year of your course. The final year rate is less than the full year rate because it does not include a notional figure to cover the summer vacation.

If you're a continuing or final year student in 2016/17, you should contact your course provider if you wish to confirm the amount of Maintenance Loan you're receiving is correct. Several rates are in operation at the moment, and which one is applicable to you depends on the date your course started and whether you have had any previous study in higher education prior to your current course.

In England, from 1 September 2016 onwards, the Maintenance Loan will be the only source of funding for living costs for you if you're a new student. (Supplementary grants for dependants, disabled students and childcare costs will still be available.) The new system of Maintenance Loans offers an increased package of support, with a further enhanced amount of loan available if you're a student who falls into one of the groups with an underlying entitlement to welfare benefits. The full rate of loan is available to students with household incomes of £25,000 or less.

Northern Ireland

In Northern Ireland, how much loan you can get depends on where you live during term-time as well as your household income. Table 5-4 describes the support available (2015/16 figures).

Table 5-4	Loans in Northern Ireland
Where You Live	*Maximum Maintenance Loan Available*
Parental Home	£3,750
London	£6,780
Elsewhere	£4,840
Overseas	£5,770

The rates of loan shown in Table 5-4 are the maximum income-assessed rates. If your household income is £41,605 or less, you can expect an amount of Maintenance Grant (or Special Support Grant if applicable) to be paid alongside your Maintenance Loan.

Scotland

In Scotland, you can apply for the non income-assessed rate of loan up to £4,750 (2015/16 rate).

The Scottish income-assessed Maintenance Loan rates depend on which bursary you qualify for (Young Person's Bursary or Independent Person's Bursary) and are as shown in Table 5-5 (2015/16 rates). (Supplementary grants for students who have a disability, dependants or childcare costs will still be available.)

Table 5-5	Loans in Scotland	
Household Income	*Young Person*	*Independent Person*
£0 – £23,999	£5,750	£6,750
£24,000 – £33,999	£5,750	£6,250
£34,000 or more	£4,750*	£4,750*

*non income-assessed rate of Maintenance Loan

Wales

In Wales, the Maintenance Loan is paid alongside the Welsh Government Learning Grant if your income is up to £50,762.

The rates of Maintenance Loan are as shown in Table 5-6 (2015/16 rates).

Table 5-6	Loans in Wales
Where You Live	*Maximum Maintenance Loan Available*
Parental Home	£4,162
London	£7,532
Elsewhere	£5,376
Overseas	£6,410

The Welsh government cancels up to £1,500 from your Maintenance Loan balance once you make your first repayment of student loan (once you have finished your time on your course and you're earning enough to make repayments). The Welsh government's partial cancellation does not apply if you have any outstanding charges or penalties in relation to your loan, or if you're in breach of the terms and conditions of your student loan agreement. At the time of writing, it is not clear whether the partial cancellation will continue to operate for new students from 2016/17 onwards.

Long Courses Loans

If you're studying on a course with an academic year lasting longer than 30 weeks and 3 days, you may qualify for additional amounts of loan in the form of the 'long courses loan' (except in Scotland).

You don't need to make a separate application for the long courses loan – its availability to you is determined according to:

- ✔ The length of your academic year
- ✔ Your household income

If your course is longer than 30 weeks and 3 days, you receive an additional weekly allowance of a long courses loan equivalent to the duration of your course up to a period of 45 weeks. If your academic year is 45 weeks or more, you're treated as though you require 52 weeks of support and you then receive a full year's entitlement.

If your household income is assessed as being £39,796 or less, the maximum amount of long courses loan is paid in addition to your standard entitlement to a Maintenance Loan. For incomes above the £39,796 threshold, the long courses loan is reduced by £1 for every complete £9.27 of additional household income.

Rates of long courses loan are as follows:

In England (2016/17):

Where You Live During Term-time	*Weekly Amount of Long Courses Loan*
Parental Home	£57
London	£113
Elsewhere	£88
Overseas	£122

In Wales (2015/16):

Where You Live During Term-time	*Weekly Amount of Long Courses Loan*
Parental Home	£61
London	£116
Elsewhere	£91
Overseas	£126

In Northern Ireland (2015/16):

Where You Live During Term-time	*Weekly Amount of Long Courses Loan*
Parental Home	£55
London	£108
Elsewhere	£84
Overseas	£117

Getting Your Hands on the Money

Your student finance is not released to you, or your course provider, until you've registered on your course. You need to do this each year of your course, not just in your first year.

Tuition Fee Loans

Your course provider is responsible for confirming your attendance on your course to the Student Loans Company. This usually occurs some weeks after the start of your academic year in order to give your course provider the opportunity to verify that you're actually attending satisfactorily.

An electronic 'Attendance Confirmation' is sent to the Student Loans Company which then releases the actual payment of your Tuition Fee Loan to your course provider. A similar 'Attendance Confirmation' is sent in the second and third terms to release the second and third instalments of the Tuition Fee Loan. If you should leave or interrupt your studies at any point in the academic year, the next Attendance Confirmation isn't sent if you're not actually in attendance. The result is that no further payment of your Tuition Fee Loan is made for the year (and the standard payment of your maintenance support is interrupted).

Your liability for your tuition fees begins on the first day of your course, and that is when interest begins to accrue on the first instalment of your Tuition Fee Loan, even though the payment is not made to your course provider until some weeks after that.

The Tuition Fee Loan is paid to your course provide in instalments of 25% for the first two terms, 50% being paid for the final term.

Maintenance Loans

If you're ordinarily resident in Scotland, your Maintenance Loan is paid to you in monthly instalments, with the exception of the first instalment (which will be of double the normal value).

In the rest of the UK, your Maintenance Loan is paid in three equal instalments at the start of the autumn, spring and summer terms.

In order for you to receive your Maintenance Loan, your course provider must submit an electronic 'Registration Confirmation' which acts as the payment trigger for your Maintenance Loan payments.

Only one Registration Confirmation is required each year, but Maintenance Loan payments are usually stopped if you suspend/intercalate/interrupt your study, or if you withdraw from your course.

Repayments

You don't usually need to make any repayments of a student loan until you have finished your time in higher education, and your earnings are over the applicable threshold. Enjoy your poverty while it lasts!

Some exceptions stand apart from this rule, however, and these arise if you leave your course early (by withdrawing, or for some other reason). If this happens, you may find yourself incurring an overpayment of student loan.

For example, you may decide in February that the course you started the previous September is really not the course you thought it was, and you're thinking about starting a different course the following September (the funding regulations allow for this – the first year of your next course would be your '+1 year'). You will have received two instalments of student finance by the time you reach this decision: one in September and one in January – these two payments will amount to approximately two thirds of your Maintenance Loan entitlement for the year. However, you won't have been in attendance for two thirds of the year, and a Maintenance Loan is only payable for periods where you're in attendance. As soon as the funding agency you've applied to is notified that you've left the course (your course provider does this, but I recommend that you notify them as well) it calculates how much of the second instalment of Maintenance Loan you're entitled to, and any remaining amount becomes an overpayment.

The usual practice for recovering an overpayment of Maintenance Loan is to deduct it from the next instalment payable – so when you start the new course the following September, your Maintenance Loan is reduced to take account of the overpaid amount. If, however, you haven't taken appropriate action to keep the Student Loans Company, one of its agencies or your course provider informed of your situation, you may find that the overpayment becomes immediately recoverable and in a lump sum.

There have been instances reported where immediate recovery of Maintenance Loans has been sought, even where students have taken reasonable action to keep their course provider and/or their funding bodies informed. If you find yourself in this situation, contact the advice service at the institution where you studied, and they will seek to assist you in exploring whether recovery of the overpayment can be challenged.

Working out what you need to repay

If you complete your course (or leave it after completing an academic year), the standard repayment procedure applies. Upon completion of your time in higher education, any Tuition Fee Loans and Maintenance Loans you have applied for are amalgamated to become your Student Loan repayment account.

Standard repayments only take place if you have finished your time in higher education and your taxable earnings are over the repayment income threshold.

You can always work out how much you need to repay as there is a standard formula which is used to calculate student loan repayments.

There are currently two repayment plans for student loans taken out since 2006:

✔ Plan 1 is relevant to you if you're ordinarily resident in Northern Ireland or Scotland and studied at any time since 1 September 1998, or you're ordinarily resident in England or Wales and your course started between 1 September 1998 and 1 September 2012.

✔ Plan 2 is relevant to you if you're ordinarily resident in England or Wales and your course started after 1 September 2012.

If any loan remains unpaid once the lifetime of the loan expires, it's written off and you don't have to make any further payments. The lifetime of the loan begins the April after you finish your studies.

Working out repayments for Plan 1

If you're making repayments under Plan 1, the maximum lifetime of your loan is 25 years. This is what you need to know about paying it back:

- ✔ You start to make repayments the April after you leave your course.

- ✔ If your income is £17,495 or less (from April 2016), you don't make repayments.

- ✔ If your income is over £17,495 (from April 2016), the first £17,495 of your income is ignored when calculating your repayments.

- ✔ Your repayments are equal to 9% of your income over the £17,495 threshold.

For example:

You earn £25,000 (before tax) a year. The first £17,495 is disregarded for repayments, leaving £7,505 to be taken into account. Nine percent of £7,505 is £675.45 – this is your annual repayment to the Student Loans Company. If you divide the figure by 12, you find your monthly repayment is £56.29.

Repayments are deducted at source by your employer in the same way as PAYE and National Insurance. If your income falls below the repayment threshold, repayments cease. Repayments are based on your personal income – if you have a partner, their income is not counted.

Working out repayments for Plan 2

If you make repayments under Plan 2, the maximum lifetime of your loan is 30 years. Here's what you need to remember about repaying it:

- ✔ You start to make repayments the April after you leave your course.

- ✔ If your income is £21,000 or less (from April 2016), you don't make repayments.

- ✔ If your income is over £21,000 (from April 2016), the first £21,000 of your income is ignored when calculating your repayments.

✔ Your repayments are equal to 9% of your income over the £21,000 threshold.

For example:

You earn £25,000 (before tax) a year. The first £21,000 is disregarded for repayments, leaving £4,000 to be taken into account. Nine percent of £4,000 is £360.00 – this is your annual repayment to the Student Loans Company. If you divide the figure by 12, you find your monthly repayment is £30.00.

Repayments are deducted at source by your employer in the same way as PAYE (Pay As You Earn, or what's usually referred to as Income Tax) and National Insurance. If your income falls below the repayment threshold, repayments cease. Repayments are based on your personal income – if you have a partner, their income is not counted.

Some students may find themselves taking out student loans which are repayable under the terms of both repayment plans. For example, you may have studied an undergraduate degree which started before 1 September 2012, and then decide to study a PGCE course which starts after that date. The loans for the undergraduate course have a lower income repayment threshold than those for the PGCE.

Loan repayments for courses starting before 1 September 1998

If you took out a student loan for study on a course which began before 1 September 1998, you make repayments on the mortgage-style loan scheme, which is based on the average income in the UK. When your income becomes greater than the average income, you're required to make repayments at a fixed rate, irrespective of how much income you have above the national average – so if you're earning £50,000 a year, you repay your loan making the same monthly repayment as someone earning £60,000 a year.

If you have a mortgage-style loan and then study a PGCE course under the new loan system, you have options available as to whether you repay your mortgage-style loan first, the new style loan first or make payments to both schemes at the same time.

In cases like this, the repayments are layered upon one another, as follows:

Assuming an income of £25,000 (gross), to calculate the repayment for the Plan 1 loans, income between £17,495 and £21,000 would be used. Nine percent of £3,505 is £315.45 (divided by 12 gives a monthly repayment of £26.29. Repayment against the Plan 2 loans would be calculated in the usual way £25,000 – £21,000 leaves £4,000, of which only 9% is used for repayments: £360. Divide by 12 to get the monthly payment of £30.00. Add £30.00 to £26.29 to find the full monthly repayment for all loans = £56.29. Note that this equates to the monthly repayment for Plan 1 loans, but some of the money is diverted to the new loan scheme.

If you're ordinarily resident in Wales, the Welsh government cancels up to £1,500 from your Maintenance Loan balance once you make your first repayment of student loan (that is, once you've finished your time on your course and you're earning enough to make repayments).

Getting Interested in Interest

Since 1 September 2012, any student loan taken out in England and Wales has been subject to a new system of repayment which includes higher rates of interest than the schemes operating before that date in England and Wales, or the current systems operating in Northern Ireland and Scotland.

If you're ordinarily resident in Northern Ireland or Scotland, or you started your current course in England or Wales before 1 September 2012, the only interest your student loan attracts is equivalent to the *Retail Price Index* (RPI) – the indicator which is usually used to measure inflation. This just means your loan debt is kept the same in real monetary terms as time passes in order to avoid depreciation.

If you applied for student loans in England or Wales for a course starting on or after 1 September 2012, a higher rate of interest is applicable, as follows:

Circumstance During Study:	*Rate of Interest*
After leaving the course and income up to £21,000:	RPI only
After leaving the course and income between £21,000 and £41,000	RPI + up to 3%
After leaving the course and income over £41,000	RPI + 3%

Chapter 6

Being Granted a Grant

*G*rants still play a major part of the student finance picture, especially if you have children, have a disability or other members of your household are dependent upon you.

Unlike student loans, grants don't have to be paid back. Most are income-assessed, but if you qualify to receive a grant, you can regard it as an entitlement and you should ensure you receive it. The Disabled Students' Allowance is not income-assessed; it's paid according to your needs.

In this chapter, I provide detailed information on the various grants available in England, Wales, Northern Ireland and Scotland.

Reviewing the Available Grants

Grants are non-repayable sources of student finance. If you're eligible to receive a grant, you really do need to ensure that you take the necessary steps in order to receive it, as a grant is effectively an entitlement that you should take every opportunity to receive.

If you are eligible to receive a grant, ensure that you take the necessary steps in order to receive it because you don't want to miss out on non-repayable funding.

This section looks at the different types of grant available to students.

Maintenance Grant

The *Maintenance Grant* is income-assessed and doesn't have to be repaid. It's intended to meet the cost of your living costs during study. The Maintenance Grant is usually paid alongside a Maintenance Loan, and when this is the case, it is counted in full for welfare benefits.

The grant is available to you if you're a full-time student who is either ordinarily resident in Northern Ireland, or if you are a student who is continuing their studies who is ordinarily resident in England and whose course started prior to September 2016. In Wales, the equivalent grant is the Welsh Assembly Learning Grant, and in Scotland the Young Person's/Independent Student's Bursary is the broad equivalent.

If you've studied previously and this results in you not receiving a Tuition Fee Loan, then your entitlement to the Maintenance Grant is similarly affected. You won't receive any Maintenance Grant payment for a year, which means that you have to 'self-fund'.

The grant available to you depends on your location, as outlined in the following sections.

England

If you're a continuing student who has ordinary residence in England, you can still be considered for a Maintenance Grant of up to £3,387 if your course began before 1 September 2016. The Maintenance Grant is income-assessed and how much you get of the full grant depends upon your income. A maximum rate of Maintenance Grant is payable on household incomes of £25,000 or less, and a partial grant is payable on household incomes up to £42,620, as shown in Table 6-1.

Table 6-1	Maintenance Grants Based on Income in England
Household Income	*Amount of Maintenance Grant (England – Continuing Students Only)*
£0 – £25,000	£3,387
£25,001 – £42,620	Partial Grant
£42,620 or more	No Grant

If you receive a Maintenance Grant, it replaces some of the maximum rate of Maintenance Loan you receive, as shown in Table 6-2 for English students whose course began before 1 September 2016 and who are in receipt of the 'elsewhere rate' of Maintenance Loan.

Table 6-2 How Your Maintenance Grant Affects Your Maintenance Loan

Household Income	Maintenance Grant (England)	Maintenance Loan – Elsewhere Rate (Maximum £5,878)	Total Student Financial Support
£25,000	£3,387	F4,185	£7,572
£30,000	£2,441	£4,658	£7,099
£35,000	£1,494	£5,131	£6,625
£40,000	£547	£5,605	£6,152
£42,620	£50	£5,853	£5,903
£42,875	£0	£5,878	£5,878

This system of payment means that if you're a student from a lower income background, you have less of your student finance paid in the form of a repayable loan, and more in the form of a non-repayable grant.

In England, from 1 September 2016, you're no longer eligible to receive a Maintenance Grant if you're a new student ordinarily resident in England. Instead, an increased rate of student loan has been introduced.

Northern Ireland

In Northern Ireland, the Maintenance Grant continues to be available to you if you're a new student, as well as if you're continuing your studies. The Maintenance Grant is paid at a higher rate of £3,475 in Northern Ireland, with the full grant available to you if your household income is £19,203 or less, with a partial grant on household incomes up to £41,605, as shown in Table 6-3.

Special Support Grant

The *Special Support Grant* is identical in value to the Maintenance Grant but is only payable to students who have an underlying entitlement to welfare benefits during their studies. It is paid to meet the costs of books and materials associated with your course, travel to and from your course or child-related costs. The special support grant is disregarded in full for welfare benefit purposes. The Special Support Grant is income-assessed and doesn't have to be repaid. No Special Support Grant is available to students ordinarily resident in Scotland (the nearest equivalent is the Lone Parent's Grant).

Table 6-3   Maintenance Grants in Northern Ireland

Household Income	Amount of Maintenance Grant (N. Ireland (2015/16 rates))
£0 – £19,203	£3,475
£19,204 – £41,605	Partial Grant
£41,606 or more	No Grant

If you have studied previously and this means you will not receive a Tuition Fee Loan, your entitlement to the Special Support Grant will be similarly affected and you will not receive any Maintenance Grant payment for a year, so you have to 'self-fund'.

If you're a full-time student ordinarily resident in Wales or Northern Ireland, or if you're a continuing student in England whose course began before 1 September 2016 and you fall into one of the following groups of students, you may qualify for the Special Support Grant rather than the Maintenance Grant:

- ✔ You're a lone parent responsible for a child or young person aged under 20 who is a member of your household, and in full-time non-advanced education; or

- ✔ You're a lone foster parent responsible for a child or young person aged under 20; or

- ✔ You've a partner who is also a full-time student and either or both of you are responsible for a child or young person aged under 20 in full-time non-advanced education; or

- ✔ You've a disability and qualify for a disability premium; or

- ✔ You've been treated as incapable of work for a continuous period of at least 28 weeks (two or more periods of incapacity with a break of no more than eight weeks counts as one continuous period); or

 ✔ You're deaf and qualify for a Disabled Students'
 Allowance; or

 ✔ You're aged 60 or over; or

 ✔ You're entitled to Personal Independence Payment,
 Armed Forces Independence Payment or Disability Living
 Allowance.

You also qualify for a Special Support Grant if:

 ✔ You're entitled to housing benefit or the housing element
 of Universal Credit; or

 ✔ You've a disability and qualify for income-related
 Employment Support Allowance

As well as being wholly disregarded for benefit purposes, the
Special Support Grant also passports you to the maximum
rate of student loan available according to where you live
(rather than reducing the amount of Maintenance Loan available to you in the way the Maintenance Grant does).

England

In England, from 1 September 2016, you're no longer eligible
to receive a Special Support Grant if you're a new student
ordinarily resident in England with an underlying entitlement
to welfare benefits. Instead, a higher rate of Maintenance Loan
has been introduced (when compared to the rate available
to new students who don't have an underlying entitlement to
welfare benefits).

If you're a continuing student who has ordinary residence
in England, you can still be considered for a Special Support
Grant of up to £3,387 if your course began before 1 September
2016. The Special Support Grant is income-assessed. A maximum rate of Special Support Grant is payable on household
incomes of £25,000 or less, and a partial grant is payable on
household incomes up to £42,620, as Table 6-4 shows.

Northern Ireland

In Northern Ireland, the Special Support Grant continues to
be available to you if you study full-time and you're a new student, as well as if you're continuing your studies. The Special
Support Grant is paid at a higher rate of £3,475 in Northern
Ireland, with the full grant available to you if your household

income is £19,203 or less, and a partial grant on household incomes up to £41,605, as shown in Table 6-5.

Table 6-4	Special Support Grants in England
Household Income	*Amount of Special Support Grant (England – Continuing Students Only)*
£0 – £25,000	£3,387
£25,001 – £42,620	Partial Grant
£42,620 or more	No Grant

Table 6-5 Special Support Grants in Northern Ireland	
Household Income	*Amount of Special Support Grant (N. Ireland (2015/16 Rates))*
£0 – £19,203	£3,475
£19,204 – £41,605	Partial Grant
£41,606 or more	No Grant

Wales

In Wales, the Special Support Grant continues to be available to you if you study full-time and you're a new student, as well as if you're continuing your studies. The Special Support Grant is paid at a higher rate of £5,161 in Wales (equivalent to the Welsh Government Learning Grant), with the full grant available to you if your household income is £18,370 or less, and a partial grant on household incomes up to £50,752, as outlined in Table 6-6.

Table 6-6	Special Support Grants in Wales
Household Income	*Amount of Special Support Grant (Wales (2015/16 Rates))*
£0 – £18,370	£3,475
£18,370 – £50,752	Partial Grant
£50,752 or more	No Grant

Welsh Government Learning Grant

The *Welsh Government Learning Grant* is the main item of grant funding you may be eligible to receive if you're a full-time student ordinarily resident in Wales.

The Learning Grant is intended to contribute toward meeting the costs of your living expenses during your studies. It's counted in full for welfare benefit purposes.

The Learning Grant is income-assessed and Table 6-7 indicates how much you can receive (2015/16 rates).

Table 6-7	Welsh Government Learning Grants
Household Income	*Amount of Welsh Government Learning Grant*
£0 – £18,370	£5,161
£18,371 – £50,752	Partial Grant
£50,753 or more	No Grant

In Wales, the Welsh Government Learning Grant is paid alongside the Maintenance Loan if your income is up to £50,752.

Young Student's/Independent Student's Bursary for Scottish residents

Non-repayable bursaries are available if you're an eligible student ordinarily resident in Scotland. Which bursary is applicable to you is determined by your circumstances.

The Young Student's/Independent Student's Bursary is income-assessed and is intended to contribute towards your living costs whilst you study. Both bursaries are counted in full for welfare benefit purposes.

If you're a college leaver, you probably qualify for the Young Student's Bursary. You may apply for the Independent Student's Bursary if you're over 25, married, living with a partner or have responsibility for a child who lives with you.

The bursary rates (2015/16) are shown in Table 6-8.

Table 6-8	Young Student's and Independent Student's Bursary Rates	
Household Income	*Young Student's Bursary*	*Independent Student's Bursary*
£0 – £16,999	£1,750	£750
£17,000 – £23,999	£1,000	nil
£24,000 – £33,999	£500	nil
£34,000 or more	nil	nil

The bursaries are paid alongside your Maintenance Loan entitlement.

Parent's Learning Allowance

The *Parent's Learning Allowance* is an income-assessed, non-repayable grant available to you if you're ordinarily resident in England, Wales or Northern Ireland.

The Parent's Learning Allowance is intended to contribute towards additional costs associated with caring for a child whilst you study. It's disregarded in full for welfare benefit purposes.

As long as you've at least one child, you're in a position to be considered for the Parent's Learning Allowance – you don't have to provide evidence of what you intend to spend the money on.

When working out your entitlement to the Parent's Learning Allowance, only your dependants' taxable income is used in the calculation (your own income is ignored). The Dependants' Grants income assessment includes your partner and any other adults or children who may depend on you financially. The Dependants' Grants income assessment is separate to the one used for your core funding. Your Parent's Learning Allowance entitlement can be affected by dependants' income of less than £25,000.

The amount of Parent's Learning Allowance payable varies across England, Wales and Northern Ireland, as shown in Table 6-9.

Table 6-9	Parent's Learning Allowance
UK Nation	*Amount of Parent's Learning Allowance*
England	up to £1,573 (2016/17)
Wales	up to £1,557
Northern Ireland	up to £1,538

Lone Parent's Grant

If you're ordinarily resident in Scotland and you're a lone parent, you can apply for an income-assessed Lone Parent's Grant. How much you receive depends on your household income.

The *Lone Parent's Grant* is intended to assist with costs associated with caring for a child whilst you study. It's disregarded in full for welfare benefit purposes.

You can apply for a Lone Parent's Grant of up to £1,305 (2015/16 rate).

Dependants' Grant

If you're ordinarily resident in Scotland and you've dependent children or adults living with you, you can apply for an income-assessed Dependants' Grant. How much you receive depends on your household income.

The *Dependants' Grant* is intended to assist with costs associated with the financial responsibility for other adults in your household whilst you study.

The Dependants' Grant doesn't cover costs associated with children, but additional assistance may be available to you by claiming Child Tax Credit or welfare benefits whilst you study.

You can apply for a Dependants' Grant of up to £2,640 (2015/16 rate).

Adult Dependants' Grant

The *Adult Dependants' Grant* is an income-assessed, non-repayable grant available to you if you're a full-time student and you're ordinarily resident in England, Wales or Northern Ireland.

The Adult Dependants' Grant is intended to contribute towards additional costs associated with financial responsibility for a partner or another adult (with a net income of £3,796 or less) who is a member of your household whilst you study. If your partner is also a full-time student, no Adult Dependants' Grant is payable.

When working out your entitlement to the Adult Dependants' Grant, only your dependants' taxable income is used in the calculation (your own income is ignored). The Dependants' Grants income assessment is separate to the one used for your core funding. Your Adult Dependants' Grant entitlement can be affected by dependants' income of less than £25,000 (and less than £3,796 if the adult dependant is not your partner).

The amount of Adult Dependants' Grant payable varies across England, Wales and Northern Ireland, as shown in Table 6-10.

Table 6-10	Adult Dependants' Grant
UK Nation	*Amount of Adult Dependants' Grant*
England	up to £2,757
Wales	up to £2,732
Northern Ireland	up to £2,695

Childcare Grant

The Childcare Grant is an income-assessed, non-repayable grant available to you if you're a full-time student and you're ordinarily resident in England, Wales or Northern Ireland.

The *Childcare Grant* is intended to contribute towards additional costs associated with using childcare whilst you study. It's disregarded in full for welfare benefit purposes.

The Childcare Grant can only be used for registered childcare provision. This means Ofsted registered childcare providers in England, Welsh Government/Local Authority registered providers in Wales, schemes and providers recognised by

Social Care and Social Work Improvement Scotland and Local Authority registered providers in Northern Ireland.

The Childcare Grant cannot be paid in addition to the childcare element of Working Tax Credit – the two schemes are mutually exclusive.

The Childcare Grant meets up to 85 per cent of the cost of eligible childcare provision. Maximum amounts of support are set per week for one child, or for two or more children (see Table 6-11).

When working out your entitlement to the Childcare Grant, only your dependants' taxable income is used in the calculation (your own income is ignored). The Dependants' Grants income assessment includes your partner and any other adults or children who may depend on you financially. The Dependants' Grants income assessment is separate to the one used for your core funding. Your Childcare Grant entitlement can be affected by dependants' income of less than £25,000.

The amount of Childcare Grant payable varies across England, Wales and Northern Ireland, as Table 6-11 outlines.

Table 6-11	Childcare Grant
UK Nation	*Amount of Childcare Grant*
England	up to £155.24 per wk (1 child); up to £266.15 per wk (2 or more children)
Wales	up to £161.50 per wk (1 child); up to £274.55 per wk (2 or more children)
Northern Ireland	up to £148.75 per wk (1 child); up to £255 per wk (2 or more children)

There is no statutory Childcare Grant in Scotland, but all higher education course providers have a Childcare Fund that you can apply to for help toward the cost of registered or formal childcare. Eligibility for the Childcare Fund requires that you must take out the maximum student loan available to you and you must be eligible to have your fees paid by your funding body.

Disabled Students' Allowance

If you're a full-time student and you've a long-term disability, mental health or specific learning difference, you may be eligible to receive a *Disabled Students' Allowance* (DSA) for additional course costs arising out of your condition. The DSA is paid according to need and is not conditional upon any income assessment.

The DSA is available if you study part-time and at least 25 per cent of the intensity of a full-time course and you're ordinarily resident in England or Wales. If you're ordinarily resident in Scotland or Northern Ireland, and you're studying at least 50 per cent of the intensity of an equivalent full-time course, then you can apply for a DSA. There are several elements to the DSA, and these are aimed at ensuring it is responsive to the various requirements which may need to be met for a wide range of disabilities. The DSA assesses your needs at an Assessment Centre – full details of assessment centres are available at the DSA-QAG website: www.dsa-qag.org.uk.

You can only make an appointment to visit an assessment centre after you've applied for your DSA (using the form on www.gov.uk/student-finance-forms) and after you've received your letter confirming your DSA has been awarded.

When applying, if you're a full-time student and you've already applied for your core student finance, use the DSA SLIM form – it's a 'slimmed down' version of the full form and much quicker to complete. If you're a part-time student or a post-graduate student, you must complete the full DSA 1 form.

The DSA contributes towards the costs of personal support and equipment recommended via the assessment centre. You receive a report with details of all the recommended support and reasonable adjustments applicable to your course once you've attended your assessment centre appointment.

The rates and allowances vary among the UK nations and are as shown in Table 6-12.

Vacation Grant for Care Leavers

If you're ordinarily resident in Scotland and you're a student who has left care who needs to pay for accommodation during the summer vacation between the academic years of your course, you can apply for an income-assessed Vacation Grant for Care Leavers of up to £105 a week during the holiday period. How much you receive depends on your household income.

Table 6-12   Disabled Students' Allowance

Nation/Allowance	Full-time Rate	Part-time Rate
England		
General Allowance	up to £1,741 per year	up to £1,305 per year
Specialist Equipment Allowance	up to £5,212 for your course	up to £5,212 for your course
Non-medical Helper Allowance	up to £20,725 per year	up to £15,543 per year
Northern Ireland		
General Allowance	up to £1,759 per year	up to £1,319 per year
Specialist Equipment Allowance	up to £5,266 for your course	up to £5,266 for your course
Non-medical Helper Allowance	up to £20,938 per year	up to £15,703 per year
Scotland		
Basic Allowance	up to £1,725 per year	pro rata by study intensity
Large Items Allowance	up to £5,160 for your course	up to £5,160 for your course
Non-medical Personal Help	up to £20,520 per year	pro rata by study intensity
Wales		
General Allowance	up to £1,785 per year	up to £1,338 per year
Specialist Equipment Allowance	up to £5,332 for your course	up to £5,332 for your course
Non-medical Helper Allowance	up to £21,181 per year	up to £15,885 per year

You need to provide a letter from your social worker or social work department confirming you were 'looked-after' or had been subject to a custodianship order throughout any 3-month period which ended on or after your 16th birthday and before the first day of your course. If you cannot provide this, a letter from a professional person (on headed paper) who knows your circumstances and can confirm that you're a care leaver is usually acceptable. Professional persons would usually include your doctor, lawyer, teacher, counsellor, student adviser or minister of religion.

The following conditions must be met in order for you to qualify for the Vacation Grant for Care Leavers:

- You must have been in the 'care' of (looked after by) a local authority or voluntary organisation or have been subject to a custodianship order throughout any 3-month period which ended on or after your 16th birthday and before the first day of your course. Only a continuous period of at least 3 months counts.

- You must be under the age of 25 on the first day of your course.

- You must not have had an assessment for your living-cost support using your parents' income.

- You must not be in receipt of full housing benefit. If your housing benefit doesn't meet your housing costs in full, the Vacation Grant for Care Leavers can be paid to you.

- You must have claimed your full student loan entitlement.

Travel Grant

If you're ordinarily resident in England or Wales, you can apply for a Travel Grant for study abroad or for medical/dental clinical placements in the UK.

If you're studying abroad as part of your course, or on an ERASMUS study or work placement, or you're a medical or dental student studying abroad or attending a clinical placement in the UK, you may qualify for the Travel Grant.

You can apply for assistance with 'reasonable costs' but you are required to pay the first £303 yourself.

How the Money Is Paid

Your student finance is not released to you, or your course provider, until you've registered on your course. You need to do this each year of your course, not just in year one.

If you're ordinarily resident in Scotland, your grants are paid to you in monthly instalments, with the exception of the first instalment (which is of double the normal value). In the rest of the UK, your grants are paid in three equal instalments at the start of the autumn, spring and summer terms.

In order for you to receive your grant payments, your course provider must submit an electronic 'Registration Confirmation' which acts as the payment trigger for your grant payments. Only one Registration Confirmation is required each year, but grant payments can be stopped if you suspend/intercalate/ interrupt your study, or if you withdraw from your course.

If you're a part-time student ordinarily resident in Northern Ireland studying at least the equivalent of 50 per cent of the intensity of a full-time course in Northern Ireland, or elsewhere in the UK, you can apply for an income-assessed Course Grant of up to £265, intended to assist with costs arising from books and materials.

Grants for part-time study

No grants are available to assist with your course costs if you're a part-time student ordinarily resident in England or Scotland and your course began on or after 1 September 2012.

If you're a part-time student ordinarily resident in Wales, you may be able to receive an income-assessed Course Grant of up to £1,155 (2015/16 rate). The full grant is available to students with household incomes up to £26,095, with a partial grant available on higher incomes up to £28,180.

If your circumstances match the relevant criteria, as a Welsh student you can also apply for part-time versions of the Parent's Learning Allowance, Adult Dependants' Grant and Childcare Grant. How much you receive depends on your household income and the intensity of your studies in relation to a full-time equivalent course. More information is available at www.studentfinancewales. co.uk

Part III

Government Funds for Specific Students

5 Ways to Specialise in Course-specific Funding

✔ Find out which professions qualify for specialised course-based statutory financial support.

✔ Check your eligibility to receive additional support based on the professional course you study.

✔ Get to grips with how course-specific funding operates alongside regular statutory student support.

✔ Gain an understanding of the different types of course-specific funds available.

✔ Find out how to apply for course-specific funding.

The government's incentives to encourage students into careers where there are shortages of professionals can be a useful boost to your financial situation. Find out more detail about the rates of assistance available for professional courses at www.dummies.com/extras/student financeuk.

In this part . . .

✔ Access detailed descriptions of the funding available for professional careers the government has prioritised.

✔ Get acquainted with how to apply for your course-specific funding to ensure you don't miss out on the financial incentives for your course.

✔ Understand how your course-specific funding interacts alongside the regular statutory student financial support system.

✔ Get an at-a-glance picture of which careers attract additional government funding schemes.

Chapter 7

Turning to the NHS

. . . .

In This Chapter

▶ Exploring eligibility for NHS Bursaries

▶ Finding out how to apply

▶ Knowing where to find out more

. . . .

*F*unding for NHS courses in England and Wales is very similar and is available from the NHS Business Services Authority (NHSBSA) in England and the Student Awards Service in Wales. This chapter focuses on the funding system in England and Wales. If you study an NHS course in Northern Ireland or Scotland, the system is markedly different, and it's recommended you contact the funding bodies directly via your course provider . In addition to the NHS funding that's available, you usually find some (non income-assessed) funding is available from the student funding agencies for the four nations of the UK as well: reduced rate student loans are available to NHS students – so ensure you apply for the loan in addition to the funding from the NHS.

NHS Bursaries have non income-assessed and income-assessed elements, but they're non-repayable – so if you qualify for one, you don't need to repay it. You need to apply for funding each year of your course, just like the standard student finance system. How much you receive depends on the course you study, what year you're studying and where you study.

In this chapter, I provide the information that you need to know on NHS Bursaries, including eligibility requirements, how to apply and the type of financial support available for students who started their courses on or after 1 September 2012.

Checking Eligibility for Funding for NHS Courses

The eligibility requirements for financial support for NHS courses are similar to the requirements for the general statutory student finance system in that they consider your ordinary residency status as well as the course/subject you intend to study.

If your course leads to a professional registration in selected professions, you may be eligible for an NHS Bursary even if you've received funding for previous study in higher education.

Residency criteria

You need to satisfy three residency requirements in order to be eligible to receive NHS Bursary funding. On the first day of the first academic year of your course, you must:

- ✔ Have been ordinarily resident in the UK, the Channel Islands or the Isle of Man for the three years leading up to the first day of your course

- ✔ Have settled status in the UK with no restriction on your stay

- ✔ Be ordinarily resident in any UK nation (for medical and dental students you need to be resident in the nation in which you're going to study)

If you're a medical or dental student and you're not ordinarily resident in the nation in which you're going to study on the first day of your course, you need to apply for student finance through the authority for the nation where you usually live.

You can access an online calculator to help you check your eligibility at: www.nhsbsa.nhs.uk/Students/3941.aspx.

Course criteria

In order to be eligible to receive an NHS Bursary, you must be accepted on an NHS-funded part-time or full-time course.

In Scotland, only nurses and midwives get separate NHS Bursary funding. If you are studying to be a doctor or Allied Health Professional, you just have access to the standard undergraduate statutory funding package. If you study to be a dentist, you can access the standard undergraduate statutory funding plus a special dentistry bursary on top of that.

In Northern Ireland, the funding works similarly to that described below but there are fewer subjects on offer: physiotherapy, occupational therapy, radiography, speech and language therapy, podiatry or dietetics.

If you're taking one of the courses listed below, all of which lead to professional registration, you may be able to apply for a bursary to help with your living costs whilst you study, but you should check with your course provider to make sure.

All places on medical and dental courses are NHS commissioned:

- Chiropody/Podiatry
- Dental Hygiene/Dental Therapy
- Dentistry*
- Dietetics/Nutrition
- Medical*
- Nursing
- Midwifery
- Occupational Therapy
- Operating Department
- Orthoptics
- Orthotics/Prosthetics
- Physiotherapy
- Practitioner
- Radiography
- Radiotherapy
- Speech and Language Therapy

If you are a medical or dentistry student, NHS Bursaries are available from the second year of study for graduate entry programmes, or the fifth year of study for undergraduate programmes. Funding in earlier years of study may be available through Student Finance England (SFE), Student Finance Wales or Student Finance Northern Ireland (via the Education and Library Boards). There is no tuition fee funding for second degrees in Scotland or Northern Ireland.

You aren't eligible for NHS funding for your course if you're on secondment and remain employed whilst attending the course. Similarly, if you're receiving sponsorship in order to attend the course, the amount of NHS funding available to you may be reduced.

Getting Funding for NHS Courses

The NHS Bursary is intended to help with your day-to-day living costs whilst you study on a healthcare course in England or Wales. A non means-tested grant is available for nursing and midwifery courses in Scotland and Northern Ireland (no grant is available for other professions).

In some circumstances you may also be able to get additional elements of financial support via the statutory student finance package from Student Finance England (or the agencies serving Wales, Scotland and Northern Ireland). NHS Bursary awards are not taxable.

If you fulfil the eligibility requirements, you can receive a bursary for each year of your training. NHS Bursaries are usually paid to you in monthly instalments.

There are no guarantees that your NHS Bursary funding will be in place each year of your course – the government issues a disclaimer stating that the rules can change from year to year.

The way your income is treated for the NHS Bursary is very similar to the method used for the standard student finance system. As a full-time student, any earnings you have during your course are disregarded, but as a part-time student they are taken into account.

You must declare any unearned income you have because this will be taken into account. Unearned income includes income from property, pensions, capital and taxable benefits.

Your parents' gross income is taken into account unless you can show that you qualify as an independent student (see Chapter 4). You qualify as an independent student if:

- ✔ You have lived independently of your parents for periods totalling 36 months before the start of your course
- ✔ You're married or in a civil partnership
- ✔ You're irreconcilably estranged from your parents
- ✔ You have no living parents
- ✔ Your parents cannot be found or it is not reasonably possible to contact them
- ✔ You have responsibility for a child under 18
- ✔ Your parents reside outside the EU and contacting them for information would place them in jeopardy or it would not be reasonably possible for them to send a contribution to the UK (not applicable to Scotland)
- ✔ You're a member of a religious order living in a house belonging to that religious order (not applicable to Scotland)

Additional *disregards* (pre-determined amounts of income which are not taken into account) apply to NHS Bursary funding which can serve to reduce the total income that is counted in your income assessment. These can reduce some elements of your income (but may not necessarily cancel them in full). These may include:

- ✔ Sponsorship for a full-time course, or income earned whilst on a part-time course
- ✔ Income from a trust deed for independent students
- ✔ Any pension or allowance for incapacity, old age, retirement, the death of a spouse, civil partner, parent or other person you were dependent upon, or for military or public service
- ✔ Any income for a single parent, a single independent student or any other student in the household which has not already been disregarded

Tuition fees

If you study an NHS course, you can receive assistance from the NHS with the cost of your fees. If you satisfy the basic eligibility for the NHS Bursary, the NHS makes a (full) contribution to the standard cost of your fees, whether you actually receive the bursary or not (your income may mean you don't qualify for a bursary). In this case, you don't need to take out a Tuition Fee Loan for any year that you're in receipt of an NHS Bursary.

The fee contribution is paid directly to your course provider in just the same way as the fee loan.

Non means-tested grant

The non means-tested grant is available to you if you're a full-time student. If you're a part-time student, you can still get a grant, but how much you receive depends on the number of years required to complete your studies, as shown in Table 7-1.

Table 7-1	Non Means-tested Part-time NHS Bursary Values
Years to Complete	*Percentage of Grant*
4 years	75%
5 years	60%
6 years	50%

You need to meet the eligibility criteria for NHS funding and have a place on an NHS-commissioned course to obtain a non means-tested grant. The non means-tested grant is only available to UK-domiciled students who satisfy the ordinary residence criteria.

The non means-tested grant is available for the years of your course which are eligible for bursary funding, and is paid in monthly instalments to your bank account alongside any NHS Bursary you may receive.

The grant is paid at one rate wherever you live whilst you're studying, and does not need to be paid back.

Means-tested bursary

The NHS Bursary is paid in monthly instalments. If you're eligible to receive the means-tested grant, both payments are made together.

The Bursary is means-tested, and how much you receive will depend on where you live whilst studying:

- ✔ London rate (highest rate)

- ✔ Outside London rate (middle rate)

- ✔ Parental Home rate (lowest rate)

If you're a full-time student, you can receive the NHS Bursary at the maximum rate. If you study part-time, you can get a reduced amount according to the number of years needed to complete the course, as shown in Table 7-2.

Table 7-2	Means-tested Part-time NHS Bursary Values
Years to Complete	*Percentage of Grant*
4 years	75%
5 years	60%
6 years	50%

If your course runs for longer than 30 weeks and 3 days in any academic year, an extra week's allowance is payable as part of your NHS Bursary. If your course lasts for 45 weeks or longer, then you get an NHS Bursary for a 52-week period.

Additional allowances

The NHS funding scheme can also include additional allowances, but availability depends on where you study. For example, in Scotland there is no Parent's Learning Allowance or Childcare Allowance.

Additional allowances include assistance with placement costs (a common feature of NHS courses) and any additional circumstances you may face as a result of having a family, partner or a disability.

Practice Placement Expenses

You may find your healthcare course includes placements. The NHS Bursary scheme entitles you to claim back some of the costs associated with attending placements (such as travel and accommodation), as long as you make a claim within six months.

Claim forms are available from the NHSBSA Student Services website (Student Awards Service in Wales, and SAAS in Scotland). Your university will need to authorise your completed claims and send the form on your behalf. A guide to completing the claim form is available from the website.

You can make a claim for Practice Placement Expenses if you're entitled to the non means-tested grant. You can only claim expenses for costs you incur whilst attending a compulsory practice placement as part of your course. You're only able to claim for the difference between what you usually pay for and the costs you face on placement.

Dependants' Allowance

If you have children or other adults who are financially dependent on you during your studies, you may be able to receive the NHS Dependants' Allowance. The allowance is means-tested using your dependants' income. This includes any dependants in your household such as your spouse, civil partner or partner, your children and any other dependent adults. Some of your dependants' income is eligible for disregards.

In addition to the income disregards, a further £1,000 is disregarded per eligible dependant in order to determine the final figure – the 'residual income'.

Your residual income is then used to calculate how much Dependants' and Parent's Learning Allowances you can receive. If your residual income is higher than the maximum allowances applicable to your circumstances, no allowances are payable to you. However, if you're applying for help with your childcare costs, you may be entitled to some assistance with these, depending on the level of your residual income when compared with the additional costs of your childcare.

If your spouse, civil partner or partner is a student in receipt of student finance (or an NHS Bursary), they cannot claim any additional Dependants' Allowances to the ones you receive.

You can share Dependants' Allowances with your spouse, civil partner or partner – but you cannot both receive full payments.

Parent's Learning Allowance

If you have children, you may be able to receive a Parent's Learning Allowance. This is calculated at the same time as the Dependants' Allowance using your dependants' residual income calculation.

How much Parent's Learning Allowance you receive depends on how many children you have and whether you have a spouse, civil partner or partner.

Child Care Allowance

You can claim a Child Care Allowance if you have dependent children aged under 15 (or aged under 17 for children with special educational needs) on the first day of the academic year and you're using registered childcare.

The Child Care Allowance is means-tested using the residual income calculation applicable to other Dependants' Allowances, but the amount of childcare you use can make a difference – the overall costs may mean the amount of allowances available to you is more than your dependants' income.

The Child Care Allowance pays up to 85 per cent of your actual childcare costs, subject to maximum weekly rates if you have one child, or two or more children.

Your initial application for the Child Care Allowance requires you to estimate the childcare costs you expect to incur over the coming academic year. You're required to verify your costs later in the year, in order to ensure that you're receiving the correct level of payments for the childcare that you're using.

You need to provide further information along with receipts from your childcare provider (your childcare provider also needs to fill in a form to verify the costs). You should make as accurate an estimate as possible when making your initial application to ensure that you do not have to repay any Child Care Allowance that you're not entitled to.

Always ensure your application is as accurate as possible to cover the actual costs you incur (provide further information if necessary if your costs are higher than your initial estimate).

Disabled Students' Allowance (DSA)

You may be eligible for DSA support if you have a disability, mental health condition or specific learning difference which satisfies the definition of a disabled person as set out in the Equality Act 2010.

You're disabled under this definition if you have a physical or mental impairment and the impairment has a substantial and long-term effect on your ability to carry out normal, day-to-day activities.

You can apply for your DSA after you've applied for your NHS Bursary online. You need to provide evidence of your disability once your DSA application has been submitted. Make sure that you provide evidence (for example, a GP's letter) in respect of all the medical conditions you wish to include in your application. If you have a specific learning difference, you must provide a post-16 (years of age) assessment report from an educational psychologist. Your GP's letter should confirm your medical condition, the effect it has on your ability to carry out day-to-day activities and whether the condition is long term (lasting longer than 12 months).

You must include a self-addressed envelope when sending your evidence in support of your DSA application. I recommend that you send documents (and arrange for their return) by special delivery so that they can be tracked if they get lost. You then receive a letter confirming whether your DSA has been approved. If your DSA has been agreed, you're advised to go for a Needs Assessment at a Disabled Students' Allowances Quality Assurance Group (DSA-QAG) approved Assessment Centre. You can find your nearest assessment centre on the DSA-QAG website: www.dsa-qag.org.uk. The Needs Assessment identifies the support and reasonable adjustments recommended to help you engage with your studies. You need your DSA letter in your hand to arrange an assessment.

Maternity Awards and Maternity Support Awards

If you're eligible for a full bursary, you're entitled to a Maternity Award of up to 12 months' maintenance in respect of any maternity leave authorised by your course provider.

Your Maternity Award can include elements of your maintenance award but not those which directly relate to your attendance on your course.

If you need to provide support to a mother and child during and after childbirth, a Maternity Support Award continues to be paid to a student for up to 4 weeks' authorised leave.

NHS Hardship Grant

The NHS Hardship Grant is for medical and dental students and is made available due to the length of those courses and the other funding that is available. It is not available to students studying in Scotland or Northern Ireland.

You can apply for a grant of between £100 and £3,000 if you can show that you're in genuine financial hardship. To be eligible for a medical and dental hardship grant, you must be:

- ✔ On a course leading to registration as a doctor or dentist
- ✔ Eligible for a full bursary (both tuition fees and non means-tested bursary)
- ✔ Unable to manage your financial situation by yourself

An application for hardship funding must include:

- ✔ Evidence of your income and expenditure
- ✔ University approval of your application
- ✔ Evidence that you've applied for all the funding available to you

You won't receive a grant if you've chosen not to take up your full student loan entitlement, or any other form of funding or financial support that is available to you.

Your application needs to be made in writing, with evidence of your financial circumstances. Your application, together with a copy of your NHS student coversheet (available from your online NHS Bursary account) needs to be submitted to NHS Student Bursaries for consideration.

Applying for Funding for NHS Courses

When making an application for your NHS Bursary, you must apply direct to the NHS through the Bursary Online Support System (BOSS) if you ordinarily live in England, Wales or Northern Ireland. If you ordinarily live in Scotland, you make an application via Student Awards Agency Scotland (SAAS).

Strict time limits apply for NHS Bursary applications – stricter than those for the standard statutory student finance package. Your application must be received no later than six months after the start of your course for the current academic year. If your application is late, it will not be processed.

Before you start the first year of your course, you need to have received confirmation of your offer of an NHS-funded place before you can apply for your NHS Bursary. Once you have the confirmation, you can create your account on the NHS Bursary Online Support Service (BOSS). Details of when you should apply, and the deadline by which your application needs to be completed, are available via the NHS Bursary Service's website. As with all student finance applications, apply as early as you can once you have received confirmation of your NHS-funded place.

Before you return to study a continuing year, you should be contacted through your BOSS account when it's time to make your next application. If your course starts in the autumn term, you can expect to receive a reminder at some point during the prior February to April period. If your course starts in the spring term, you can expect to receive a reminder at some point during the prior October to January period. You're required to re-apply online through your BOSS account.

If you make an application, but you have not supplied all the relevant documents to support your application, this is likely to lead to a delay in your funding reaching you.

Whether you're a new or continuing student, if you do not provide supporting documentation within the six-month deadline after the start of the academic year, your application will be rejected. This means that you don't receive any tuition fee or living cost support (Bursary, non means-tested grant or additional allowances) for that year.

Check the progress of your application through your BOSS online account and keep checking back to ensure that there are no delays in the process. If your application remains 'pending' after you have sent all your documentation, you may need to take further action to check your application is complete and all the necessary information has been received.

Once your application is processed, you receive a notification through your BOSS account (an email will be sent to you to let you know about the notification) giving details of the elements of support you have been assessed to receive. The notification also confirms the dates of any payments you will receive.

As well as applying for the funding available via the NHS Bursary scheme, you can also apply for a non income-assessed student loan from Student Finance England, or the similar agencies for Wales, Scotland and Northern Ireland.

If you're studying a postgraduate NHS-funded course, check to see whether additional loan support is available to you from Student Finance England, or the similar agencies for Wales, Scotland and Northern Ireland.

Chapter 8

Teachers Needed, Funds Available!

*I*f you're interested in a career as a teacher once you've finished your studies, you may be able to get financial support to help you along via the Teaching Bursary scheme.

The Teaching Bursary scheme is an incentive for students to train for a career in teaching. The support available has been subject to change over recent years but the current package of bursaries is the most generous ever.

How much you receive depends on where you study, where you live, the subject you plan to teach and the classification you achieved for your first degree (indeed, if you have any postgraduate qualifications, these can also influence the rate of bursary you can receive).

In this chapter, I provide information introducing the Teaching Bursary scheme, including eligibility requirements, how to apply and which courses and subjects attract Bursary funding.

Funding for Initial Teacher Training Courses

If you begin a teacher training course, you're able to access the same undergraduate statutory support packages as other undergraduates, but you may also be eligible when studying certain postgraduate courses (as an undergraduate qualification is an entry requirement, it's 'ignored' when it comes to additional financing). This section looks first at the funding available to undergraduates and then at the choices available to postgraduates.

You aren't eligible for student finance if you study for an employment-based course, such as Salaried School Direct, an Assessment Only employment-based route (available to trainees with teaching experience but who do not hold QTS) or the Graduate Training Programme (GTP) in Wales.

Undergraduate courses

Wherever you study an undergraduate initial teacher training course in the UK, full-time or part-time, you can apply for the standard student finance package from Student Finance England, Student Finance Wales, Student Awards Agency for Scotland or Student Finance Northern Ireland.

The usual residency, course and course provider requirements apply, as explained in Chapter 3.

In addition to the standard undergraduate student finance package, the following additional funding is available in England and Scotland only.

If you're studying in England:

- ✔ If you're starting study in 2015/16 onwards, a non repayable bursary has been introduced for undergraduate maths and physics courses leading to qualified teacher status (QTS).

- ✔ The bursary is paid in equal monthly instalments during the final year of your course.

If you are ordinarily resident in Scotland and you study part-time, you may qualify for an Individual Learning Account from Skills Development Scotland.

Postgraduate courses

You're usually eligible for the standard student finance package for postgraduate initial teacher training courses, as previous study (your undergraduate degree) isn't taken into account. The funding for a postgraduate course is entirely separate and you need to apply as if you were applying as a student for the first time.

All nations of the UK make student finance packages available for postgraduate initial teacher training courses. These are broadly similar to the undergraduate equivalent.

 A postgraduate course is treated as entirely separate from your previous studies. If the student finance regulations have changed since you started your undergraduate studies, you switch over to the new funding system when you start your postgraduate course – this could affect the amount or type of funding available to you.

The type of course you study on determines whether student finance is available to you or not. The following types of course usually qualify for the standard student finance package:

- Postgraduate Certificate in Education (PGCE)
- Schools Direct (non-salaried)
- Postgraduate Diploma in Education (PGDE)
- Schools Centred Initial Teacher Training (SCITT)

Employment-based courses do not qualify for any student finance or additional funding incentives. This is because you're regarded as an employee on these courses, rather than a student.

The initial teacher training routes which do not attract student finance are:

- ✔ Salaried School Direct

- ✔ Graduate Training Programme (GTP) in Wales

- ✔ Assessment Only employment-based routes (available to trainees with teaching experience but who don't hold QTS)

England

If you're ordinarily resident in England, you can apply for the following in addition to the standard statutory student finance package:

- ✔ For EYTS routes, you can get a grant for your tuition fees, so you don't need to apply for a Tuition Fee Loan.

- ✔ For all PGCE routes (Primary, Secondary, EYTS, non-salaried School Direct and SCITT), you may qualify for an income-assessed Maintenance Loan which can be paid at a higher rate than usual because PGCE courses last longer than most undergraduate courses.

- ✔ Bursaries are available from the National College of Teaching and Leadership (NCTL). These are not income-assessed, but depend on which subject you study and the classification of your first degree (or another postgraduate qualification you already hold). More information is available at: getintoteaching. education.gov.uk/bursaries-and-funding.

- ✔ You need to get at least a 2:2 to qualify for a bursary, but this only applies to limited subjects. If you get a 2:1 or higher, you can expect to qualify for a bursary. The highest rate bursary is paid if you get a 1st.

- ✔ Scholarships are available if you study a PGCE Secondary course in Maths, Physics, Chemistry or Computing. (You need to apply direct to the professional body overseeing these subjects.)

- ✔ If you have recently left the armed forces, and you're already eligible to receive a bursary, you can apply for a 'Troops to Teachers' uplift to increase the amount of bursary available to you – ask your course provider for more details about applying.

- ✔ NCTL Bursaries are non-repayable and tax-free.

Wales

If you're ordinarily resident in Wales, you can apply for the following in addition to the standard statutory student finance package:

- ✔ For all PGCE routes, you may qualify for an income-assessed Maintenance Loan which can be paid at a higher rate than usual because PGCE courses last longer than most undergraduate courses.

- ✔ Bursaries are available from the Welsh government. These are not income-assessed, but depend on which subject you study and the classification of your first degree. More information is available at: teachertrainingcymru.org/node/16.

- ✔ You need to get at least a 2.2 to qualify for a bursary, but this only applies to limited subjects. If you get a 2:1 or higher, you can expect to qualify for a bursary. The highest rate bursary is paid if you get a 1st.

- ✔ Tuition Fee Grants are available alongside the Bursary scheme.

- ✔ If you speak Welsh, and you're studying a Secondary subject, you can apply for extra funding from the Welsh Medium Improvement Scheme.

- ✔ Welsh Government Bursaries are non-repayable and tax-free.

Northern Ireland

If you are ordinarily resident in Northern Ireland:

- ✔ You can access the equivalent NCTL bursaries available to English students if you study in England.

- ✔ PGCE courses in Northern Ireland attract the equivalent of the undergraduate student finance package.

Scotland

If you are ordinarily resident in Scotland:

- ✔ Tuition fee support is available as long as you haven't already received previous statutory support for postgraduate study.

✔ Support is available if you're studying a postgraduate teaching course for particular subjects, even if you've already studied at postgraduate level. For more information visit: `www.teachinscotland.org/getintoteaching/financialsupport/introduction.asp`.

✔ If you're a PGDE student, you can apply to SAAS for the equivalent of undergraduate student finance.

Eligibility for Funding

Wherever you study in the UK, you need to meet the required residency criteria before you qualify for financial support for a teacher training course.

The following criteria apply if you're studying an initial teacher training course and are a UK national:

✔ On the first day of your course, you must be ordinarily resident in the nation in which you are going to study in the UK. You must also have settled status in the UK. Note that for Scotland, the first day of the course is 1 August, but for all other countries in the UK it's 1 September.

✔ You must also have been ordinarily resident in the UK and Channel Islands or the Isle of Man for the full three-year period before your course begins.

Additional rules apply to EU nationals, and migrant workers who are nationals from within the European Economic Area. If you're in one of these groups, contact an adviser at your course provider in order to discuss your situation in full and find out what support may be available to you. EU nationals can qualify for the additional funding specific to teaching courses.

If you study an initial teacher training course and access specific funding for that course, you're expected to work in the UK upon completion of your studies.

Additional funding in England and Wales

Additional funding is available to postgraduate initial teacher training courses in England and Wales, provided that you do not already hold certain qualifications.

✔ You must not be on an employment-based training route such as Salaried School Direct or Assessment Only QTS or EYTS routes.

England

✔ You mustn't already hold Qualified Teacher Status (QTS) or Early Years Teaching Status (EYTS).

Wales

✔ You mustn't be on an employment-based training route such as the Graduate Training Programme.

Applying for Funding for Teaching Courses

If you're going to study an initial teacher training course, you can make an application for the statutory student finance online in the same way as undergraduate students apply (see Chapters 3 and 4 for more details). You should find courses of initial teacher education are listed when you select your course details for the application.

If you're applying for a postgraduate course, you still need to provide details of your previous study, but this won't count against you when it comes to funding, as an undergraduate qualification is required to begin a postgraduate course of teacher education.

You need to apply as if for the first time, so you need to provide proof of identity as well as residence just like you were required to when you applied for student finance for the very first time.

Always apply for student finance as early as you can (applications usually open in the January before your course starts) and if you do not hear anything after 6 to 8 weeks, check your online account for any correspondence. If necessary, make a phone call to the agency assessing your application to find out if there is a problem.

Your application for a bursary from NCTL in England, or the Welsh government, is made directly via your course provider – contact them for more details.

The bursaries available from NCTL and the Welsh government are paid in equal instalments on a monthly basis during your course of study. Your course provider can confirm the arrangements for you, as the funding bodies pay the money to them so they can pay it to you. You usually need to provide evidence of your student finance entitlement, your first degree classification (plus any postgraduate qualifications you may already hold) and your bank details as part of the application.

Chapter 9

Finding Funds for Social Work

• •

In This Chapter

▶ Looking for social work courses with funding

▶ Discovering eligibility criteria

▶ Getting in your application

• •

*T*he Social Work Bursary scheme was introduced as an incentive for students to train for a career in social work. Different schemes run in the four nations within the UK.

The national number of bursaries is determined on the basis of available funding, with a higher priority being given to postgraduates rather than undergraduates.

In this chapter, I provide information introducing the Social Work Bursary scheme, including eligibility requirements, how to apply and the type of financial support available.

Courses Attracting Social Work Funding

Your course needs to be approved by the relevant body for the nation in which you study. These are the Health and Care Professions Council (HCPC), the General Social Care Council (GSCC), the Scottish Social Services Council (SSSC), the Care Council for Wales or the Northern Ireland Social Care Council (NISCC).

In England, in order to qualify for a Social Work Bursary, you must not be studying a 'joint discipline' with another subject, such as nursing.

If you're studying a joint degree, you need to apply to the NHS Bursary Unit.

You won't be eligible for a Social Work Bursary if you study for an employment-based course, including direct Open University courses.

Undergraduate courses

In England, Wales and Northern Ireland, Social Work Bursaries are available. The number of available bursaries is limited and is set by the government each year.

England

If you're ordinarily resident in England:

- ✔ No bursary is payable for the first year of an undergraduate course – but you're able to apply for loans and grants from Student Finance England (SFE) instead, subject to the standard eligibility criteria.

- ✔ Social Work Bursaries don't count as NHS or Department of Health Bursaries; in the second and third year of the course, you may qualify for a bursary which is paid in addition to the support you receive from SFE.

- ✔ A non income-assessed Basic Grant (for living costs) is payable based on the location of your university. This grant is available if you don't qualify for the Social Work Bursary, and includes a fixed amount of Placement Travel Allowance (PTA). Part-time students are paid a pro rata amount of Basic Grant and PTA.

- ✔ The Bursary funding is paid in three equal instalments.

Northern Ireland

If you are ordinarily resident in Northern Ireland, the following funding support may be available:

✔ The Student Incentive Scheme is specific to the part-time and full-time undergraduate degree in social work.

✔ Grants are available each year of study.

✔ Additional amounts are available for work-based learning expenses.

Wales

If you are ordinarily resident in Wales, the following funding support may be available:

✔ A non income-assessed bursary per year (up to three years)

✔ Practice Learning Opportunity Allowance paid at a standard rate per practice learning opportunity day (covering costs such as travel costs which you may incur when you attend a work placement)

Scotland

In Scotland, no undergraduate Social Work Bursary is available, but you can apply for financial support from the Scottish Awards Administration Service (SAAS) for all years of your course.

Postgraduate courses

Availability of Social Work Bursaries is limited for postgraduate courses, and numbers are set by government each academic year. You may not get a bursary even if you have a place on the course.

England

If you are ordinarily resident in England, the following financial support may be available:

✔ A non income-assessed Basic Grant is payable based on the location of your university. This includes a fixed amount of Placement Travel Allowance (PTA). Part-time students are paid a pro rata amount of Basic Grant/PTA.

✔ An income-assessed Maintenance Grant.

✔ Income-assessed Adult Dependants' Allowance, Parent's Learning Allowance and Childcare Allowance (based on your dependants' income).

✔ Disabled Students' Allowance.

✔ A contribution towards tuition fees.

Northern Ireland

If you are ordinarily resident in Northern Ireland, there are no social work bursaries available for postgraduate study in Northern Ireland.

Scotland

If you are ordinarily resident in Scotland:

✔ A Maintenance Grant and contribution towards tuition fees is available.

✔ Part-time students can access a part-time fee grant.

Wales

If you are ordinarily resident in Wales, the following support may be available:

✔ A non income-assessed bursary per year (up to two years), which includes a contribution towards tuition fees.

✔ A Practice Learning Opportunity Allowance at a standard rate per practice learning opportunity day (covering costs such as travel costs which you may incur when you attend a work placement).

✔ You may also be able to apply for additional funding that is available to Masters Degree students in Wales.

Assessing Eligibility for Social Work Funding

The eligibility requirements for financial support for social work courses are similar to the requirements for the standard student financial support available from the Student Loans

Company (England and Wales), Student Awards Agency for Scotland and Student Finance Northern Ireland.

There are additional requirements which are there to ensure that your course provider allocates the bursaries to those students who are prioritised under the scheme. These are described in the next few sections of the chapter.

Residency criteria

Wherever you study in the UK, you'll find residency criteria which you need to meet before you can qualify for financial support for a social work course.

The following criteria apply if you are studying a social work course and you are a UK national:

- ✔ You must be ordinarily resident in the nation within the UK in which you intend to study on the first day of your course and have settled status in the UK. Note that for Scotland, the first day of the course is 1 August, but for all other countries in the UK it is 1 September.

- ✔ You must also have been ordinarily resident in the UK and Channel Islands or the Isle of Man for the full three-year period before your course begins.

Additional rules apply to EU nationals, and migrant workers who are nationals from within the European Economic Area.

If you're in one of these groups, contact an adviser at your course provider in order to discuss your situation in full and find out what support may be available to you.

Inclusion criteria

Each year, only a limited number of bursaries are made available, so there is no guarantee you will be awarded a bursary even if you have a place on a social work course. The general rule is that priority is given to allocations for postgraduate courses rather than undergraduate courses (although the Northern Ireland scheme is for undergraduates only).

You need to be included on your course provider's bursary selection list in order to be prioritised for either an undergraduate or postgraduate bursary. Your place in the list is based on a ranking during the admissions process.

If you're an undergraduate student, the ranking can be adjusted during year one of your course based on attendance and/or your performance in the 'readiness to practice' and year one exams.

Your course provider should consider other factors such as their obligations for widening participation under the Equalities Act 2010. A long-list of students is required so that bursaries left unclaimed or unallocated in the original selection process may be re-allocated to students on the long-list, in line with the prioritisation criteria.

Other criteria

You also need to satisfy additional criteria before accessing financial support for a social work course, once again dependent on your location.

England

The criteria for England are as follows:

- ✔ You must not hold a higher education qualification in social work; and

- ✔ You must not be receiving other funding for your social work education training (this requirement ignores funding through Student Finance England, and discretionary funds or bursaries from your course provider).

Northern Ireland

In Northern Ireland, the criteria are:

- ✔ You must be undertaking a Northern Ireland Social Care Council (NISCC) approved programme of study in Northern Ireland leading to the Degree in Social Work from September 2006 onwards; and

✔ You must be currently registered with NISCC on the relevant part of the Register; and

✔ You must not be employed as a Regional Social Work Degree Trainee.

Wales

In Wales, you must not be receiving a financial incentive to train from an employer.

Applying for Social Work Funding

You need to apply for funding as early as possible to maximise your chance of receiving a grant.

If you're a postgraduate student, make sure you register your interest in the bursary with the institution you want to join.

The government decides how many bursaries will be available in the months leading up to the start of the course, so getting updates from websites and institutions is advisable.

Sorting out how and when to apply

The method of applying for a bursary is dependent on where you are currently resident. The following sections provide information for each nation of the UK.

England

If you are ordinarily resident in England, you can check your eligibility at: www.nhsbsa.nhs.uk/Students/835.aspx. Additionally, application forms are available at: www.nhsbsa.nhs.uk/Students/986.aspx. You need to provide photographic ID confirming your residency – usually your passport.

There are strict deadlines for applying in England:

- ✔ Applications open on 1 May.
- ✔ If your course starts in the autumn, you must apply by 30 November.
- ✔ If your course starts in the winter, you must apply by 14 February.

Scotland

If you are ordinarily resident in Scotland, apply to SAAS for financial support for undergraduate courses. Also, contact the Scottish Social Services Council for more information about funding available for postgraduate study at `bursaries@sssc.uk.com`.

Wales

If you are ordinarily resident in Wales, information is available at `www.ccwales.org.uk/student-funding`. Bursaries are allocated to each course to ensure a fair distribution, and if you are a nominated student, you should receive an application form and guidance booklet from June onwards.

You need to complete your application electronically and return it by email; the deadline for applications is 1 September. You should hear whether your application has been successful within 6 weeks of applying.

Northern Ireland

If you are ordinarily resident in Northern Ireland and studying an undergraduate social work course, you can apply for the Student Incentive Scheme. Information is available at: `http://www.nidirect.gov.uk/student_incentive_scheme_leaflet.pdf`.

Your course provider will send you the application form along with the enrolment information for your course. Once you have completed the form, it needs to be sent to the Office of Social Services (an addressed envelope is provided with the form). The first of your two annual instalments will usually be paid to you during November.

Chapter 10

Financing Studies After Your First Qualification

Student finance is generally only available in order for you to obtain your first degree. You may initially study a lower level qualification, such as a Higher National Diploma or a foundation degree – in which case you may later decide to study at a higher level and obtain an Honours degree.

Any course you've studied in higher education can be counted as 'previous study' when you come back to study another course, even at a higher level. How your previous study is treated can be quite complex, as you may find your available funding reduced. In some cases, however, your previous study may not be counted at all.

In this chapter, I provide information about how previous study can affect your funding for a new course, and what level of entitlement to student finance may remain as a result.

Financing a Second Degree

You may find yourself considering study for a second undergraduate course. This could be for a variety of reasons, but a common one in recent years, in light of the downturn in the economy, has been as a result of the need to retrain for a new career.

The student finance system does not make a priority of you if you're in this situation, except in some professions which are seen to be of necessity to the UK economy (such as NHS careers, teaching and architecture). Therefore, incentives do exist for some professions, whereas rules are relaxed a little for others.

Understanding the basics

Student finance is generally available to you if you're an eligible student (satisfying the ordinary residence and course criteria) and you're studying for your first degree. This usually gives you access to student finance for the duration of your course, plus one year of additional study.

In effect, the government intends you to have funding available in order to study (and complete) an undergraduate first degree. The 'plus one year' is included as a safety net, in recognition that sometimes students transfer to another subject, or may need to retake a year because of re-sits.

If you've already studied in higher education and you've obtained an equivalent or higher level qualification to the one which you propose to study, this can lead to future funding being reduced. This is the case even if you've not accessed any funding previously in the UK, for example, by studying for a degree overseas. Any year, or part of a year, that you were registered on a previous course can have the effect of reducing the number of years' full support available for your new course.

The number of years of previous study you undertook on a previous course and whether you obtained a qualification can have an effect on the way any future entitlement is worked out. Whether your previous course was full or part-time can also be an important factor in determining future entitlement.

Any years where you're required to 'self-fund' mean you don't receive a Tuition Fee Loan for that year. If you're studying for a higher-level qualification than one you already hold, you may still be able to apply for a Maintenance Loan, even if you cannot access a Tuition Fee Loan, and you can still receive any targeted support applicable to your circumstances (dependants' allowances and the Disabled Students' Allowance). See Chapter 5 for more on these loans.

Being aware of exemptions

If you wish to return to study after doing a first degree, obtaining financial support is easier for some courses leading to professions which are prioritised by the government.

Postgraduate initial teacher training courses (full-time or part-time) are an example where previous study is ignored for a further course of study. You're able to obtain a full package of support equivalent to that which is available to full-time or part-time undergraduate students. This means you can get tuition fee, living cost and targeted support (for dependants and/or disability) as a full-time student, and tuition fee support only as a part-time student. In addition, extensive incentives are available to you in the form of Teaching Bursaries (some as high as £25,000) if you choose to study (either full-time or part-time) for a PGCE qualification in England or Wales. By making this funding available, the government hopes to encourage you to consider a career in teaching (where there are significant shortfalls in recruitment at present).

If you're a graduate entry medical or dental student, student finance is available on the following basis. You will need to fund the first £3,465 of tuition fees yourself in your first year of study. As long as you satisfy the usual eligibility requirements (covered in Chapter 3) you can access a Tuition Fee Loan of up to £5,535 for the remaining fees. You can also apply for a Maintenance Loan in your first year of study (but not a Maintenance Grant).

After you are in your second year of study, you can access the NHS Bursary scheme for funding that can cover the first £3,465 of your tuition fees, in addition to the Tuition Fee Loan available to cover your remaining tuition fees. From your second year onwards, you can apply for the reduced rate non income-assessed Maintenance Loan usually available to undergraduate NHS students.

In addition to postgraduate teaching, exemptions apply to full-time courses in medicine, dentistry, veterinary science, architecture, social work and undergraduate initial teacher training. In Scotland, similar exemptions apply to Allied Health Profession, Divinity and Theology programmes (you should check for additional criteria with your course provider).

These exemptions open up the opportunity for partial further student financial support. If you're studying a full-time second degree in one of these subjects, you're able to access a Maintenance Loan despite you already holding a first degree (or higher level) qualification. Further Tuition Fee Loan support isn't available to you (but you're still able to access any targeted support applicable to your circumstances).

In addition to the exemptions applicable to full-time study, the government has also introduced exemptions for part-time Honours degree courses in STEM subjects (Science, Technology, Engineering and Maths) in England. Subject to the usual eligibility requirements, you can obtain further Tuition Fee Loan funding (and a Disabled Student's Allowance, if applicable) for part-time study in these specific subjects in England. Your part-time course must be an Honours degree and satisfy the subject and designation requirements. You must also be studying at least 25 per cent of the intensity of a full-time equivalent course in each year of study.

Returning to Study For an Honours Degree

If you had to leave your original Honours degree course, or you obtained a lower-level qualification (such as a Certificate of Higher Education, Diploma of Higher Education, Higher National Certificate, Higher National Diploma or a foundation degree) then you may be eligible to receive further funding to obtain an Honours degree qualification.

However, any further funding that may be available to you is reduced according to how many years of study you've undertaken on your previous course, or courses. As a consequence, you may have to make careful decisions about the kind of course you study, especially in terms of the number of years of study required to complete it.

Returning to a Non-Completed Course

If you left a course without completing it, a number of factors need to be considered if re-applying or taking on a new course.

Restarting your course

If you left your original course of study without a qualification, any years or part years you were registered on that course usually count as full years of previous study. For student finance purposes, one day's registration on a course can count as a whole year in terms of previous study.

If you previously studied on a part-time course and now wish to study a full-time course (or vice versa) and you left the original course without obtaining a qualification, the years of previous study don't count and you can obtain full funding for your new course. This only applies if you switch from part-time to full-time, or vice versa.

If you're a full-time student and you leave your course part way through the year, you can incur an overpayment of student finance for any period you're not in attendance. This usually leads to the immediate recovery of any grants you receive. Any overpayment of student loan is recoverable in a lump sum from your student finance entitlement if you return to study in a future academic year.

If you've not notified your course provider and the student finance agency you apply to of your decision to leave your course, you may even be asked to repay the full amount of loan overpayment with immediate effect.

Full-time students

If you studied full-time on your original course and wish to return full-time, upon your return to your original course (or when you start another course) your entitlement to student finance will be calculated.

The following formula is used:

$$(OD+1) - PC$$

Where:

- ✔ OD = Ordinary duration of your new course
- ✔ PC = All years of study on your previous higher education course

If you had spent two years on your original course, and you now wish to start a three-year Honours degree from year 1, your entitlement would be:

$$(OD(3)+1) - PC(2) = (3+1) - 2 = 2$$

You would have two years' funding for your new course. The student finance regulations require that the first year of funding is applied to the final year of your course, the second to the penultimate year of study and so on. In this example, you would need to 'self-fund' year one of your new course because the two years of funding would be assigned to the second and third years of the course.

The term *self-fund* only refers to tuition fee funding – you would still be eligible to receive a Maintenance Loan during the first year of the new course – as long as the qualification you're seeking is at a higher level than one you already hold. Any targeted support (Dependants' Grants and Disabled Students' Allowance) applicable to you would also be available in your first year.

Part-time students

If you studied part-time on your original course and wish to return part-time, upon your return to your original course (or when you start another course) your entitlement to student finance is calculated as described in this section.

If you're a part-time student on a course which started on or after 1st September 2012, you have funding available for up to four times the period ordinarily required to complete the full-time equivalent course. For a three-year full-time course, this would give you up to 12 years' part-time funding.

How much funding you require depends on the intensity of your study. For a three-year full-time equivalent course, the following fully funded study patterns are possible:

- ✔ 25% intensity = 12 years
- ✔ 50% intensity = 6 years
- ✔ 60% intensity = 5 years

If you've studied part-time on a previous course, those years of funding are taken into account. If your future study pattern allows you to complete within the maximum allowable period (after your study intensity is taken into account) then you can still access the Tuition Fee Loan.

The amount of time in which you expect to complete the course is assessed every time you make an application for a Tuition Fee Loan for your course.

Compelling personal reasons

If you were a full-time student and an unexpected situation led you to leave, or interrupted your course, you can make a case for compelling personal reasons. This could be due to illness or a caring responsibility – but is not necessarily limited to these situations. You usually need to write a letter describing your situation in detail, and provide documentary evidence of the circumstances (usually from an independent source).

If your compelling personal reasons are upheld, any funding you received during the year when the circumstances arose is ignored when calculating your entitlement to future funding.

 Applying for compelling personal reasons can be a key strategy to use if your studies are affected by circumstances beyond your control, as doing so can help safeguard your remaining entitlement to student finance so you can complete your studies.

Improving Your Qualification

You may decide to get a better qualification from the one you already hold. If you do, then you need to consider what sources of funding are available to you.

Looking at ways of funding your 'top-up' course

The way your previous study is counted varies in the four nations of the UK where you obtain a qualification such as a Certificate of Higher Education, a Diploma of Higher Education, a Higher National Certificate, Higher National Diploma or a foundation degree.

England

If you studied full-time or part-time and gained a lower level qualification on a higher education course, then you're usually able to access funding to 'top-up' your qualification to a higher level.

Your previous study is taken into account to find out how many additional years of student finance are available to you. Where you've previously obtained a qualification, all years of study on that course and any other full-time higher education courses you may have studied are all taken into consideration.

If you've a lower-level qualification, the following formula is used:

$$(D + X) - PrC$$

Where:

- ✔ D = the greater of 3 and the number of academic years that make up the ordinary duration of the course.

- ✔ X = 1 where the ordinary duration of the course was less than three years, and where the ordinary duration of the preliminary course (or preliminary courses in total) was three years or more, the ordinary duration minus 1.

- ✔ PrC = the actual number of years you've studied on previous courses (not counting any repeat years of study for compelling personal reasons).

If you had spent two years studying a foundation degree, and wish to 'top-up' to an honours degree after gaining the qualification, the calculation would look like this:

$$\big((D=3)+(X=1)\big)-(PrC=2)=(3+1)-2=2$$

This would give you enough funding to complete the ordinary duration of your course, and have a year to fall back on should you need it.

If you wish to progress from a lower level qualification to a higher level qualification that is not an Honours degree, the alternative formula of (OD+1) – PC is used (as described earlier in this chapter).

Northern Ireland

If you're studying to top-up a lower level qualification, you aren't eligible for a Tuition Fee Loan or any income-assessed grants if you enter the first year of a degree course. Entry to any other year is usually fully funded.

If you studied a part-time Level 4, Level 5, Higher National Certificate, Higher National Diploma or foundation degree, you're eligible for full support from year one of a full-time first degree.

Scotland

If you obtain a lower level qualification, you're then able to progress to year two, or higher, of a degree course. If you join the degree in the first year, you don't receive any funding for that year.

Wales

In Wales, the standard previous study rule applies where you've a lower level qualification. Your future entitlement would be determined using the $(OD+1)$ – PC formula.

Going from an ordinary degree to an Honours degree

If your studies to date have resulted in you achieving an ordinary degree, you can usually access further funding to top-up your ordinary degree to Honours degree level.

England

When calculating your entitlement to funding for a year in which you top up to Honours, the $(OD+1)-PC$ formula is used. However, the ordinary duration of the 'top-up' year should be treated as being three years in order to allow you the chance to top up to an Honours degree qualification.

Northern Ireland

When calculating your entitlement to funding for a year in which you top up to Honours, the $(OD+1)-PC$ formula is used. If you hold an ordinary degree, you can usually receive further funding to top-up to Honours degree level.

Scotland

You may be eligible to apply for full support for a year in which you top up to Honours, providing that:

- ✔ You study an Honours year in the same subject as the one you studied for your ordinary degree (you can choose to study at a different university to the one where you studied your ordinary degree); and

- ✔ You've not already received funding for a topping up to Honours year.

You're not required to do the Honours year immediately after the year you graduate with an ordinary degree – you can have a break in study if you wish.

Wales

When calculating your entitlement to funding for a year in which you top up to Honours, the $(OD+1)-PC$ formula is used.

Financing Postgraduate Courses

If you wish to study a postgraduate course, it's largely your responsibility to gather together the funds you need to cover the cost of your tuition fees and to support your living cost expenses.

At the time of writing, if you're a full-time or part-time postgraduate student, no formal statutory student finance scheme exists for postgraduate courses in England, Wales or Northern

Ireland, with the exception of subject-specific support for postgraduate courses in initial teacher training, social work and medicine or dentistry.

In Scotland, some statutory support is available from the Student Awards Agency for Scotland. You can obtain a Tuition Fee Loan for vocational courses (usually at postgraduate diploma level), and there are also limited opportunities to get funding to study a course anywhere in the UK, as long as a similar course does not run in Scotland. More information is available at: www.saas.gov.uk/full_time/pg/eligibility.htm. No statutory support is available for taught Masters or research degrees.

The lack of a formal statutory student finance scheme has meant that postgraduate students often explore part-time modes of study, so that they're able to work to support themselves whilst studying. As a part-time student, you're able to claim welfare benefits (although you may be required to undertake to actively seek work in order to do so).

Professional and Career Development Loans

In terms of a national scheme, the closest thing at present is the Professional and Career Development Loan (PCDL) which is covered in detail in Chapter 13. The PCDL can be a very useful method of funding postgraduate study, as it can be used to pay for both your tuition fees and your living costs – the amount you can apply for ranges from £300 to £10,000, so it can be an extremely effective source of funding if it's available to you.

Some basic criteria need to be met in order to be able to apply for a PCDL:

- ✔ You need to be aged 18 or over.

- ✔ You need to have been ordinarily resident in the UK for the three-year period before the start of your course.

- ✔ You must have settled status in the UK (no restriction on your residency in the UK).

- ✔ You must not have funds already available to you which could be used to pay for your studies.

✔ You must confirm that you're planning to work in the UK, the European Union or the European Economic Area upon completion of the course.

In addition to your personal eligibility, the course you're studying must also qualify under the PCDL scheme:

✔ Your course must ordinarily last up to 2 years (or 3 years if it includes 1 year of work experience).

✔ Your course must be either a part-time or full-time vocational course.

Other funding for postgraduate study

Whether or not you're able to obtain a PCDL, you may find it useful to explore whether there are any educational trusts or charities which may be able to help you. You normally need to show that you've made provision for the bulk of the costs associated with your course, but some of these sources may be able to help you with relatively small amounts of funds (awards are typically worth a few hundred pounds).

Many universities have discretionary funds available which are open to applications from postgraduate students as well as undergraduates.

As is the case with educational trusts and charities, university discretionary funds usually require you to make arrangements for the bulk of your financial requirements.

The standard system of assessing postgraduate applications for discretionary funds (as set out in the Access to Learning Fund guidance published by the National Association of Student Money Advisers, in association with the National Union of Students) requires that a National Postgraduate Income (NPI) figure is used in order that costs are met. The NPI figure is used regardless of what your actual income is – you usually only receive assistance for any shortfall in your income when compared to your expenditure after this figure, and any other additional income such as your partner's income is taken into account.

You should also check with your course provider to see if they offer any scholarship or bursary schemes for the course you're interested in. These can be limited in number, and may only apply to specific subject disciplines, but you should enquire to find out what is available. This is especially true at the level of postgraduate research degrees, where universities can offer non-repayable stipends to support students engaging in research.

> ✔ Your course provider must be registered with the PCDL scheme on the scheme's Register.
>
> ✔ You must not be eligible to receive any other form of statutory student finance for your course.

The vocational requirement of the PCDL scheme means it can be restrictive for some postgraduate courses which do not include vocational elements leading directly to a specific career.

Postgraduate loans

At the time of writing, the government is consulting the higher education sector on a scheme to introduce postgraduate loans in England.

In 2014, the government announced a new loan system for postgraduate taught Master's students, which should be in place from September 2016. The scheme is aimed at students aged under 30 studying a postgraduate taught Master's course in any subject. This loan is an income-contingent loan (similar to the Tuition Fee and Maintenance Loans available to under-graduates) of up to £10,000.

The loans are intended to be used for both tuition fee and maintenance purposes, but the final detail of how the scheme will work in practice has yet to be decided.

In addition to the proposed loans available for Master's study, in 2015 the government announced its intention to introduce a further package of support for students engaging in post-graduate research. This includes an intention to introduce income-contingent loans of up to £25,000 for students study-ing a postgraduate research degree. One loan would be made available for the duration of the course (which usually lasts for up to four years).

Research Councils

If you're studying a postgraduate research or Master's course, you may be able to obtain a studentship from a UK Research Council.

Studentships are limited in number each year and are mostly aimed at postgraduate research programmes. The process of applying for Research Council funding is competitive and so you need to make a high level of preparation for it to be successful. You should also be aware of the timeframes and deadlines because the process can be very lengthy. For example, application to the Arts and Humanities Research Council can take up to 30 weeks to be completed.

Each of the Research Councils has a dedicated website for its own subject area:

- ✔ Arts and Humanities Research Council (AHRC): www.ahrc.ac.uk/

- ✔ Biotechnology and Biological Sciences Research Council (BBSRC): www.bbsrc.ac.uk

- ✔ Economic and Social Research Council (ESRC): www.esrc.ac.uk

- ✔ Engineering and Physical Sciences Research Council (EPSRC): www.epsrc.ac.uk

- ✔ Medical Research Council (MRC): www.mrc.ac.uk

- ✔ Natural Environment Research Council (NERC): www.nerc.ac.uk

- ✔ Science and Technology Facilities Council (STFC): www.stfc.ac.uk

Each of the Research Council websites contains full information about how to apply for funding, together with details of deadlines and application processing times.

You can find out which courses attract a studentship by visiting the Research Councils UK website: http://www.rcuk.ac.uk/funding/

If you've the opportunity to apply for a studentship, you need to do this through your course provider, rather than direct to the Research Council. If you're successful in making an application for a studentship, any support you receive is non-repayable, and additional allowances are available for dependants in your household, and if you've a disability.

Part IV

Finding Financing from Other (Non-Statutory) Sources

Top 5 Ways to Supplement Your Student Finance

- ✔ Check whether your course provider can assist you financially.

- ✔ Research whether your circumstances allow you to tap into additional financial support.

- ✔ Identify whether alternative sources of income may be available to you.

- ✔ Get to know how additional sources of income can be accessed, and how they are paid to you.

- ✔ Structure your strategy to additional financial sources so that you maximise your income and reduce the chances of missing out on available funds.

Accessing non-statutory financial support can give your financial situation a real lift. Access tips to realising those additional pounds and pence at www.dummies.com/extras/studentfinanceuk.

In this part . . .

- ✔ Explore the range of additional financial support available through your course provider.

- ✔ Find out where to access information about additional financial support.

- ✔ Get to know the basics of which students can access welfare benefits during their studies.

- ✔ Gain an understanding that additional financial support is also made available as a mixture of grants and loans.

Chapter 11

Finance From Universities

• •

In This Chapter

▶ Considering the types of funding available

▶ Figuring out how to apply

▶ Understanding typical eligibility criteria

• •

*I*n addition to any statutory student finance available to support you in your studies, your course provider should have information on additional sources of funding available which you may be able to make use of.

Bursaries, scholarships and discretionary funds are widely available at course providers throughout the UK, so check which additional sources of financial support may be available to you.

In this chapter, I give an overview of the typical characteristics of the various kinds of financial support most commonly available, and how to access them.

Finding a Bursary

Bursaries are now a well-established part of the student finance landscape. They're usually provided as a means of targeting additional financial assistance at specific groups, such as students from low-income backgrounds. Bursaries exist in a variety of forms, and you need to check what is on offer at each of the course providers you're thinking of studying at.

This section concentrates on bursaries available from course providers, and does not cover other forms of bursary which relate to specific subjects, including NHS Bursaries, General Social Care Council Bursaries and National College of Teaching and Leadership Teaching Bursaries. These forms of bursary are covered elsewhere in this book in Chapters 7, 8 and 9.

Whereas scholarships may take the form of fee waivers, this is less likely to be the case with a bursary. A *bursary* usually takes the form of a payment that assists with your living costs. It could be a direct payment to your bank account, or take the form of a payment for accommodation or a voucher scheme that can be used as payment for campus facilities.

If you have the choice, a 'cash' option is usually the best to take because this is the most flexible for you. You can then decide how the money is best spent according to your needs.

Amounts available through bursary schemes vary between course providers, so you need to check for details. Where a tuition fee exceeding £6,000 per year is charged, an Access Agreement is required which should include financial support for students from low-income backgrounds. Many bursary schemes are detailed within Access Agreements, and these can be found (and compared) at the Office for Fair Access (OFFA) website: www.offa.org.uk.

Looking at your eligibility

By far the most common criterion used to determine bursary eligibility is your level of household income. Many course providers use similar income thresholds to those which feature in the statutory student finance system.

Here's an example of how bursaries work: students with household incomes of £25,000 or less may qualify for a higher rate of bursary than those with incomes between £25,000 and £42,620. A scheme like this would provide support to all students receiving a Maintenance Grant, which is payable on incomes up to £42,620.

In addition, you may find that your ordinary place of residence outside term-time could restrict whether you qualify for a bursary – the bursaries available through OFFA Access Agreements are specific to students from England (although your course provider may have a scheme which extends support to other nations in the UK).

When you apply for your student finance online, look out for the check box asking if you would like to share your information with your course provider so that they can check out your bursary entitlement. The check box should default to allowing information to be shared – doing so means the Student Loans Company shares the information needed to work out whether you're entitled to a bursary. Check your course provider's website to find out if there is anything else you need to do to apply.

Additional amounts of bursary may be available depending on your circumstances. All bursary schemes differ, but check to see if you qualify for a higher rate if:

- ✔ You have children
- ✔ You live in an area with a low participation in higher education
- ✔ You're a student from care (care leaver)
- ✔ You're disabled

Understanding how bursaries are paid

Bursaries tend to be paid as cash payments, but can take the form of direct payments to your rent account for halls of residence, or may be paid as a voucher scheme for on-campus services and facilities.

Whichever form of payment you receive, the bursary is often paid in instalments. This is because your course provider usually uses instalments of tuition fees to fund the payments. As the fees are paid to course providers (by the Student Loans Company) in three instalments during the year, you may find the bursary payments follow a similar pattern.

If you're required to apply for a bursary via your course provider, they ask you to include your bank account details so that they can make payment direct to you.

Bursaries and the Student Loans Company

If your course provider uses the HEBSS system provided by the Student Loans Company, you should find the payments are made direct to the same bank account where you receive your student finance payments.

As tuition fee payments tend to dictate the cash flow for bursary payments, you may find that your bursary payments reflect the proportion of fees paid by the Student Loans Company during an academic year.

The structure of fee payments is as follows:

Autumn term	25%
Spring term	25%
Summer term	50%

You may find your bursary payments follow a similar pattern to the above, meaning the bulk of your bursary is paid towards the end of the year. You may need to factor this into your budgeting plan for the year.

Check the information your course provider publishes about its bursary scheme to find out when payments are made and how much each instalment is worth – this helps you with your budgeting over the year.

Finding Out More About University Finance

Make sure that you check your course provider's website for information on the full range of financial support it provides. Look out for different forms of funding – you may be able to make more than one application to a number of different funding routes.

If, having read the information, you're left in any doubt, call in to the student services department and ask a member of staff to see if there is any additional funding you have missed – they can ensure that you get all the information about the available funding.

Studying Scholarships

A *scholarship* is usually defined as financial support which is dependent on academic success. A notable exception to this was a recent government scheme called the National Scholarship Programme (it wasn't national and wasn't a scholarship by the usual definition) but this was abolished in 2014, so is no longer a concern. However, the scheme does indicate that terms are not always universally applied, so you may just want to check what the qualifying conditions are for any scholarships offered by your course provider.

Scholarship amounts are likely to vary depending on course provider, and an individual scheme may have a flat rate available or a number of rates based on levels of academic achievement.

Understanding the deadlines

Deadlines are highly variable between course providers, just as the schemes are themselves. You need to make sure that you look at information available online for dates, or enquire at your advice service.

Be sure to use Open Days, or just make a telephone enquiry to find out details of what scholarships your course provider has on offer – that way you can make sure that you don't miss out if you're eligible to receive one. Ask about the closing dates for applications.

Take care to find out whether there are any additional scholarships available provided by external organisations. These are usually aimed at supporting study in specific subject areas, so check if any such funding is available for your course. Your course provider usually publicises such scholarships on its website. Deadlines for these kinds of scholarships can be more demanding – you may need to make an application in advance of the start of your course, and funds may be limited, so be sure to make enquiries as early as you can.

Looking at your eligibility

Qualifying conditions for scholarships can vary in a number of ways, so check the details of the schemes where you're studying. Available scholarships may depend on your entry grades (usually A levels) or may be according to your performance on your course (for example, at the end of your first year).

Some scholarships may be available for some subjects or qualifications and not others – this depends on the strategic priorities of your course provider, so you need to check on its website.

You may be required to provide a written statement describing why your circumstances are particularly deserving of a scholarship, or you could be invited to an interview to give you the opportunity to talk through your achievements and suitability for a scholarship. A panel may consider the information presented to determine which applications have been successful.

Your course provider's website usually gives details of the application process.

Finding out how scholarships are paid

Scholarships can vary in terms of the financial support they provide. The amount you can get depends on the individual scholarship you apply for. The way the amount is paid to you also varies from scheme to scheme. Some may provide you with direct financial support which you can use to assist with your general living costs, others may be available in the form of a fee waiver, reducing the amount of fees you need to pay in order to study your course.

Some scholarships are paid directly by the course provider to you – these tend to be schemes that the university or college has direct control over. Alternatively, your course provider may use the Higher Education Bursary and Scholarships Scheme (HEBSS) from the Student Loans Company (SLC) to administer your payment. This money can be used for fee waivers or direct payments to you. Where a payment is made to you, HEBSS can facilitate this because the Student Loans Company usually already holds your bank details for the core statutory student finance they pay to you (your course provider pays the money to the SLC so that they can then pay you).

If you have applied for a scholarship that is run by an organisation that is independent of your course provider, you may be required to provide your account details to them so they can pay you (although they may issue a cheque).

Delving into Discretionary Hardship Funds

Discretionary Hardship Funds is the generic term given to pots of money aimed at helping students to remain engaged with their studies. No course provider wants to lose the students it has recruited due to purely financial reasons, so it's very common to see funds set aside to assist with difficulties caused by unexpected costs, or other circumstances which mean finances become strained.

The assistance from these funds is unlikely to be an 'entitlement' – your student services team usually make an assessment based on the circumstances you describe, and any financial assistance they give may be a contribution towards your situation, rather than one that resolves it outright. Usually they use their discretion to offer meaningful assistance to target the priority costs you are facing.

Access to Learning Funds

In recent years the government provided a ring-fenced budget to higher education providers in England so that they can deliver a national discretionary fund scheme, the Access to Learning Fund (other schemes exist in the other nations of the UK, such as the Financial Contingency Fund in Wales). This fund allowed course providers to ensure additional financial assistance was available to students facing unexpected hardship, or those who were in priority groups, for example, student parents, students from care, final year students or students with other caring responsibilities.

As part of the government's recent 'austerity' agenda, the Access to Learning Fund (ALF) budget was cut, and replaced with a 'recommendation' that some of the grant funding that is still paid to course providers be used for the purposes of making discretionary funds available to students in hardship.

At the time of writing in 2015, the future of other, similar funds in the other nations of the UK remains uncertain – but all are similar in nature to the 'discretionary funds' described in this chapter.

These developments mean there is now a devolved approach to the delivery of discretionary funds in England, and each course provider can determine the extent of support it provides to its students. Some have retained the description 'Access to Learning Fund' or something similar; others may have new names for their discretionary funds, but they're likely to be similar in nature.

The National Association of Student Money Advisers (NASMA) has taken steps to preserve and develop the guidance which formerly governed the ALF across all course providers. Although still regarded as a 'best practice' approach to delivery of discretionary funds, this recommendation is only guidance, and course providers do not have to follow it. They can also adapt it to support their own strategic priorities.

If you find yourself facing unexpected costs, perhaps as the result of an accident or a theft, make sure you check for the availability of discretionary funds – they may help you. Similarly, if your situation is 'non-traditional' ('traditional' students are defined as those whose family has a history of engagement with higher education, who are single and have started their course at the age of 18 straight from college) you may also be able to access additional financial support from a discretionary fund.

Discovering how discretionary funding works

Discretionary funds usually offer two different kinds of support – emergency short-term loans and non-repayable 'awards' (or *grants*).

Short-term loans

Emergency short-term loans usually provide assistance to students when their statutory student finance is delayed or hasn't been paid for some other reason. These loans can even help you if you're unable to obtain funding because you should have made a repayment on a loan you had for a previous course, but didn't do so. The short-term loan can sometimes be made available to help you settle your debt to the Student Loans Company so that funding for your new course can be released for payment.

More typically, if your student finance is delayed, short-term loans are made available as a means of ensuring you have some money available for essentials such as food and laundry until your funding gets paid to you. Upon receipt of your first instalment of student finance, you are usually expected to repay the loan to the discretionary fund. This means the short-term loan is not actually extra money – just a means of giving you access to some of your student finance before it's actually paid to you.

Short-term loans are typically a couple of hundred pounds in value, although they may be higher if you have children. They're not usually sufficient to deal with large items of expenditure like rent, so you may need to talk to your landlord about negotiating a delay in paying your rent until your student finance arrives (this is quite a common situation and most student landlords are patient in these circumstances).

Discretionary awards

Under the recommendations of the ALF guidance, once you have received the first instalment of your student finance, you can make an application for non-repayable financial support from your course provider's discretionary fund. This is either an online process or a more traditional paper form, usually with associated guidance to help you make an effective application (although there is also usually help on hand from the advisers at your course provider's advice service).

Discretionary awards are usually more likely to be made to 'priority groups' such as:

- ✔ Students from care, or living in a Foyer housing scheme
- ✔ Student parents
- ✔ Students who are carers
- ✔ Disabled students
- ✔ Final year students
- ✔ Students with pre-existing debts

Priority circumstances are more likely to result in a successful application where you can show they have arisen unexpectedly. Instances of theft or fire are classic examples, but if you've additional costs arising out of your 'priority' circumstances (such as child-related costs) then these can make an award more likely.

If you have any kind of priority debt (rent, council tax arrears, fuel debts) then you should definitely explore the possibility of financial assistance from a discretionary fund, even if you do not fit into one of the priority groups.

The team which oversees the discretionary fund is likely to be looking at all available opportunities to apply discretion in your favour so that they can offer some form of assistance.

Don't wait until your course begins to find out more about the discretionary funds your course provider has available – make enquiries as early as you can, even if you're still only applying for a place on the course. Then you can make sure that you're aware of the additional sources of support available and get all the details of how and when to apply.

Making an application

The usual process for making an application to a discretionary fund relies on you having received the first instalment of your student finance, but there are some exceptions to this rule (any rule worth its salt has an exception!).

You may be able to make an application to a discretionary fund at any time if:

✔ You're applying for a short-term loan

✔ You have a debt to the Student Loans Company meaning your student finance payments are blocked (you can apply for a short-term loan)

✔ You require funding to meet the cost of a diagnostic test so you can then apply for a Disabled Student's Allowance

✔ You require help with the £200 contribution for IT equipment recommended as part of your Disabled Student's Allowance

The final two types of application shown in the preceding list may even be made in advance of the start of your course. They may be income-assessed, or may require you to make some contribution to the costs as well – check with your course provider.

All applications are likely to require you to provide personal information about yourself, so course providers are required to make reference to data protection protocols to safeguard the information you provide.

You usually find that the discretionary fund is made available via a confidential service – all of which should help to reassure you that the information you provide is secure. Providing this personal information is crucial because, generally speaking, your application is far more likely to be successful the more information you provide.

There are usually some minimal information requirements to support your application for financial assistance:

✔ A fully completed application form

✔ Copies of your student finance notification for the relevant academic year

✔ Your most recent 3 months' bank statements for all accounts held by you (and your partner if you have one)

✔ Documentation which confirms your regular priority expenditure (for example, a rent agreement, utility bills)

Whilst these items of information may be required, if you have any further information and/or evidence you feel is relevant to your application, you should include this as well – providing more information gives the person assessing your application more opportunity to explore the discretion that they have available to them.

Sometimes submitting electronic copies of evidence, or photocopies, may be possible – check with the service responsible for overseeing the fund to find out what they can accept. If you do have to provide original copies of important documents (the birth certificates of your children, for example), you can usually ask for a copy to be made and retained so that you can keep the original after it has been seen.

Make sure that you check your application is complete when you submit it. As well as checking it yourself, you can ask a member of staff to check it. That way, if there is anything else required, you can obtain it quickly. You may find that your application isn't looked at for several days (or even weeks) and you may then be advised that more information is required before a decision can be reached.

Usual processing times differ between course providers. Most use the national recommended processing period of up to 20 working days, but some with larger dedicated teams have much quicker turnaround times. The time of year you apply may also determine how quickly your application is dealt with.

The budgets allocated to discretionary funds can be limited, so you should make an application as early in the academic year as you can to ensure that you get the support you require.

Looking at how discretionary funding is paid

Discretionary awards are usually paid to you directly either in instalments or as a lump sum. This award may be in the form of a cheque, but electronic payments made direct to your account are increasingly common, as this is usually more efficient.

Students who have an eligibility to receive welfare benefits (usually lone parents, student couples with children or some disabled students) usually receive a lump sum payment – the benefit rules allow lump sum payments like those from discretionary funds to be disregarded for 52 weeks.

You may also find instances where there is a recommendation that the money be paid to a third party on your behalf – typically where there is a debt of a priority nature which needs attention (such as rent). Agreeing with such a recommendation is usually in your best interest because it's a convenient means of settling such a matter – but the decision on how the money which has been awarded to you is paid is usually your choice.

If you have applied for a short-term loan from the discretionary fund, and this has not been repaid by the time you make a successful application for a discretionary award, you usually find that the short-term loan is recovered from the award of financial assistance made to you.

Finding out more

Discretionary funds are usually offered by your course provider, so you should normally contact your students' services team rather than the Student Union for information about how to apply (although your Student Union welfare team may be able to assist you in making an effective application).

 The last published version of the Access to Learning Fund guidance chapters is available at www.practitioners. slc.co.uk in the policy pages of the website. These have since been revised by the National Association of Student Money Advisers (NASMA) in association with the National Union of Students (NUS) – and your course provider may have published its own adapted guidance since the budget was devolved to individual institutions – check your university or college website for details.

Chapter 12

Trying Out Educational Trusts and Charities

In This Chapter

▶ Investigating educational trusts and charities

▶ Finding out how to apply

▶ Discovering where to find out more

*Y*our statutory student finance is likely to be your main source of income during your studies, but you should also take time to explore what additional funds might be available to support you in your studies. Doing some fairly straightforward research could unlock the door to funding opportunities you would otherwise miss out on.

Educational trusts and charities are highly diverse categories of financial assistance – they are so varied in terms of their scope, funds available and eligibility criteria that it's only possible to give a broad overview here.

This chapter provides some typical characteristics of trusts and charities to give a flavour of how to access them, what factors they consider and the type of support they provide.

Knowing the Basics of Trusts and Charities

Educational trusts and charities are probably the most diverse type of student finance available in the UK. Thousands of small pots of money are distributed throughout the UK, all aimed at helping students to engage in, or to complete, their studies. The funding on offer from these sources is almost always a non-repayable grant.

The type of trusts and charities this chapter focuses on tend to provide relatively limited amounts of funding to an individual – the amount you receive is most likely to be supplementary to the core statutory student finance available to you.

Another common characteristic is that trusts and charities often target their funding towards the final stages of your course (many trusts and charities measure the impact of their funds in terms of the number of students they have helped to complete their studies).

Educational trusts and charities have comparatively small budgets from which to offer assistance each year – this means there is likely to be a high level of competition for each one, even with a relatively small number of applications. Research which ones are most likely to apply to you as early as you can so that you give yourself the best chance of making a successful application.

In most cases, a successful application to an educational trust or charity is likely to realise financial assistance of a few hundred pounds. This makes them a worthwhile avenue to consider – but clearly you are unlikely to get by using them as a sole source of income. In fact, many trusts and charities require evidence that you have the majority of your finances in place already, and that any additional assistance they provide is required in order to complete your course successfully.

On the other hand, some trusts and charities only provide funding if you're unable to access statutory student finance for your studies, and then only release their funds where no government funding is available. This just emphasises how different these sources of finance can be.

The trust or charity you apply to usually expects you to have exhausted all available funding routes before making an application to it. Make sure:

- ✔ You have applied for all the statutory student finance available to you

- ✔ You have asked your course provider about any possible financial assistance they can provide to you

If you still require financial support after exploring these steps, you can take the next step and start making applications to educational trusts and charities.

In some cases you may need to apply for support before your course even begins, so applying for all statutory student finances beforehand may not be possible – check the deadlines for applying to each individual trust or charity.

Take the time to do some online research to see if you can identify any trusts or charities that are available to help you. Knowing that they exist at all puts you at an advantage – they don't receive any great degree of publicity, so many students complete their course without exploring whether any additional funds might be available to them.

Checking Eligibility for Trusts and Charities

Don't underestimate just how many and varied educational trusts and charities are when you consider the national picture.

This section looks at some of the typical factors that can play a part in helping to determine whether a trust might be available to help you. Note that whilst a list of various criteria is given here, some trusts or charities may require a number of criteria to be met before you can apply, not just one.

When considering making an application to a trust or charity, be careful to select only those for which you meet the eligibility criteria. Their funds are often run on very limited administrative budgets, perhaps even on a voluntary basis, so speculative or otherwise inappropriate applications can be a big drain on the resources available. More often than not you'll find that you've simply wasted your own time, as your application is simply rejected (without a response) if you don't meet the required criteria.

Subject of study

Your chosen field of study can be a determining factor as to whether some trusts or charities are able to help you.

For example, if you're studying for a profession such as teaching, you may find that there are a number of education-related organisations that you can apply to.

Your subject doesn't necessarily have to be a 'profession' in its own right – you may be studying a more generalised discipline, such as a modern language or one of the 'Arts', and find that there are trusts and charities with links to your subject.

Parental occupation

Surprising as it may seem, the jobs your parents have worked in could well have an influence on the additional funding opportunities available to you. Classic examples here are occupations such as the armed forces and the police service – each of which has well-established programmes of support for the families of those who have served.

Other traditional occupations with established 'benevolent' funds include mining, textiles and transport industries – often with a heritage going back to 19th-century philanthropists who wished to establish a legacy of ensuring education for future generations.

 Check to see if your parents' careers may have opened doors to funding for you, as there are plenty more examples of qualifying occupations.

Personal circumstances

Various aspects of your own circumstances might open doors to eligibility to money from an educational trust or charity. Covering the wide variety of attributes various trusts might consider is almost impossible, and this section can only give a flavour of the most common issues the trusts and charities tend to focus upon.

The following sections are commonly used by websites offering search facilities for trusts and charities. Although some trusts might have additional personal attributes they are interested in, the factors discussed in the following sections are usually considered by the vast majority.

Age

Trusts and charities often target their available financial resources to a particular age group. Just as some may target younger students (typically up to the ages of 21 or 25) others may be aimed at those studying at an older age. Make sure that you check whether there are any age requirements for any trusts or charities you apply to.

Disability

Once again, the range of circumstances which might qualify for financial assistance is vast. Various trusts and charities exist, some of which may be aimed at a general definition of disability, whilst others might be more focused, for example, on sensory impairments or specific learning differences.

In general, being disabled increases the likelihood of there being some additional funds available from these sources to help support your studies.

Carers

If you are a carer, taking on the responsibility of looking after a relative or loved one, your situation is all the more challenging, not only in terms of balancing that responsibility with the requirements of your course, but also due to the fact that carers who are full-time students are also ruled out of being eligible to receive carers' benefits like Carer's Allowance.

In recognition of this, if you're a carer, you may be able to obtain funds from an educational trust or charity, and whilst there may not be many exclusively dedicated to the needs of those taking on caring duties, a detailed description of your circumstances is highly likely to add significant weight when applying to a more general fund (but be careful to ensure you meet the eligibility requirements before you apply).

Religion and belief

If you have religious affiliations or other connections, these can be valuable when seeking funding. Many churches seek to promote educational and learning opportunities and have a rich tradition in doing so. So remember to check if your religion has any trusts or charities affiliated with it.

Furthermore, there are some educational trusts and charities which have religious origins but which provide additional support to those of all faiths, and none. So, even if you don't have a faith allegiance, this avenue could still provide you with some support.

Gender

One gender in particular can benefit from support from educational trusts and charities. Some are set up with the express purpose of providing women with the opportunity to pursue an education, largely due to the fact that women are more likely to have set their own careers aside due to caring responsibilities for their family.

This bias is reflected in a number of trusts and charities which focus on women as their sole client group, with philanthropists, educational foundations and worldwide organisations amongst those responsible for providing the funds for the grants available.

Location

Where you live or were born may be decisive factors in determining eligibility for assistance from trusts and charities.

Hundreds of trust funds have been set up by local philanthropists or organisations in order to further the educational achievement of people from a specific area.

Criteria concerning location are (you guessed it) just as varied in nature as all other aspects of these sources of funding. They can depend on residence (or birth) within a particular region, county, city, town, village or parish. They may be based on electoral wards or even on ancient boundaries which no longer have a practical purpose.

If any educational trusts exist relating to locations relevant to you, they can be an extremely worthwhile option to consider as they are far more likely to have 'general' eligibility criteria to promote the education of people from that area, and in that sense are less specific than the other categories listed here.

Career

Just as your parents' occupations may qualify you for assistance from trusts and charities, so may your own career ambition be relevant if your studies are specific to a particular profession or vocation.

There are many examples of careers (for example, the arts, medicine and teaching) which have trusts and charities aimed at assisting students in completing their studies (and any associated professional qualifications) in order that upon graduation they're equipped to make successful progression to that career.

Figuring Out What Funding is Available

The typical assistance that you can expect to receive from an educational trust or charity usually comes in the form of a one-off non-repayable grant. Amounts can range from the relatively small (for example, £250) to amounts closer to £1,000 – although higher-end grants are much less common. Grants of up to £500 are fairly typical.

Any grant from an educational trust or charity is likely to be made to you with a specific purpose in mind. These grants are often to meet costs to help you through the final stages of your course, but support may be available for specific items such as course materials or childcare costs occurring at any time during your course.

The amounts awarded by trusts and charities are expected to have a meaningful impact upon your situation. Wherever possible, the trustees deciding on the allocation of their funds wish to see those funds being as effective as possible in resolving the circumstances of the applicant. A successful application often results in a useful amount, and this is what makes it worthwhile seeking funding from these sources.

Making an effective application

The budgets of trusts and charities tend to be very limited. Most of them are relatively small trust funds aimed at a particular locality, or sometimes they're national (or international) organisations with a high level of applications.

Add the fact that a trust or charity's own administrative resources for dealing with applications may be extremely limited, and you can soon see how competitive applications can become. This competition for funds makes it all the more important to apply as early as you can, and to make as effective an application as possible.

Your first step in making an effective application is to ensure that you've accessed all other opportunities for funding available to you in the first instance – many trusts and charities operate on the principle that they won't replace statutory funding that is available for your studies, and that the funds they release are meeting a genuine need.

Once you have identified an educational trust or charity for which you meet the eligibility criteria, you should contact the trustee (sometimes called 'the respondent') responsible for administration of the applications. In doing so, you'll probably receive the relevant application form (if there is one) and full instructions on how to apply. Pay particular attention to the instructions so that you can make sure that your application meets all the requirements (you may have to include documentary evidence of your income and priority expenditure, for example).

When you complete the application form or provide information in a letter, you'll probably be required to describe your income and expenditure in detail. Either use the forms in the budgeting chapter of this book or contact your course provider's advice service if you need assistance with this. Give a full description of your circumstances and do not miss out any obvious items of income or expenditure, as doing this can jeopardise your application.

Having given an overview of your financial situation, you're probably required to write some form of personal statement which explains the circumstances that have led you to make your application.

Providing as much detail as you can is important, as this enables the trustees who consider your application to use whatever discretion is available to them. Provide a full account of your situation, but remember to keep the details relevant – don't let your description wander into unnecessary details.

Of equal importance is a description of how the situation has come about – unexpected and unforeseen circumstances are far more likely to result in a successful application than circumstances which could have been planned for in advance. Do bear this in mind when making your application – any applications based on circumstances which are deemed to be avoidable are less likely to be successful.

Whilst you're expected to provide full details of the income you have available to you from all sources when you make your application, there's nothing to prevent you from seeking assistance from more than one trust or charity simultaneously. A good strategy is to identify all those which match your circumstances, and make an approach to each one in accordance with their individual requirements.

Declaring the other trusts and charities you have already approached is good practice (some may require you to repay financial assistance if you have secured funds from elsewhere).

Make sure you refer back to the instructions for your application. It may be necessary for an advice service (or other third party) to submit your application for you – where this is required it's usually so that someone in a position of responsibility can check that you're eligible to make an application (this helps the trustees to know that they only receive qualifying applications). Check for requirements such as this, otherwise you may make the mistake of making a direct application when you shouldn't.

Checking deadlines

The various educational trusts and charities throughout the UK each have their own individual requirements when it comes to application deadlines, so check the instructions you receive about how to apply to find out what is required for that particular application.

Sometimes you may find a trust requires you to plan ahead of the start of your course, so it's always a good idea to research those trusts and charities that are relevant to you as early as you can. You don't want to miss out on applying to those with early deadlines. Equally, there are other examples where support may only be available towards the final stages of your studies – in which case you should set a reminder for yourself so you do not forget to apply when the time comes around.

Other trusts and charities may have several deadlines a year, maybe on a quarterly basis. These sources provide a more flexible approach, but some may only have one annual deadline, so try not to miss out.

Referees

Applications to educational trusts and charities often require you to provide referees in support of your application. Check the information you have received about how to apply to find out who is deemed acceptable as a referee. Some applications may allow you to include a family member as a referee, others may not. Almost all require you to include a referee who is seen as an independent, objective third party – this could be an adviser or a teacher/lecturer.

Check to see if there are any specific forms a referee should use, or if they're required to include any particular items of information about you. Consider whether the people you're approaching to be your referees are in a position to provide the required information.

Make sure you give your referees all the relevant information they need so that they can support your application effectively. You may be approaching extremely busy professionals for assistance, so you want to make sure that they get the reference right first time so that you can get on with applying.

Supporting evidence

You will be required to provide as much information as you can about your situation to ensure the trustees considering your application can reach a reliable decision.

Usually, the more information you provide, the more likely your application will be successful – but make sure the information is focused and relevant.

As well as describing your situation in a personal statement, the trust or charity often wants to see documentation to back up what you're describing. Typical documentary information which may be required can include:

✔ Confirmation of personal identification (birth certificate/passport)

✔ Confirmation of your student status (this may be required through one of your referees)

✔ Details of all sources of income (student finance, wage slips, benefit/tax credit letters)

✔ Bank statements – usually for all accounts you hold, check what period they need to cover

✔ Details of priority expenditure (rent, fuel bills, travel costs)

✔ Accurate estimates of regular household expenditure (for example, food, clothing) – make sure these are as realistic as you can get them

✔ Details supporting the main reason for your application (for example, medical evidence in the case of illness)

✔ References – check the information you have received to see who is suitable, and how many referees you need to support your application

Ensure that you include all the documentation that is required to support your application, as it may be treated as incomplete (and may not be processed) without it. At best, this can lead to further delays for your application and at worst, those delays can lead to you missing a deadline, or remaining funds being allocated to other applicants.

Finding Out More

Information about trusts and charities is available online. There are two main sources giving access to databases of available sources of funding (and these are both charities):

✔ Turn to Us: `grants-search.turn2us.org.uk/`

✔ Family Action: `www.family-action.org.uk/what-we-do/grants/educational-grants/`

Turn to Us offers an online search facility which allows you to enter details about your personal circumstances – this information is then used to conduct a search for those trusts and charities that may be relevant to you. You still need to check that you meet the eligibility criteria for each funding source the search finds, but the results are usually accurate enough to give you some options to approach.

Family Action's database works in a slightly different way and requires that your application is submitted via your course provider's advice service. The database is only available to you if your course provider is an affiliate of Family Action's Educational Grants Service.

As well as exploring the above, speak to your course provider's advice service – they may hold details of useful trusts and charities which either support local students or are relevant to the subjects studied at that university or college. They may also be able to provide access to the Directory for Social Change's Educations Grants Directory, which is a comprehensive resource listing many of the trusts and charities providing more extensive levels of financial support.

Research what additional sources of funding are available to you as early as you can and identify a timetable for making applications to each one.

Chapter 13

Professional and Career Development Loans

*T*he Professional and Career Development Loan is an alternative form of student loan which may be available to you if you're studying a *vocational* course (one which leads directly to a career).

These loans are different to the standard student loan from the Student Loans Company, and are only available where no other form of statutory student finance is available to you.

In this chapter, I provide an overview of the Professional and Career Development Loan scheme, including eligibility requirements, how to apply, what is paid and how repayments work.

What You Need to Know

Professional and Career Development Loans (PCDLs) are commercial loans available from high street banks. They offer reduced rates of interest and the government covers the cost of the interest on your PCDL whilst you're studying.

 PCDLs are another example of a government-subsidised loan scheme – but marked differences exist between PCDLs and the student loans available from the Student Loans Company.

You can apply for a PCDL in order to cover the costs of your tuition fees, course materials and your living costs. The course you are studying will need to be vocational – you need to show that it directly leads to a job, or otherwise helps you in your career.

At the time of writing, two banks offer this loan scheme (Co-operative and Barclays). You are not guaranteed a loan even if your course qualifies and you meet the basic eligibility criteria – whether you get a loan comes down to the bank's own discretion as a lender. Most likely, the bank will require you to go through a credit-scoring process before it agrees to provide a PCDL to you.

Before deciding which bank's scheme to apply for, compare the products on offer. Each bank may operate its own credit-scoring system, so if you are declined by one, it may be worth-while trying the other.

If you're in receipt of welfare benefits, a PCDL can count as income, so tell your benefit office(s) if your application for a loan is successful.

Applying for a PCDL

When you apply for a PCDL, you should do so at least three months before the start of your course to ensure that the bank you apply to has sufficient time to process your application. You should also bear in mind that certain times of year can be far busier than others, leading to delays in processing times.

Ask the National Careers Service about when might be the best time for you to apply when you enquire about a PCDL.

In the first instance, contact the National Careers Service helpline on 0800 100 900. The helpline is open 7 days a week, from 8am to 10pm. You can arrange for them to call you back if they are not available to answer your call straight away.

The National Careers Service provides you with impartial advice about the PCDL scheme, as well as the course(s) you might be interested in studying. Their advice helps you to make an informed decision before undertaking further study. The helpline informs you of the banks currently involved in the PCDL scheme as well as arranging for an application form to be sent out to you.

When you receive the application form:

1. **Complete the form and return it to the bank you're applying to.**
2. **The bank considers whether you meet the eligibility criteria to receive a PCDL.**
3. **The bank then considers your credit history and decides whether to offer you a loan.**

If your application is successful, you then need to complete the process by signing up to the loan agreement, agreeing to abide by its terms and conditions.

Eligibility for a PCDL

Not every student will be eligible to apply for a PCDL.

There are some basic criteria you need to meet in order to be able to apply:

- ✔ You need to be aged 18 or over.
- ✔ You need to have been ordinarily resident in the UK for the three-year period before the start of your course.
- ✔ You must have *settled status* in the UK (no restriction on your residency in the UK).
- ✔ You must not have funds already available to you which could be used to pay for your studies.
- ✔ You must confirm that you're planning to work in the UK, the European Union or the European Economic Area upon completion of the course. In practice, this may amount to you giving an indication 'in good faith'.

In addition to your personal eligibility, the course that you're studying must also qualify under the PCDL scheme:

- ✔ Your course must ordinarily last up to 2 years (or 3 years if it includes 1 year of work experience).
- ✔ Your course must be either a part-time or full-time vocational course.

   ✔ Your course provider must be on the Professional and Development Loan Register. You need to know your course provider's registration number to complete your application – contact your course provider for the details. (If your course provider has not already registered your course with the scheme, they may be able to do so.) The Register exists to ensure that PCDLs are only available for courses delivered by course providers with a proven track record – so you're protected from your loan being used to meet the cost of a 'sham' course. Your course provider is required to have clear refund and complaints policies in place.

   ✔ You must not be eligible to receive any other form of statutory student finance for your course.

Dealing with the Bank

The National Careers Service helpline provides you with up-to-date information about the banks participating in the PCDL scheme.

When making an application for a PCDL through one of the participating banks, be aware that part of the process involves you being taken through a credit check. Your credit score is an important factor in increasing the chances of your application for a loan being accepted.

Take steps to familiarise yourself with your credit report before you apply for a PCDL. Ensure that you're registered on the electoral register, and establish a reliable track record of making payments through your bank account to help improve your credit report.

Take time to ensure that your application for your loan is realistic. Applying for costs associated with your tuition fees is relatively straightforward, but trying to make a realistic estimate of how much money you require for your course materials, and in particular how much you will need for living costs, is not so easy. The bank expects you to base your loan application on reasonable expenditure, so make sure that you can justify the amounts that you request.

Understanding the Differences Between PCDLs and Student Loans

The main differences between the PCDL scheme and Student Loans Company loans concern the amount of money you can apply for, how the loans are repaid and the way that they attract interest. This section looks into these areas in more detail.

Amounts available

If you meet the personal and course eligibility requirements, you may be able to apply for a PCDL for any amount between £300 and £10,000. The amount you receive depends on the bank's credit checks, including your ability to repay the amount requested.

You can apply for a loan in respect of the amount of funding you need for your tuition fees, and how much you expect to require to meet other costs, such as general living costs (the loan will cover up to 80 per cent of the amount you require).

The amount you apply for needs to be based on your estimated actual expenditure. Your tuition fees can be confirmed by providing information from your course provider. But also work out how much money you need for key items of expenditure such as rent, bills and food. Be sure to use a realistic amount for each item, otherwise the bank may view your application less favourably.

Repayments

If you've borrowed it, you do – sadly – need to pay loaned money back at some point!

PCDLs do not have to be repaid whilst you are studying. Repayments usually begin approximately one month after you leave your course.

Your repayments are fixed (regardless of your income once you have finished study) at the time you apply for the loan, and can range from a period of 12 to 60 months. Make sure that you're fully aware what your future obligations are going to be at the time you take out your loan.

Interest

The government covers the interest on your loan during your period of study and for one month after you leave your course. This makes the loan interest-free to you whilst you study.

Once repayments begin one month after you leave the course, you make repayments on the loan with interest. Repayments need to be made whether you completed your course or not, and regardless of your income (of lack thereof!).

You may wish to contact the bank for details of the interest rate applicable to your PCDL. The rate will be pro-rated over the entire period of the loan – the length of the course plus the repayment period. The repayment period will be fixed when you apply for the loan.

Finding Out Where to Get More Information

To find out more contact the National Careers Service helpline on 0800 100 900. The helpline is open 7 days a week, from 8am to 10pm.

You can arrange for them to call you back if they're not available to answer your call straight away.

Once you have contacted the National Careers Service and have obtained a PCDL application form, you need to contact the banks participating in the scheme.

If your application for a Professional and Career Development Loan is unsuccessful with a particular bank, ask them why. Their answer may help you prepare an application to another bank participating in the scheme.

Chapter 14

Students and the Welfare System

In This Chapter

▶ Discovering which students can claim benefits

▶ Claiming the right benefits

▶ Treating student finance as a taxable and assessed benefit

*M*ost full-time students are not able to claim welfare benefits, but they are available to some and also to part-time students. And all students are able to receive support from tax credits if their circumstances mean they qualify for them.

The rules surrounding welfare benefits are complex, and a variety of welfare benefits may be found within the system, all of which make it advisable to contact an adviser for information and guidance to ensure that you're claiming only those benefits available to you. See the later section 'Finding Out More' for ways of obtaining advice.

In this chapter, I provide an introduction to the most common benefits within the UK system, and describe how they apply to part-time and full-time students.

Understanding Student Finance and Welfare Benefits

Being a student, the benefit system automatically assumes that you have applied for, and will receive, the maximum student finance available to you including all loans and grants.

If you haven't applied for a Maintenance Loan, or you haven't applied for the maximum amount, any benefit calculation will use the maximum loan amount available to you, irrespective of whether you have actually applied for it.

The academic year for benefits

Your academic year is split into *relevant quarters* for benefit purposes. The quarters are set out as follows, if your course begins in the autumn term:

- ✔ Quarter 1: 1 September to 31 December
- ✔ Quarter 2: 1 January to 31 March
- ✔ Quarter 3: 1 April to 30 June
- ✔ Quarter 4: 1 July to 31 August

If your course begins in the spring or summer terms, then the dates applicable to the start of your course are 1 January or 1 April respectively. The rest of your academic year uses the quarters in sequence, using the same time periods as described above in order to make up a complete year.

Note that the quarters are not equal. Your student finance is counted as income over three quarters, but is not counted in the quarter in which the summer vacation falls. The only exceptions to this rule are any additional items of funding for professional courses (for example, NHS or Social Work Bursaries). In these instances, bursary funding is taken into account over 52 weeks.

Disregarded income

You need to check which items of student finance that you receive are not counted for benefit purposes.

Broadly, in terms of the current student finance system, these are:

- ✔ Any amount paid for tuition fees
- ✔ Any amount paid in respect of a dependent child or young person

▶ Any amount paid in respect of childcare for a dependent child

▶ Any amount paid in respect of travel costs to attend the course

▶ Any amount paid in respect of books and equipment

▶ The Special Support Grant

▶ The Parent's Learning Allowance

▶ Any lump sum amount paid from discretionary hardship funds for costs other than everyday living costs is disregarded as capital for 52 weeks (if paid for everyday living costs, the amount counts as capital straight away)

▶ The higher education bursary for care leavers (paid by your Local Authority)

Usually, this leaves the Maintenance Loan, the Maintenance Grant and the Adult Dependants' Grant as items of student finance that can count as income for benefit purposes (unless you're on a course where specific subject-related funding is available, for example, NHS, Social Work, Postgraduate Teaching); however, the Adult Dependants' Grant is being replaced (see the later sidebar, 'Bye bye Dependants' Grants').

Additional disregarded income includes what you spend on books, equipment and travel. If you have a Maintenance Loan, this is also disregarded.

Working out your student loan calculations

In order to work out how much of your Maintenance Loan counts for benefit purposes, I'm going to show you a calculation – don't worry, it's not quite as terrifying as a return to GCSE Maths!

In this example, I'll use a Maintenance Loan assessed at a maximum rate of £4,000 for the academic year for a continuing year of study.

The calculation assumes that you're in receipt of the maximum Maintenance Loan available to you, even if you have not applied for the full amount.

Here goes:

1. **Work out how many benefit weeks apply. You need to identify the period of benefit weeks as follows:**

   In your first year, the period begins with the week that includes, or immediately follows, the start date of your course until the last day of the week that starts with, includes or is immediately before 30 June.

   In a continuing year, the period begins on the first day of the week that starts with, or follows, 1 September until the last day of the week that starts with, includes or is immediately before 30 June.

   In your final year, the period begins on the first day of the week that starts with, or follows, 1 September until the week that starts with, includes or is immediately before the last day of your course.

   In practice, this usually works out as a period of 43 weeks for first and continuing years, and a period of 39 weeks for final years.

2. **Apply the books/equipment and travel disregards. The following amounts are deducted from the maximum loan as allowances:**

   Books/equipment = £390

   Travel = £303

   $$£4,000 - (£390 + £303) = £3,307$$

3. **Divide the remaining loan by the number of benefit weeks:**

   $$£3,307 \div 43 = £76.91$$

4. **Apply the weekly disregard of £10:**

   $$£76.91 - £10.00 = £66.91 \text{ per week}$$

So, a £4,000 loan in your first or second year would count as £66.91 per week for an income-based benefit. (Note that in your final year, the rate of loan is a lower amount divided by fewer weeks (39), which gives a comparable outcome.)

Check the benefit calculation for any income-based benefit you receive to ensure that your student income has been taken into account correctly. This situation can arise if you live in an area without a large student population, as the benefit office is less likely to be familiar with the special rules relating to student income.

Fortunately, most benefit letters provide you with a break-down of the calculation including the figure used for student finance – so you can compare that with your own figures. If you think the benefit has been worked out incorrectly, and you want to get a second opinion, the advice service at your course provider can check the figures before you take any further action.

Factoring in Vacation versus term-time

Your entitlement to welfare benefits can change during the course of the year. Different rules apply to your income at different times.

The long vacation (usually during July and August) is one such key period. For benefit purposes, the majority of student income is only taken into account during term-time. The only exceptions to this rule are the Adult Dependants' Grant (which is being replaced at the time of writing) and some additional grants or bursaries payable for professional courses such as NHS or Social Work courses. This means you may not have any student income to take into account during the long vacation, which can increase the amount of benefit available to you.

For example, your student income may mean that you don't receive income support during term-time, so reducing the amount of housing benefit that you're entitled to. In the long vacation, the fact that you've no student finance for benefit periods means that you may well qualify for income support during the two summer months – and even if you get just a penny of income support, full housing benefit is payable along with income support (see later in this chapter for more info on both).

Note that these benefit rules appear to contradict the student finance system – under the student support regulations, you're paid higher rates of loan in the first year, and any continuing years, in order to provide you with money for the long vacation. However, student support regulations, and the rules governing welfare benefits, are set in two separate areas of legislation which do not mesh together neatly. Therefore, instances such as this highlight rules of one system appearing to contradict the other.

Try not to get too concerned about these inconsistencies – the important thing to remember is always provide accurate information about your circumstances when applying for any kind of student finance or benefits.

Changing your circumstances

The welfare benefits system, in particular, requires you to report any changes in your circumstances to the benefit offices responsible for the administration of the benefits you receive.

The responsibility always rests with you as the claimant to ensure such information is provided in an accurate and timely fashion. Whilst some communication can occur between benefit offices (if your Income Support or Jobseeker's Allowance claim comes to an end, your housing benefit office will usually be notified automatically), there is no substitute for you notifying the offices yourself. Always keep the necessary contact details to hand so that you can keep them up to date with your circumstances.

A number of occasions exist where you may need to notify your benefit office of a change in circumstances. Here are some examples:

- ✔ When you become a student (part-time or full-time)

- ✔ When you start the long vacation

- ✔ When you rejoin your course after the long vacation (remember the quarters applicable to your academic year)

- ✔ If you change address

- ✔ If you start or finish paid employment

> ✔ If you become responsible for the care of a child
>
> ✔ When you move in with, or leave, a partner or spouse
>
> ✔ If you become disabled
>
> ✔ If you start care duties for another person
>
> ✔ When you leave or finish your course

All of the above (with the exception of your change of address) can have some bearing on the amount of benefit you receive. Some changes in circumstances may mean you receive more benefit, others may mean that the amount you receive is reduced. Whatever it means in terms of the money you receive, you must ensure that up-to-date information is provided.

If you fail to provide information to a benefit office, it's possible that you may find yourself facing fraud proceedings – as your failure to inform them of a change of circumstances may be interpreted as a deliberate act to obtain benefits that you're not entitled to. This would be a 'worst case' outcome but underlines the need for you to report information that is relevant to your claim.

Because of the serious implications of not making accurate and timely reports of changes in circumstances, it's often best to ensure that you make your report in writing, so that you can show that you took the correct course of action. Letters or emails are much easier to produce as evidence compared to phone calls or face-to-face conversations.

Even if you're not deemed to have committed fraud, if you don't provide information when your circumstances change, you may receive payment of benefits that you're not entitled to. Any such payment that you receive is known as an overpayment of benefit, and you usually have to pay it back.

Overpayments

You should try to avoid situations where overpayments of benefit occur if you can, because any overpayment you receive may be recoverable immediately, or at the very least your future payments of benefit may be cut until the amount is recovered in full.

Overpayments can occur very easily for students, particularly full-time students, because of the way that your student finance is taken into account at different times of the year. For example, if you're unaware of the need to renew your claim for benefits at the beginning of September each year, and carry on receiving benefits on the same basis as during the long vacation, you're likely to incur an overpayment.

'Not knowing' that you were supposed either to renew your claim or advise the benefit office of a change in circumstances is rarely a defence in the eyes of the benefits system. As a claimant, you're expected to know what your responsibilities are.

If, however, you have informed the benefit office of a change, and they fail to act on it, you may have a defence if you can show it was the office's 'official error' that led to the overpayment. However, even in situations like these you're expected to know that a change in circumstances would change the amount of benefit you receive – so you would still be expected to take action if your benefit was not reviewed after you gave over the information. In instances of official error, the overpayment is still deemed to exist, it's just that it may no longer be recoverable because of the benefit office's part in the error.

The most common issues to arise around overpayments of benefit are at the start of the course and at the start of the academic year.

Always be sure to notify every benefit office where you're claiming benefits as a part-time or full-time student when you start your studies, and at the beginning of each subsequent academic year. Where possible, always provide a copy of your student finance notification letter so that they're able to review the calculation of your benefit.

If you haven't notified the benefit office of a change in circumstances and you realise that you should have done so, contact them as soon as you can. The response is likely to be far more favourable if you can show that you've taken action to address your error, rather than remaining silent and continuing to receive amounts of benefit that you may not be entitled to.

If you're concerned about an overpayment, or the possibility of an overpayment arising, you may wish to contact the advice service at your course provider – they can give you all the relevant information and advise you on the options available to you.

At the end of your course

The last day of your course is the end of your 'period of study' for benefit purposes. The next day you're no longer a student.

This means that, if you have been unable to claim benefits as a full-time student, or the amount of benefit you have been able to receive has been reduced due to your student finance, you no longer have such restrictions and (if you have no other source of income) you're able to make a claim for benefits.

If you're not starting work immediately, you should consider claiming Jobseeker's Allowance, as you may have an entitlement for the period between the last day of your course and when your employment begins. If you currently live in rented accommodation, or plan to do so, you may qualify for housing benefit as well.

If you have a disability, are unable to work due to illness, have responsibility for a child or are caring for someone, you may need to claim other benefits such as Income Support, Employment and Support Allowance or Carer's Allowance – you can claim these benefits once your course is at an end.

One issue which can arise is a question mark over the final date of your course. The Department for Work and Pensions has a data-sharing arrangement with the Student Loans Company, which it uses to determine the end dates of courses. If the information on the Student Loans Company database is incorrect, this error can affect your ability to claim.

If such an issue should arise, contact your course provider – any letter from them will override the information from the Student Loans Company, as the course provider (the 'educational establishment') is regarded as the authority on matters such as start and end dates of its courses.

Looking into Non Student-specific Benefits

Whether you're able to claim welfare benefits (or tax credits until Universal Credit is fully introduced) is determined by the nature of your circumstances whilst you study.

Generally speaking, most part-time students are usually in a position to claim and receive income-based welfare benefits as long as they (or their partner) do not have income from elsewhere which cancels out the entitlement. Another possible complication is your potential for becoming 'unavailable for work' due to your study commitments – and this can affect your entitlement to Jobseeker's Allowance.

Part-time students who started their course after September 2012 usually only qualify for tuition fee support and no maintenance support (although part-time teacher education students who qualify can receive the NCTL Teaching Bursary, which can be taken into account by benefit offices). Tuition fee support is ignored when calculating income for benefits, so the only income usually taken into account would be from a partner, other benefits or any paid work the student is doing. In principle, therefore, a part-time student may receive payment of benefit during their studies.

Full-time students, on the other hand, are usually ruled out of receiving income-based welfare benefits, although there are some important exceptions:

- ✔ Lone parents, or lone foster parents with responsibility for a child or young person in full-time 'non-advanced' (for example, primary/secondary school or Sixth Form) education

- ✔ Couples who are both full-time students and have responsibility for a child or young person in full-time 'non-advanced' education

- ✔ Students in receipt of disability benefits like Disability Living Allowance or Personal Independence Payment, or who are registered blind

- ✔ Students treated as incapable of work for a continuous 28-week period (if two periods of incapacity are separated by a period of 8 weeks or less, they can be treated as continuous)

> ✔ Deaf students who qualify for the Disabled Students'
>   Allowance
>
> ✔ Students aged 60 or over at the start of their course
>
> ✔ Students waiting to rejoin their course after a period of
>   illness or caring responsibilities

If you live with a partner who is not a student, they may be able to make a claim for you both as a couple. Their claim will be a standard, 'non-student' claim – but remember your student income (along with your partner's income) will still be taken into account.

Even if you're in a group that can claim a benefit, you may find that you're not entitled to receive a payment because of the student finance you receive – but as student finance is only counted for some of the year, there may be a period when you can receive payment after all, outside of the period for which your student finance counts. (One thing to understand about welfare benefits is the rules are far from straightforward!) Add to this that the rules can vary from benefit to benefit and it's easy to see why some students miss out on the money they can claim during study.

One rule that we can start with is how an academic year is defined for benefit purposes – suffice to say it rarely equates to the dates of the academic year as published by your course provider:

> ✔ **In the first year of your course:**
>
> The academic year begins on the day your course starts and finishes the benefit week in which 30 June falls
>
> ✔ **In the final year of your course:**
>
> The academic year begins in the benefit week in which 1 September falls, and finishes with the final day of the course
>
> ✔ **In any other year:**
>
> The academic year begins in the benefit week in which 1 September falls, and finishes the benefit week in which 30 June falls

Whichever year of your course that you're in, one of the above applies in order to determine the number of weeks your student income is counted as income for benefit purposes (and your income is divided over those weeks).

This means that if you can claim benefits during the summer period, this usually equates to the weeks between 1 July and 31 August. Then, in a continuing year of study, you're treated as if you're in receipt of your student finance from the start of September, even though you might not receive it then. Geddit? As I say, these things aren't always as straightforward as we'd all like.

In order to try and make all the complex rules around benefits as easy to understand as possible, this chapter goes through the current benefits one by one . . .

Income-based benefits such as Income Support and Jobseeker's Allowance are 'passport' benefits – if you receive any amount of them, then you can also receive housing benefit if you live in (qualifying) rented accommodation.

If you're in receipt of benefits before you begin your course, make sure that you declare your change of circumstances to all of the offices which handle your benefit claims when you become a student. You're required to do this, and taking action means you can prevent money being paid to you which would need to be paid back if there is an overpayment due to a change of your circumstances.

Jobseeker's Allowance

This benefit is probably the most well known earnings-replacement benefit. There are two versions of it:

- ✔ *Contributions-based Jobseeker's Allowance* (JSA) is paid if you have previously made enough National Insurance contributions to qualify – it is then paid for 6 months regardless of any other income you (or your partner) may have coming in. (But you only qualify to receive it during the summer vacation if you or your partner have claimed Universal Credit).

- ✔ *Income-based JSA* is identical in value, but will only be paid to you if your income is below the relevant threshold that applies to your circumstances. The threshold (called the applicable amount) is made up of various premiums reflecting your status, for example, single, a couple or a lone parent. This means some students might receive more benefit than others.

If you're a part-time student, you're usually able to claim and receive JSA, whether it's contributions-based or income-based – the latter depends on what income you have coming in from other sources. However, in claiming the benefit, you're required to sign up to a 'jobseeker's agreement' which means that you may have to take up work whilst studying – the agreement gives you an opportunity to nominate days when you're available for work. Therefore, in this case it's in your interests to find work allowing you to strike a balance between study and employment.

If you study full-time, the default position is you cannot claim income-based JSA (although you remain entitled to contributions-based JSA for the period it is payable). Exceptions to this rule do exist; for example, if you are:

✔ A full-time student and a lone parent, you may qualify for Jobseeker's Allowance during your studies. How much you get depends on the age of your children (over 5 years), whether they're in 'non-advanced' education, the student finance you receive and when you claim during the year (usually you only receive payment for JSA during the summer vacation). If you or a member of your family has a disability and/or your youngest child is younger than 5 years, you should claim Income Support instead.

✔ One of a couple, both of whom are full-time students and you have responsibility for a child or young person in 'non-advanced' education, in which case you may be able to claim Jobseeker's Allowance during the summer vacation (but not during the academic year).

✔ Waiting to rejoin your course after a period of illness or caring for someone, you may be able to claim JSA once those circumstances have ended. You're only able to claim for the period up until the start of the next academic year.

In addition to the above, you must satisfy the basic requirements for eligibility for Jobseeker's Allowance (for example, being available for, and actively seeking, work). Contact your course provider's advice service for more information.

Income Support

Income Support is similar to income-based Jobseeker's Allowance in value (see the previous section), but is payable in fewer circumstances. The main difference between the two benefits is that Income Support has no requirement for you to be available for work.

Full-time students aren't usually in a position to claim Income Support. Part-time students usually can if they fulfil the eligibility requirements. Income Support is aimed at people who are lone parents with young children, or who are sick or disabled.

If you're in one of the groups that are eligible to receive Income Support, it's possible to receive payments throughout the year. These circumstances allow you to claim Income Support if you're:

- ✔ A full-time student who is a lone parent, and your youngest child is younger than 5 years and in 'non-advanced' education (basically this refers to primary/secondary school or Sixth Form). The student finance you receive, and the time of year when you claim, affects your claim. Usually you only qualify for payment of Income Support during the summer vacation. However, if you or a member of your family has a disability, you're more likely to receive payments all year round.

- ✔ A full-time student who is a lone foster parent of a child under 16. The student finance you receive, and when you claim during the year, will affect your claim. Usually you will only qualify for payment of Income Support during the summer vacation. If you or a member of your family has a disability, this may mean you're more likely to receive payments all year round.

- ✔ A member of a couple with responsibility for a child where both of you are full-time students, and you would qualify for Income Support if you were not a full-time student; you can claim during your summer holidays.

- ✔ In receipt of long-term Incapacity Benefit; you can claim Income Support as a full-time student.

Employment and Support Allowance

Two types of Employment and Support Allowance (ESA) may be applied for: contributory ESA and income-based ESA. Both types of ESA are available to part-time students. Employment and Support Allowance was introduced to replace Incapacity Benefit. If you're still in receipt of Incapacity Benefit at the time you become a student, you're required to declare your change in circumstances – doing so can mean that your claim is reviewed and you may find you have to claim ESA instead.

Contributory ESA is available to you if you are:

- ✔ A full-time student and you have a disability, or

- ✔ Unable to work through illness, and you have worked and made sufficient National Insurance contributions.

If you're unable to claim contributory ESA, then you may be able to claim *income-based ESA* if you're in receipt of:

- ✔ Disability Living Allowance

- ✔ Personal Independence Payment

Note that you will not be able to claim income-based ESA if you're unable to work due to illness.

An integral part of claiming ESA is the Work Capability Assessment. You can only get ESA if you satisfy the requirements of the assessment. If you're in receipt of ESA before becoming a student, you need to declare your change in circumstances, and this can bring about a review of your claim – particularly if there are elements of your study which suggest a conflict with the information in your Work Capability Assessment (for example, your course requires you to undertake periods of work placement).

Housing benefit

Housing benefit is paid to assist with costs for commercial rent. If you rent from a close relative, you may not be able to claim housing benefit. Part-time students can claim housing benefit, subject to the income assessment and other eligibility requirements.

As a full-time student, you may be able to claim housing benefit if you're:

- ✔ In receipt of Income Support, income-based Jobseeker's Allowance or income-related Employment and Support Allowance

- ✔ A lone parent or a lone foster parent with responsibility for a child in non-advanced education

- ✔ A member of a couple, both of whom are full-time students with responsibility for a child in non-advanced education

- ✔ In receipt of a disability benefit such as Disability Living Allowance or Personal Independence Payment

- ✔ Eligible for a Disabled Students' Allowance because you (or your partner) are deaf

- ✔ Eligible for a Disabled Students' Allowance because you (or your partner) are registered blind

- ✔ Treated as incapable of work for a continuous 28-week period (if two periods of incapacity are separated by a period of 8 weeks or less, they can be treated as continuous)

- ✔ Waiting to rejoin your course after a period of illness or caring responsibilities

- ✔ Over 60

How much housing benefit you receive depends on your student income, whether you have any other adults living in your household (this would not usually include other students you might share a house with) and the Local Housing Allowance (based on market rents in the local area).

You may qualify for housing benefit, but you normally have to make your own contribution towards the full value of your rent. This is far more likely in term-time, when your student finance is taken into account. It does not count during the summer vacation – meaning that you may get the full amount of housing benefit payable (but this may not cover the full cost of your rent).

Council Tax reduction

Council Tax reduction schemes vary from one district council to the next, so you need to check the details based on your term-time address.

Full-time students are exempt from Council Tax liability, but need to apply for the exemption. This is usually done by obtaining a Council Tax exemption certificate from your course provider, and sending it to the local district council of the property that you're living at during term-time. There may still be a bill for the property if you share a house with one or more non-students, but you're not liable to make any payment towards the bill. If you live with only one non-student, they can make a claim for a 25 per cent single person's discount, in the same way as if they were living in the house alone.

Part-time students are not exempt from Council Tax, so you may need to make a claim for Council Tax reduction if you (and your partner if you have one) are on a low income – contact the local district council for details.

Disability Living Allowance and Personal Independence Payment

The times, they are a'changing. Disability Living Allowance (DLA) is being replaced by a Personal Independence Payment (PIP). If you're making a new claim, or renewing a claim, then you must claim PIP. If you already claim DLA you can continue to receive it, but it is not possible to make a new claim – you have to claim PIP instead. Even if you're still in receipt of DLA, you can expect to be transferred to PIP in future.

You can get either DLA or PIP as a part-time or as a full-time student, as long as you're eligible to receive these benefits. DLA and PIP are working-age benefits – so if you're under 65 and have a disability and you require support in terms of your personal care or mobility, you may be eligible to receive one of them.

Just as is the case with ESA, if you're already in receipt of either DLA or PIP at the time you become a student, this change in your circumstances may prompt a review of your claim. You're required to inform your benefit office of the change in your circumstances, and if the requirements of your course conflict with any of the information held in connection with your claim, your claim may be reviewed.

DLA and PIP are paid according to need and are universally disregarded as income – they cannot be taken into account for any other benefit, and they are not classed as income for student finance. DLA and PIP do not have any income-based elements, so they're payable regardless of your financial circumstances.

If you're over 65 you can claim *Attendance Allowance* (AA). AA is also universally disregarded as income in exactly the same way as DLA and PIP, and is paid to assist with personal care requirements. Both part-time and full-time students are able to claim AA if they meet the eligibility requirements.

Carer's Allowance

Carer's Allowance (CA) is a benefit paid to you if you're looking after someone else with 'substantial care needs'. The person does not have to be a relative, nor must you be living with them.

CA is not available to full-time students. Part-time students can claim CA. You must, however, be caring for the person for at least 35 hours a week – so you need to show your studies do not interfere with this requirement.

If you receive any income-based benefits, your CA counts as income and is likely to reduce the amount of the other benefits that can be paid to you.

Universal Credit

Universal Credit (UC) is a new benefit being introduced across the UK at the time of writing. Its aim is to simplify the benefits system and replace six benefits (income-based JSA, income-based IS, income-related ESA, housing benefit, Child Tax Credit and Working Tax Credit) with one. UC is designed to offer incentives for people to take up work. The main difference between it and the existing benefits it replaces is that it is paid monthly rather than weekly.

The roll-out of UC is behind schedule. Until 2014, it was only operating in a number of pilot areas, but new areas have been included during the course of 2014. The government's plan is that this phased roll-out will continue until all areas are covered – its aim is to achieve this during 2016.

However, as far as students are concerned, the introduction of UC is likely to take longer. At the moment, those areas where UC is in place are only handling claims for people whose circumstances are relatively straightforward (for example, single unemployed people). Whilst more complex claims (for example, claimants with children) are being handled in some areas, student claims are not yet being considered due to their complexity (for example, student finance has to be taken into account).

The current expectation is that student claims will not be considered until 2017 at the earliest. Students are expected to be amongst the last groups of claimants to be included in the scheme. At some point in the future, all income-based benefit (and tax credit) claims will switch to UC, as the system currently has cross-governmental support.

Even though this is the current situation, it is feasible for you to be caught up in the roll-out of UC if your partner makes a claim for UC, or if you move in with a partner claiming UC during the course of your studies.

Knowing About Other Benefits

Other benefits are available from the UK Government. For example, Child Benefit is probably the most common benefit not already covered in this chapter. Child Benefit is not affected by your student status and you can continue to receive it. It will not affect your student finance or vice versa.

By and large, these other benefits tend to continue to be payable to full-time and part-time students, as they tend to be contribution-based or payable due to specific circumstances.

If you're in receipt of a benefit not covered in this chapter, the best course of action would be to contact the advice service at your course provider, and they are likely to be able to confirm whether it will continue to be payable, or be otherwise affected by your student status.

Bye bye Dependants' Grants

When tax credits were introduced in 2003, their appearance marked the departure of the then Dependants' Grant – tax credits were payable instead, and the Parent's Learning Allowance was introduced (at a lower rate compared to the Dependants' Grant it replaced).

Tax credits have been a feature of the financial support available to student parents since their introduction. The only item of student finance taken into account for tax credit purposes is the Adult Dependants' Grant – all other loans and grants are disregarded. The Adult Dependants' Grant is not, of itself, sufficient in value to affect your tax credits claim, but it is taken into account alongside any other income your household receives, so can have an effect if your total income exceeds the relevant tax credits assessment threshold.

Tax credits are available to people with children, and those who work over 30 hours a week (24 hours a week if you're in a couple and both of you are working). If you use registered childcare, or if you have a disability and are working, you may be entitled to receive additional elements of tax credits. They replaced the previous benefit of Dependants' Grants (see the nearby sidebar for more detail), and are perhaps the most common benefit applied for.

Tax credits are income-assessed, and are designed to be paid to people on low incomes. If you fulfil the eligibility criteria, then qualifying for a payment of tax credits is usually much easier than is the case with welfare benefits.

Finding Out More

If you need more information about benefit entitlements, including actual amounts you can expect to receive, contact your course provider's advice service or the advice service at your student union. They usually give you bespoke information based on your own circumstances.

It's a good idea to check with your advice service when you have made a claim for benefits – they can check over the calculations and make sure that you're getting all that you're entitled to.

Information is also available at your local Citizens Advice Bureau, or online via the website: www.gov.uk/browse/ benefits.

The Child Poverty Action Group (www.cpag.org.uk) produces wide-ranging information resources on welfare benefits, and Turn 2 Us (www.turn2us.org.uk) offers resources for students on its website.

Information on tax credits is available from HM Revenue and Customs: www.gov.uk/browse/benefits/tax-credits and information on how to claim is available via the Tax Credits Helpline: 0345 300 3900 (textphone: 0345 300 3909).

Part V

Managing Money and Maximising Income at University

Top 5 Ways to Make Your Money Work For You

✔ Get yourself financially capable by planning your strategy for managing your money throughout your studies.

✔ Familiarise yourself with your finances by using budgeting tools to get a realistic overview of how much money you have.

✔ Understand the range of things that need paying for during your studies – but always consider how you can get the same for a little less.

✔ Consider how to supplement your student finance – with additional sources of funding, and with employment.

✔ Think about the credit option – don't just go for any type of loan, as some are more suitable for you than others.

Planning your finances is highly likely to make them go further during your studies. Access some online budgeting tools and a handy income/expenditure sheet to get you started at www.dummies.com/extras/student financeuk.

In this part . . .

- ✔ Explore how to plan your finances, recognising priorities and identifying different kinds of expenditure within your budget.

- ✔ Consider tips for reducing your essential costs and managing your expenditure on non-essentials. Recognise how exploring your expenditure in detail helps you to uncover opportunities for making savings.

- ✔ Explore opportunities for additional income, including taking out credit – but only use credit if you can afford it and if the credit product suits your circumstances.

- ✔ Find out where to go for help if your financial situation takes a turn for the worse.

Chapter 15

Getting to Know Your Money

*T*he more information you have about your income, the better placed you are when making decisions about how it should be spent. You should also consider how to supplement your main sources of income, and try to find out as much as you can about the costs which may arise during your studies so you're prepared for them.

Planning ahead is a great way of safeguarding your money during your studies. Budgeting identifies what money is available to you, and how you need to use it to your best advantage.

In this chapter, I provide information to enable you to plan your budget and show you how to get the most from your student finance and additional sources of income.

Counting Out Your Budget

Planning ahead gives you a realistic appreciation of how much money you have and helps you understand your spending patterns.

The first step towards successfully managing your money during your studies is to gain a thorough understanding of how much you have available to you.

Planning a budget

Very few people are filled with excitement at the idea of examining their finances in depth (probability dictates there must be someone somewhere who enjoys doing it!), but the majority recognise the benefits of undertaking this approach. The act of preparing a budget gives you a hands-on experience of what your finances look and feel like in real terms – in short, budgeting is a really useful eye opener, putting your finger on the pulse of your money.

Budgeting tools

Happily, the Internet has seen the development of a number of online budgeting tools which take some of the tedium out of the task of reviewing your budget. These online tools have the significant advantage of covering all kinds of typical items of income and expenditure – so you can be reassured that you're including items that you may not have thought to include otherwise. An online budgeting tool can be a powerful ally in taking the first steps towards taking control of your money, and getting it to work for you.

Use a free online budget planner that suits your circumstances. Some are aimed directly at students, others are for more general circumstances (which may suit students who have a partner and/or children). Brightside and the Money Advice Service provide the following budget planners which are free and easy to use:

- ✔ studentcalculator.org
- ✔ moneyadviceservice.org.uk/en/tools/budget-planner

If you prefer to work offline, you can make your own budget planner easily enough. Contact your course provider in the first instance, as their advice service may have a pro forma budget planner which you can use. If that option is not available, you just need to follow the following steps:

1. **Identify all your sources of income and note them down individually.**

2. **Identify all the items you spend money on – use helpful headings such as:**

   - Food
   - Utility bills
   - Phone/Internet
   - Accommodation
   - Course materials/costs
   - Health
   - Household goods
   - Clothing
   - Travel
   - Sundries (for example, newspapers)
   - Entertainment
   - TV licence
   - Insurance
   - Credit card/loans
   - Court fines
   - Other

   There may be additional items applicable to you, but the above list is a helpful starting point. Most importantly, make sure that you identify which of the above items you must prioritise – doing so helps you identify where you may have some options to adjust your expenditure.

3. **Use a standard time period so that all your items of income and expenditure can be compared accurately.** Use monthly or weekly figures because these are more memorable and practical.

4. **Review your items of income and expenditure and ask yourself:**

   - Have you included everything you need to?
   - Are the amounts you have written down representative of what you actually spend?

The second of these points is really important. The act of writing down what you spend on various items makes you reconsider how you wish to spend your money – you need to begin with a true picture of your spending patterns. Only by doing this can you take the time to reflect on how to spend your money wisely, and then to identify what spending habits you may need to adapt. Anything less than a 'warts and all' approach is unlikely to do you any favours in the long run, so try and be as honest with yourself as you can.

5. **Once you're satisfied that you've included all the items of income and expenditure, and that the figures are accurate:**

   • Total all your items of income

   • Total all your items of expenditure

   • Subtract your expenditure from income to work out how much money you have spare

If following the above procedure results in a positive figure this is great – your finances balance and you've some spare cash which you can use to your advantage. Think about what you can do with it.

If the calculation balances, you're just doing enough to get by – but you need to be careful to ensure that your financial position doesn't deteriorate.

When the budget doesn't balance

If your budget calculation produces a negative figure, you need to go back over the figures and begin to think about how you can change your spending patterns so that your finances balance, or identify additional sources of income so that you can afford everything you consider essential. If you've done this and you still can't get your budget to balance, consider seeking some advice from an experienced money adviser – contact your course provider's student services team for free, confidential and impartial advice.

Adding Up Your Income

How much income you have available to you as a student is largely determined by your own personal circumstances. A number of variables can affect how much income you have, including:

- ✔ Your age
- ✔ The course you're studying
- ✔ Where you usually live when you're not studying
- ✔ Where you live during term-time
- ✔ Whether you have children or adult dependants
- ✔ Whether you have a disability
- ✔ Whether you're working part-time
- ✔ Whether your course is full- or part-time

The above list is not exhaustive, but it illustrates just how many factors can combine to determine how much income you may have as a student.

The main source of your income is likely to be the statutory student finance available via the Student Loans Company but bear in mind that other sources of income exist as well and can often play an important role in supplementing your student finance. Additional sources include:

- ✔ Tax credits (for students with children, or working at least 16 hours per week and having responsibility for a child, or having a disability)
- ✔ Welfare benefits (for students with children, or some disabilities)
- ✔ Part-time employment
- ✔ Educational trusts and charities
- ✔ Bursaries and other financial assistance from your course provider

Additional sources of income rarely affect the amount of student finance you receive – any additional income you can access usually has a direct and positive effect on your finances. For example, any income a student has from employment is ignored for student finance purposes – this is a direct incentive to encourage students to seek work during their studies.

Realising when equal instalments aren't equal . . .

Your student finance is likely to be your major source of income each year you're a student. You receive a student finance notification as the outcome of your application for student finance, and this gives you details of the student finance you have been assessed to receive and when it will be paid to you during the year. This information is available from your online student finance account.

A quick glance at the payment timetable (which is part of the student finance notification) shows that your student finance is paid as three instalments of approximately equal value during the year. This sounds straightforward enough – but look more closely at the payment dates for each instalment. You'll find that these dates match the term dates your course provider uses to deliver your course.

 Typically, the autumn and spring terms at most universities and colleges are twice the length of the summer term – this means that your budget planning may not be as accurate as you had at first thought.

Using student finance of £4,000 a year as an example, you may have adopted a monthly figure in your budget planner as follows:

$£4,000 \div 12 = £333.33$ per month

The accuracy of this figure depends on your interpretation of a year for student finance purposes. If you define a year in terms of the length of an academic year, this is usually around 8 months long (October until the end of May). This can vary between institutions – it could be longer or may be even shorter, so you need to check with your course provider. This leaves what could be as much as a 4-month period for the long summer vacation when you may be available for work. In practice, this is commonly the interpretation students use when working out their budget, so your planning needs to reflect this:

$$£4,000 \div 3 = £1,333.33 \text{ per term}$$

Now look at how that figure breaks down over each term . . . here is our typical academic year:

Autumn term (October to December)	14 weeks = 3.2 months
Spring term (January to March)	13 weeks = 3 months
Summer term (April to May)	8 weeks = 1.8 months

Autumn term	$£4,000 \div 3$	$= £1,333.33 \,(\text{autumn term payment})$
	$£1,333.33 \div 3.2$	$= £416.67 \text{ per month}$
Spring term	$£4,000 \div 3$	$= £1,333.33 \,(\text{spring term payment})$
	$£1,333.33 \div 3$	$= £444.44 \text{ per month}$
Summer term	$£4,000 \div 3$	$= £1,333.33 \,(\text{summer term payment})$
	$£1,333.33 \div 1.8$	$= £740.73 \text{ per month}$

You can see from the above that, in real terms, the amount of money available to you during the weeks of the academic year fluctuates from term to term.

The picture becomes more complicated when you factor in some of the typical costs you may face – the biggest single item of expenditure in a year is likely to be your accommodation. For our purposes here, a figure of £2,700 represents the cost for the year. This is payable in equal instalments of £900 each term.

Each term, you need to deduct £900.00 from the £1,333.33 instalment in our example, leaving £433.33 available to you

Autumn term	$£433.33 \div 3.2 = £135.41 \text{ per month}$
Spring term	$£433.33 \div 3 = £144.44 \text{ per month}$
Summer term	$£433.33 \div 1.8 = £240.73 \text{ per month}$

You can see from the above that your budget planning can become more sophisticated the more you interrogate your situation. You should play around with the figures so that you gain a thorough understanding of your finances, not only in one year of your course, but during the entire length of your studies.

Maximising your income

Budgeting can be very challenging, largely due to so many costs competing for a slice of your income. Some of them are essential, others may be highly desirable – and the choices you make as to the lifestyle you live have direct consequences on your financial well-being.

One strategy to try and alleviate the pressures on your budget is to look at opportunities to maximise your income. There are several ways of doing this, and the effects can be dramatically effective if you're successful in realising an opportunity to increase the amount of money you have coming your way.

 Every extra amount of income you utilise is going to help your financial situation overall. Don't underestimate the importance of even the smallest amounts because they can all add up and make a positive contribution. It really is a case of 'look after the pennies and the pounds will look after themselves'.

 A good place to start is to look at the sources of income you have identified on your budget planner. Are you absolutely certain you're getting all the money you can from these sources? Take student finance as an example. Have you had your financial notification checked over for accuracy? An error may have been made in your application or the assessment of your student finance, meaning that you have entitlement to additional funds that you're not receiving. There are several commonly occurring reasons why this may be the case:

- ✔ Incorrect course details
- ✔ Incorrect term dates
- ✔ Incorrect address
- ✔ Being in receipt of non income-assessed funding when your circumstances mean income-assessed funding is available

The above list is not exhaustive, but is indicative of a number of the reasons your student finance could be incorrect. All of the above can lead to underpayment of student finance, and all are relatively easy to correct so that more funds are released. A relatively quick call into the advice service at your course provider can lead to a thorough exploration of your student finance entitlement, so this is highly recommended.

You may be in receipt of income from additional sources – here are two examples of checks that you can make against various types of income to make sure that you're getting all the income you should have:

✔ Wages – check what deductions are being made. If you're paying income tax (PAYE) check your tax code to see if you're on an 'emergency code'. If so, you can usually apply for a rebate, as students usually earn well below the threshold for paying income tax. More information is available from the website of the Low Incomes Tax Reform Group (LITRG): http://www.litrg.org.uk/ and http://www.taxguideforstudents.org.uk.

✔ Welfare benefits – some benefit offices automatically turn down claims from students, even though some categories of student are eligible to claim. If you are a lone parent or a member of a couple and both of you are full-time students with responsibility for a child, or you are a disabled student, make sure you check whether you can make a claim. Housing benefit (which is being replaced by Universal Credit) has been particularly problematic for students because it is handled by local district council offices – if you live in a district with a low proportion of students, the assessment of your claim could be incorrect if the office is not used to dealing with the special rules on how to treat student income. Again, you can check with the advisers at your course provider who can usually identify any errors in a benefit calculation – because all they deal with are student-focused calculations.

As well as the income you already receive, check to see if there are any additional sources of income you can tap into. Additional funds are likely to be available through your course provider such as:

✔ Institutional bursaries

✔ Scholarships

✔ Discretionary Hardship Funds

✔ Emergency short-term loans

Bursaries and scholarships usually have specific eligibility criteria – check what they are (the details should be on your course provider's website) and see if you think you may qualify. If so, make enquiries. Some course providers automatically allocate their bursaries/scholarships, others may expect you to make an application. There could even be a blend of approaches in operation. Make enquiries via the student services team – you can soon find out if there is any additional money available.

Even if bursaries/scholarships are allocated using an automatic system, it is still worth making an enquiry because automatic systems can sometimes get it wrong! Don't assume you are not entitled because you haven't yet heard anything – make the enquiry and make sure.

If you've looked at ways to maximise your income but you haven't been able to make any progress, and/or your budget is still worrying you, make an appointment with a money adviser at your course provider's student services department.

Understanding Expenditure

As well as scrutinising your income to see how you can maximise it, you should take a look at the 'expenditure' side of your budget plan to identify opportunities to cut down on your costs.

Some items of expenditure are easier to amend than others. Your rent is likely to be a fixed cost you can do nothing about. You may be able to save money on household bills by switching energy provider (check the price comparison sites online).

In this section, we consider typical costs you can expect during your studies, and consider how you may reduce those costs to a minimum, so they take less of your income away.

Typical costs you can expect

Accommodation is likely to be your largest single item of expenditure in any one year. How much you spend on accommodation is fixed as soon as you sign up to a contract, so researching the options available to you is extremely important – and compare them before you sign.

Never feel that you must rush into making a decision about where you live – if you find a landlord is putting pressure on you to make a decision, that can be an indicator they're not the best person to be doing business with. You would be extremely unlucky to be left without any alternative options, so if you feel you're being put under pressure, it's often best just to walk away.

There are some typical areas of accommodation contracts which you can focus on in order to compare and see which one is best for you. Consider:

- ✔ **Rent:** Rates can vary, so check this first.

- ✔ **The period of the tenancy:** Agreements are often for a fixed term, so check how long it is for. A monthly or weekly rent may look cheaper than a competitor, but if you're required to pay the rent for a longer period, it could work out more expensive overall.

- ✔ **Bills:** Is the rent inclusive of bills? If so, is there an additional 'fair usage' clause? Check these details to assess whether the arrangement may work out cheaper than other options.

- ✔ **Type of contract:** Is it specific to one room, or is it joint and several? If the latter, you could be taking on liability for more than your share of the rent, so take care to check.

If your accommodation contract requires you to take responsibility for household bills, there are a couple of strategies to consider to reduce the costs you can be held liable for:

- ✔ Consider changing energy supplier via a price comparison website (you may need your landlord's permission to do this, but this is usually just so they are kept informed of any changes).

> ✔ Make sure all the names of the people you're sharing your property with are on the bill – this makes it much easier for you to only pay your share of the bill, and encourage the billing company to pursue those who haven't paid in the event of any bills going unpaid.

If you pay rent for a room only and have a TV in your room, you need a TV licence. If you have a joint-tenancy, this is likely to mean you live with your housemates as one household, in which case you will be covered by one licence for the whole household. At the time of writing, TV licences are only applicable to devices which receive live TV, and are not required for 'catch-up' TV. Consider whether you can watch TV via catch-up – if so, you may only need to pay your fair share towards a communal TV licence for the shared areas in your house. Also, ensure you claim any refunds for any periods of the year where a TV licence is not required, for example, if you move out of the house during the summer months.

Try and be as creative as you can with your approach to essential costs – you can usually identify a cheaper alternative, and every change you make can add up to a considerable amount when you multiply weekly savings over the years you're studying on your course.

Typical costs you may not expect

In recent years there has been a call for transparency in the higher education sector to ensure all costs associated with study are clearly communicated in advance to all students. It is worth noting that some costs may not be the responsibility of your course provider.

Deposits for accommodation are required by private land-lords, as well as for some university halls of residence (some of which are managed by universities on behalf of private companies). Make sure you check whether a deposit typically needs to be paid before you move into your room, before your course begins and before you receive any student finance.

Disabled students need to be mindful of a recent change to the assistance available via the Disabled Students' Allowance (DSA). If IT equipment is recommended as part of your needs assessment, you are required to contribute to the first £200

of that equipment. Peripheral items such as connecting leads and printers are no longer supported by the DSA from 2015/16 onwards – so this places more of a financial burden onto you. Check with your course provider to see if they have made any financial support available to help meet these costs – some have already made such support available, often targeted at students from lower-income backgrounds.

Your course provider may require you to pay for a Disclosure and Barring Service check, to check your criminal record. This is almost certainly going to be required if your course involves placements working with children or vulnerable adults. Additionally, if you're going to be studying a course that leads into a profession, you may be required to pay fees for membership of a professional association – it's always worth enquiring about this if you haven't already been notified and you think it may apply to you.

If there are practical elements to your course, you may be asked to pay 'laboratory fees' or similar – these are costs associated with the upkeep or access to specialist facilities. These costs really should be made clear to you in advance, but do check if you haven't had any information.

Many course providers charge for on-campus facilities such as car parks and gyms – don't assume that they're going to be free because you're a student studying there. If you do use these facilities, ask about the payment options available – season ticket and membership schemes are quite commonplace and these can help reduce the costs for regular users.

Have a look at the information on your chosen course on the Unistats website (`unistats.direct.gov.uk/`) – costs associated with study are a required part of the 'Key Information Set' for all courses listed, so you can gain access to the information and compare with different course providers.

Setting up a budget

Once you have completed a budget plan, you have before you a useful benchmark when spending your money. Whenever you make a transaction, bear your budget in mind. This is a really useful life skill to learn – it doesn't just apply whilst you're a student. You can use this approach whatever your circumstances so you get a better appreciation of your financial position. It's a great skill to master before you set out on your graduate career.

You may even find it helpful to keep a spending diary so that you capture the most accurate picture of where your money is going.

Make sure you use your budget plan as a 'living document'. If your circumstances change, or some unexpected costs arise, go back to it with an update and see what this means for your finances overall.

Gaining an insight into your budget means that, if you've had a more expensive week than usual, you understand straight away that you need to make some adjustments to your up and coming spending pattern so that your finances are brought back into balance. If that's not possible, you need to think about what alternative strategies are available to you.

The key thing is that you can identify a 'ball-park' figure upon which you can plan your spending. Knowing your budget allows you flexibility – and it also means you're in a position to be in control.

Once you've planned your budget, it is time to put it into action. Think about what strategies you can adopt to ensure you stick to the levels of expenditure you've identified. Are there any opportunities for you to save small amounts of money (these can add up surprisingly effectively over time)?

These are some approaches you may consider to ensure you stick to your budget:

- ✓ Set up standing orders for essential costs such as rent and utility bills to ensure that they're paid.

- ✓ Set weekly or monthly cash limits for yourself, to make sure you stay within your planned budget.

- ✓ Set reminders on your phone to review your budget plan at regular intervals – doing so helps give early warnings when you may be facing difficulties with your money.

- ✓ Use regular and small amounts of cash rather than paying using plastic – this helps give you a real appreciation of how much money you're spending.

✔ Take time to check over your bank statements every month so you can review your expenditure and identify opportunities to spend your money more effectively.

✔ Get into good habits when using 'hole in the wall' cash machines (ATMs) – always check your balance before withdrawing cash (and ALWAYS cover your PIN).

✔ Always be on the lookout for opportunities to reduce your essential costs – if you have an insurance policy up for renewal, compare prices online. Check whether your household insurance is already covered by a parent's policy. Remember to check whether switching energy provider can save you money.

✔ Check for the availability of weekly, monthly or seasonal passes for travel schemes to see if they're cheaper than paying for individual trips.

✔ Make use of your NUS card whenever you can to make savings.

✔ Always remember to seek advice if you discover your financial situation is looking fragile.

Where to Seek Budgeting Advice

Most course providers make money advice available in some form or other on campus. Advice may be available via the Student Services team at the university or college, or via the welfare team at a Students' Union. Either way, you can usually expect to gain access to professional and experienced money advisers who are ready to help with an assessment of your situation, and provide options you can choose to explore.

Getting advice from a money adviser can be beneficial not only because they are usually able to give you some useful tips, but also because they can provide reassurance and support in more serious situations. You don't have to feel that you're alone trying to sort out your money.

A money adviser can:

✔ Identify priorities

✔ Try to maximise your income

> ✔ Discuss options to reduce your spending
>
> ✔ Suggest a strategy for your finances

 Details of money advisers at universities throughout the UK can be found on the National Association of Student Money Advisers website (www.nasma.org.uk). Check to see if a NASMA money adviser is available at your course provider.

If your course provider doesn't have a money adviser on campus, or the assistance they can provide is limited, then check the services available at your local Citizens Advice Bureau. Citizens Advice have an excellent reputation for delivering free, confidential, non-judgemental and impartial advice throughout the UK, so there is likely to be a bureau near your course provider. Citizens Advice often make dedicated money advice services available to the general public in the local area. Sometimes these services can be very busy as a result, so be prepared for the possibility of long waiting times for an appointment.

Citizens Advice (www.citizensadvice.org.uk), StepChange (www.stepchange.org), National Debtline (www.nationaldebtline.org) and the Money Advice Service (www.moneyadviceservice.org.uk) all have informative websites giving free advice online. Their resources can be a useful place to start when putting together a strategy to deal with your finances.

Chapter 16

Making the Most of Your Money

*S*tudent finances can be extremely challenging, and sometimes, paying for essential outgoings may leave you with no money for the other expenditure you face. This being the case, you should always seek opportunities to maximise your income and reduce your costs wherever the opportunity arises.

Putting your budget into practice means you need to develop your strategy for dealing with choices when they arise – you'll need to be informed as to how much money is available and what you can afford.

In this chapter, I provide some examples of ways you can reduce your spending on essentials like rent and food, and better manage your decisions on buying things you may like rather than need.

Spending Money on Essentials and Non-Essentials

In order to put your budgeting skills into practice, you need to be able to recognise the difference between costs which you *need* to pay for, and those which you may *want* to pay for.

Think of this dilemma by using the concept of *opportunity cost.* This is a bit of economics jargon which simply means that when you spend your money on one thing, you can't then use it to pay for something else.

Opportunity cost is an easy concept to describe, but not always so easy to put into practice. If you can exert the discipline to ensure that you weigh up what you need as opposed to what you want, you're doing yourself no end of financial favours.

You need to establish which costs should be treated as what's known as *priority expenditure.* The reason these costs are treated as a priority is because the consequences of non-payment are usually direct, and can be serious. For example, if you choose not to spend money on food, you can easily imagine that it won't be long before you're feeling hungry. Table 16-1 lists the typical priority costs for students, and indicates the consequences of the costs not being met.

Table 16-1	Priority Costs and Consequences
Cost	*Non-Payment Leads To*
Rent/Mortgage	Homelessness
Food	Hunger and ill health
Energy bills	No heating/cooking/hot water
Council Tax	Imprisonment
Clothing	Limitations to social engagement
Travel	Inability to get where you need to be
Tuition fees	Non-continuation/completion of study
Childcare	Loss of nursery place for child

 Don't underestimate the psychological effects of making provision for the costs associated with your basic needs. Taking the time to ensure that you meet these costs not only gives you the best chance of managing your finances in the long run, it also provides you with peace of mind, and even some satisfaction that you've established a basic quality of life on which you can aspire to build further. This will, in turn, put you in the best position to devote your energies to your studies, so that you can look forward to a future career beyond your studies.

Non-payment of priority expenditure can have immediate and longer-term effects. If you don't pay a bill, you may find your energy supply gets cut off. The immediate effect can be you no longer have the use of your heating, cooker and hot water. If you do nothing to resolve the situation, you can then find the matter is taken to court (which usually adds further costs to what you already owe) and you can end up with a judgement against you. So, not only do you not have the use of the energy, you have a debt situation which can damage your reputation to the extent it rules you out of pursuing certain careers (in the legal profession, for example).

Finding Ways to Reduce Spending on Essentials

Although your priority expenditures must be paid for, remember that you don't always have to pay the most expensive rate for the essentials in your life. In this section, I consider how it may be possible to pay less for the things you can't avoid purchasing.

Dealing with initial purchases

You may find that several 'up-front costs' may need to be considered even before you arrive at university. Below I consider some of the best ways to tackle them.

Deposits

If you plan to use rented accommodation (either from the university or a private provider), check to find out whether a deposit is required in advance. Deposits can be used to secure your room so that it's ready for you to move in to, and are often a feature of setting up an accommodation contract. How much you're required to pay varies according to the type of accommodation you use, and its geographical location (housing in London is more expensive than other areas of the UK).

Where an accommodation provider takes a deposit, it must be registered with the Tenancy Deposit Scheme (TDS) – this helps ensure your deposit is handled appropriately, and the TDS acts as a mediator in the event of any dispute between you and your landlord. If your landlord doesn't abide by the requirements of the scheme, you can qualify for financial redress.

Savings

Whilst not strictly an initial purchase as such, if you have the opportunity to put together some savings before your course begins, you'll usually find this a really helpful safety net to fall back on.

Unfortunately, students often experience a delay in their student finance reaching their bank account at the start of term – so if you have some money set aside in savings, this helps you get by whilst you wait for your funding to reach your account.

Laptop

At the time of writing, a laptop is arguably still the most effective tool for completing your coursework when you aren't working on campus. Whilst tablets are extremely intuitive, not to mention cool, they don't have the same processing power as a laptop, so the latter is probably the best investment if you haven't got one already.

Here are a few points to keep in mind when shopping for a laptop:

- ✔ As with all consumer products, shopping around to get the best deal you can is very important.

- ✔ If at all possible, be patient and save up for a machine rather than buying one on credit – your student finances are under enough pressure without you starting your studies owing money under a credit agreement.

- ✔ Don't feel obliged to purchase any additional insurance cover for the product – you may be covered already, and there's always your statutory rights under the Sale of Goods Act – which offers protection for a number of years for consumer durables.

And whilst I'm on the subject, try and take a frugal approach with any other mobile devices. Can you really afford the monthly mobile phone contract for the best phone on the market – or would it make more sense to go for a more modest handset on a pay-as-you-go scheme so you only pay for what you need? Also try to take advantage of free wi-fi hotspots wherever you can (but be mindful of security!), so you don't end up using a data allowance you have to pay for.

A cookbook and a larder

For many students, the start of a university course is also the time when they start to live independently. This is a skill in itself and purchasing a reputable cookbook (I won't name names, the choice is yours; but be sure to buy a book that tells you how to make more than just cake!) not only provides you with a comprehensive choice of recipes, a crash course in the skills you need and ways to make best use of on-hand ingredients, but it also gives you details of what should go in a basic larder to allow you to develop your cooking skills.

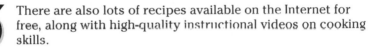

There are also lots of recipes available on the Internet for free, along with high-quality instructional videos on cooking skills.

For more tips on all things kitchen and food related, see the 'Feeding yourself' section later in the chapter (with a disclaimer that I can't turn you into Jamie Oliver).

NUS card

One of the first purchases you have the opportunity to make during the process of enrolling for your course is an NUS card. Don't make the mistake of thinking your Students' Union is taking advantage of the process of enrolment to get hold of your cash – the NUS card more than pays for itself in terms of the multitude of discounts available at a host of high street stores, supermarkets and fast food shops. So look upon your NUS card as an investment because it unlocks plenty of savings for you – just remember to keep it with you and use it regularly. Check out the 'Picking up a welcome pack' sidebar in this chapter for related money-saving discounts.

Picking up a welcome pack

Your university may offer 'welcome packs', particularly if you're moving into a hall of residence. Check out what may be on offer, as the university probably orders the contents of the packs wholesale so that they can pass the savings on to students – so you may be able to get some basic essentials such as bedding and a starter pack for your kitchen much cheaper than if you were to buy the goods yourself.

Feeding yourself

Food is one of those purchases which isn't going to go away – this one will be with you constantly! So don't forget to factor it in. Typically, you should be setting aside around £35 a week for a food shop (which includes your housekeeping expenditure for cleaning products, toiletries and general 'household' items), but you can adopt some strategies to save you a little money, or make your money go further.

Don't shop hungry

The first rule of food shopping is never go to the supermarket when you're feeling hungry – your eye will catch sight of all sorts of goodies which you really don't need. Worse still, you can find yourself having a feast of perishable items when you get home and then have nothing to eat for the rest of the week! Much better to plan your shop so that your ingredients can complement one another and be as flexible as possible (your cookbook helps you with this!).

Shop and cook as part of a household

The second strategy you can use is to shop as part of a household – if you can get together with other students who live nearby, or you share accommodation with, and agree meals you all enjoy, you can share the costs of a household shop.

Generally speaking, it's easier and cheaper to cook for two people or more than for one person.

Planning for a meal for four people may seem daunting at first, but give it a go and you'll soon get used to it – roast dinners are very popular with guests and surprisingly easy to serve up. Ideally, if you can get into a routine with friends all taking turns to cook, you can save money, improve your cooking skills and even get the odd day off!

 If you really do need to cook only for yourself, remember to use your freezer. You can cook larger meals designed for more than one and freeze individual servings for later. This approach generally saves you money on a per-meal basis and saves time during the week as you simply take the meal out of the freezer and reheat it – a healthy, homemade approach to fast food. (Just don't be tempted to eat larger portions!)

Opt for meat-free meals

If you're a vegetarian, you're already in prime position to be making savings – so even if you have carnivorous tendencies, try going meat-free for a few days a week – it'll help vary your diet and save you money.

Look past the premium brands

It's important to eat well, but don't feel compelled to buy the premium brand all the time. Does it really matter to you that you use the leading brand of cleaner or toilet roll, or how about tinned food, or staples like rice and pasta, or salt? Most supermarkets offer perfectly acceptable alternatives to the leading brands.

I know of colleagues who have given 'taste tests' to students and it is a revelation how often the cheaper brands come out on top. In addition, in many cases, supermarkets use the same suppliers to create their own brand products as the more expensive premium brands.

So give them a go and save some money as a result. Taking this approach amounts to a lot of savings over the years.

Eat away from home for less

It's reasonable to expect you won't be eating all your meals at home – some days you won't be able to get back for lunch, so you'll need to eat out. Whilst many universities try to offer cheap catering to their students, you can save even more money by making a packed lunch for yourself. And even if that isn't convenient all the time, do at least try to save money on buying soft drinks. Buy yourself a re-usable bottle and fill it with tap water or your preference. Staying off the fizzy drinks has health benefits as well. Doing this saves you at least £1 every time: that's £260 a year if you do this Monday to Friday!

Checking out your clothing and laundry

Clothing can be one of the more emotive of the items on the essentials list. You obviously want to look good and there's always pressure to keep up with the latest fashion trends. But when putting clothing on your essentials list, you need to put aside any aspiration of keeping up with the latest trends.

Ultimately, always try and keep a practical head when purchasing clothing, rather than indulging your more extravagant desires.

Identify a shortlist of wardrobe essentials

Your initial consideration should be to identify a shortlist of essential items in your wardrobe, and then work out what you can do to bring the cost of that list to a minimum. Think about the various situations you expect to find yourself in and the clothes you may need. Here are a few suggestions:

- ✔ Everyday casual attire for studies and meeting friends
- ✔ Kit for keeping fit
- ✔ Something more formal if you have a part-time job, going to interviews or your course requires you to go out on placement

Wherever possible, consider whether some items may serve dual purposes on your list. Do this before you head out shopping!

Hunting for bargains

Once you're satisfied that you've identified your needs, then you can start your bargain-hunting. Be aware that some bargains may not be all they seem. Paying 50 per cent less for an item may not be the bargain it seems if the quality means it wears out in no time. You may also hold ethical views about

which clothing manufacturers or retailers you're prepared
to shop at. These are all important considerations which you
need to weigh up.

Whilst looking out for bargains in the sales is always a good
idea, do keep a budget in mind. You've not really saved any
money if you're looking to buy one item, but buy two in a
'buy one get one half price' deal that takes you over the
budget you've set. Also, just as with food shopping, plan your
purchases rather than get to a point where you have to buy
something – that way you'll have the best opportunity to find
a real bargain.

Making more significant purchases

Occasionally, you may need to make a more significant
purchase like shoes, or a suit for work. Try to save up for
these eventualities (they will happen from time to time). If you
can't save, make sure you offset the expenditure against the
clothing allowance you've given yourself over the next few
weeks or months.

Consider opening a catalogue account for your clothing
needs. This is a useful way of spreading the cost of more
expensive purchases, but do be aware that this is a form of
credit – always ensure that you have the money available
to meet the costs on a monthly basis. And don't forget that
the goods may cost you more than if you'd purchased them
outright. Also, don't be tempted to buy more than you need –
use the same rules as when you're out on the high street and
don't be tempted to buy items that aren't essential. (For more
on managing credit and debt, see Chapter 18.)

Keeping things clean

When it comes to taking care of your clothes, check out the
laundry services that are local to you. Your university may
even have some on campus. If you have to use a launderette,
take time to shop around for the cheapest and most reliable –
you can probably get word-of-mouth recommendations from
other students you meet. If you have the use of your own
laundry facilities, don't forget to weigh up whether you really
need to buy the premium brand products, or are the supermarket own brands sufficient for your needs? Clothes have a
habit of wearing out from time to time, but you may consider
whether there are opportunities to repair them before you

discard them completely – it may be cheaper to get a repair done and use for a different purpose than go straight out and buy a replacement.

Finding appropriate accommodation

Your housing costs are likely to be the single most expensive priority cost you face each year. Students often leave home for university and move straight in to halls of residence. This is usually a fantastic opportunity to meet others in exactly the same situation and you begin to build a circle of friends outside of those you meet on your course. Living in halls usually means you have access to well-kept facilities, and bills are usually included in the rent (there may even be free wi-fi), all of which can add up to an attractive package. Living in halls can have plenty of advantages, and at the same time there may also be opportunities to save money.

Some universities offer a variety of housing options. Some may be university owned, some may be owned by one or a number of private providers. En-suite rooms are usually the most expensive option, so you may find cheaper alternatives if you can manage with shared facilities. Take the time to find out what options exist at the university – you can usually find out more information through the university's accommodation office.

University accommodation teams are usually very helpful and have useful details of the range of local housing available, including lower-price alternatives.

The accommodation office can also advise you of the various ways in which you can pay for your accommodation. These days, the common approach is to set up a direct debit arrangement which regularly takes rent direct from your bank account (usually at a time which coincides with your student finance payments), but some rent agreements give discounts if you pay for rent up front. You may also be able to find somewhere cheaper to live in the private-rented market, but don't forget to factor in bills if they aren't included in the rent.

Whether you rent from a university or a private landlord, you should check some key points in the contract before you sign.

Make sure you consider what period of time the accommodation contract covers. This will help you understand how much it will cost you in total.

Some agreements are approximately equal to the length of an average academic year – about 30 weeks. Some are longer than this and effectively cover the summer period, usually up to around 48 weeks. So, you need to decide what period you actually want to live in the property for, and if this differs from what is in the contract, you may need to think about negotiating with the accommodation provider.

The contract is a rental *agreement* – both parties need to be comfortable with what they sign up to. You may find the landlord is willing to alter the terms in their standard contract, so always ask if there's something you'd like to explore.

You should also check what the requirements are for payment of energy bills – this can often become a messy area if you don't follow some basic tips (but we'll discuss this in more detail later).

When renting accommodation in the private sector, you need to pay special attention to the contract you sign up to. Be watchful for phrases like *'joint and several liability'* as these contracts can be potentially more expensive. That said, such arrangements are extremely commonplace, so don't let the phrase put you off moving in altogether – you just need to be aware of what it means. Joint and several liabilities mean that each tenant named on the agreement is equally responsible for the entire rent due under the agreement.

Take this example:

> House for Rent: 6 bedrooms
>
> Weekly rent: £420.00 exclusive of bills
>
> All tenants named in this agreement will be jointly and severally liable for the rent.
>
> For a fixed term of 48 weeks

Let's assume six tenants move in to the property. The weekly rent can then be divided by six so that each occupant pays £70 for their room. Seems fair enough doesn't it. But what if one moves out? Common sense would suggest the landlord would have to chase the absent tenant for the rent, but under a joint and several agreement the landlord can obtain the rent from the remaining tenants – it would be up to them to take action to recover the additional rent they're having to pay from the tenant who left. So, in the above example, each tenant is potentially liable for up to £20,160 (the full rent due under the agreement over the fixed term).

If you sign up to a joint and several tenancy, do so with people you know and trust, and even then ensure that you have permanent contact details for each of them so that you can get hold of them if needs be. In practice, leaving one tenant with the entire liability would be most unusual, but the above example serves to illustrate how this kind of agreement helps a landlord get the best security possible from the possibility of tenants defaulting on rent payments.

Having the contact details for the people you're sharing with can help assist the landlord in the event of a tenant effectively doing a runner – and this can lead the landlord to be less insistent that you pay the additional share of the rent.

Some contracts are specific to a single room – these are usually preferable because they put a limit on the liability you can be asked to pay. They are easily identifiable because the contract usually only has your name on it, and specifies the rent you personally are required to pay. Another advantage of this kind of contract is the transparency of what you and everyone in the household is expected to pay.

Imagine if, in the 'joint and several' example previously discussed, one of the tenants got the master bedroom, and another found themselves in a box room – is it really fair that they should pay the same amount of rent each? (Under the joint and several agreement, any such dispute would be down to the tenants to work out.) Where a contract is per individual room, the landlord has usually already considered these kinds of issues in the first instance. So, as well as limiting the amount of rent you're actually liable to pay, you may also have one less argument with the students you're living with!

It's also worth mentioning you may need to check whether your landlord requires you to nominate a guarantor for your rent (this will usually be a relative who agrees to cover the cost of any rent you don't pay). This can be a requirement for joint tenancies, and if all your housemates have their guarantors in place, you might find it an awkward moment when you announce you haven't got one sorted out.

Adding up your bills

Just as is the case with rental agreements, joint and several liability can become an issue with household bills – except this time it is usually the desirable option, especially if only your name is on the bill! If you move in to shared accommodation, and you take it upon yourself to set up the bills in your own name, then it is you who will be liable to settle the account. If, however, the account is in joint names, all of the tenants living with you are liable as well

Ensure all those sharing in your household have their names on the bills.

Have discussions to ensure everyone is clear on how much they are obliged to pay on a monthly basis. Situations can sometimes arise where one tenant claims they haven't been using a service, for example, the Internet, and so don't need to pay the broadband bill; these arguments can often be extremely difficult to resolve, so it is far better if all agree to what they will pay for at the outset – this helps you identify what your regular outgoings will be.

In most instances, you need to obtain your own TV licence if you have a device capable of receiving a TV signal (this includes a laptop) and your rent agreement is for a room that is for your sole occupancy. If you have a joint tenancy, or there is only one TV in a shared area used by all, then you only need to buy a TV licence as a household. Not having a TV licence is a criminal offence, so it pays to get one – you can take advantage of payments by direct debit so that you don't have to pay the full amount up front – and remember that you may be able to get a refund if you're not at the address for the full year.

Energy

Energy costs are nearly constantly in the news, with costs steadily increasing each year. Consider switching energy provider, either to take advantage of a duel fuel contract or just simply to get a cheaper tariff than the one you're on. Always keep your landlord informed of any changes to the energy supply, but be aware that you have the right to change the supplier you deal with (unless you're in a rental agreement which is inclusive of bills). The act of switching provider can often be a simple means of saving some money.

Be careful of fixed-rate tariffs because these may tie you into a contract for several years, and you may not be planning on being at the address that long.

If you find yourself in financial difficulty with an energy bill, you may be able to get assistance from a trust fund. Several utility companies offer this kind of financial assistance and you can find out more about these schemes from the Energy UK website: `http://www.energy-uk.org.uk/customers/help-with-your-energy-bills.html`.

If your rent agreement is inclusive of bills, but your landlord wants to charge you an additional amount for energy, the first thing you need to do is check your rental agreement. Some include 'fair use' clauses whereby a standard charge is levied, but the landlord has discretion to charge more if the bills come in higher.

If this situation comes about, you should ask to see proof that the bills exceed the fair use charge. If there is no fair use charge, you can dispute paying any additional amount – but you may want to seek advice about this before doing so.

Internet

It is becoming increasingly common for university accommodation to include a free wi-fi package, but you should also be aware of other opportunities to use the Internet for free, rather than paying for it.

University campuses usually have excellent Internet connections – you just need to make sure you're abiding by the campus fair use policy.

Identifying local wi-fi hotspots can also be a useful way of keeping costs to a minimum, but always be careful of the security risks – avoid making transactions or accessing sensitive information (such as your bank account) unless you're confident no one else can access your connection.

If you're living in a privately rented property, you may wish to set up a broadband account. Always take the time to find out which providers are in your area and shop about to see which package suits you best. If you're opening an account as a household, make sure everyone is clear about their obligations before the contract is signed.

 The Student Loans Company has reported phishing scams every year since it launched its online application service.

If you're targeted by such a scam, you can report it via http://www.slc.co.uk/students/online-safety/phishing. Organisations you have an account with will *never* contact you by email to ask you to verify your account details. Always ensure you're accessing their website from a bona fide address and not a link from an email (scammers have created very convincing copies of websites) and always check for an 'https' prefix to any address where you're accessing your secure account information.

University fees and related expenses

Universities are required to set their fees in accordance with the limits set by the Office for Fair Access (OFFA). You can find how much a university plans to charge for a particular course by checking its Access Agreement at www.offa.org.uk/access-agreements. The Access Agreement also provides information about financial support available – so as well as telling you what you need to pay, it tells you what you may receive as well.

Whilst the Tuition Fee Loan is usually the most convenient means of paying for tuition fees for undergraduate courses (and PGCEs and some integrated Masters), don't assume it's fool proof. Errors can occur in the systems which operate between universities and the Student Loans Company that can result in you being charged a higher fee than you actually should be. If these errors go undetected, you can end up being charged interest on a higher amount of Tuition Fee Loan than is necessary – and whilst it's usually possible to rectify an error, the interest accrued as a result may go unnoticed by the parties concerned. For this reason, double-checking the information on your Student Finance Notification letter is vital *when you receive it* to ensure it is as you expected.

If you're unsure about any details of your student finance, contact the advice service at your university, or the agency assessing your application (Student Finance Wales, for instance, if you're usually resident in Wales).

If you have any other costs to pay alongside your fees, such as professional memberships or field trips, always enquire to see if any payment options are available. Universities are acutely aware of the financial position students can find themselves in, so are usually open to making more favourable payment arrangements upon request – contact the university's finance department for more details.

Travel

The easiest way to save money at university is not to have a car. The cost of fuel, insurance, and road tax can take a serious chunk out of your available income. So, if you can find a way of doing without, that is probably for the best. Of course, some students have no choice but to use a car – perhaps they have childcare commitments, a mobility impairment, caring responsibilities or simply live somewhere that isn't serviced by public transport.

Public transport is usually a much more financially viable alternative, particularly if you don't have to travel every day of the week.

Use your NUS card to obtain student discounts on trains and some bus services (check locally). The NUS card is a gateway to big savings on travel.

You may occasionally find yourself in a situation where the only option is to travel by taxi. If you have to use a taxi, try and do so with friends, so you can share the cost between you. However, don't let the cost put you off using a taxi if you're alone late at night – your personal safety must come first. Always ensure that you're using a reputable taxi company – arrange one in advance if at all possible.

Whilst public transport is becoming a cheaper and greener means of travelling, the cheapest and most environmentally friendly is getting about under your own steam. If you plan to cycle during your studies, it's a good idea to make sure you have insurance cover and the appropriate security measures against theft. Unfortunately, bike theft is still a very common occurrence, so if you want to keep pedalling, do pay attention to where you keep your bike, at home and when out and about.

Those that are able to have the option to walk save even more money – with the bonus that walking helps to keep you fit (just always be mindful of your personal safety and walk around with friends, particularly at night).

Taxes and students

Student finance (loans, grants, bursaries and so on) are not taxable items of income, but students don't get special treatment in the income tax system. The government has recently increased the personal allowance (the amount you can earn before tax) to £10,600 (set to rise again to £11,000 in April 2016), so you may think students would usually be unaffected by tax issues. But this isn't necessarily the case. You can finish your first year on your course, and then use the summer to find full-time work.

You may find a job that pays £15,000 a year for a full-time worker, but you are probably only working for two or three months. Your employer wouldn't take this into account when working out your wages though – they treat you as a standard employee, so the assumption is that your earnings can reach £15,000 by the end of the year. That means £4,400 of your income would be taxable (at 20 per cent) and the resulting tax bill would be apportioned on a monthly basis. So, by the time you finish working at the end of the summer, you may have been taxed up to £250. Now, as your earnings will have effectively ceased, and you are not in a position to earn the full £10,600 personal allowance, this means you can apply for a tax rebate and get back the money you paid in tax. If you have no other taxable income, you can apply to get a tax rebate for the current tax year. If you have some other form of taxable income, such as a welfare benefit, you need to apply once the tax year has finished (at the end of March). You have a time limit of four years in which to make your claim for a refund.

Most full-time students are exempt from paying Council Tax – as long as they live with other full-time students. If you live with a part-time student, or someone who isn't a student at all, a Council Tax liability applies to the house you live in. The thing is, as you're a full-time student, you still have no liability for the bill – the bill becomes the responsibility of the person(s) who is not a full-time student. If there is only one such person in the property, they can apply for a 25 per cent discount to their bill, as they are treated as living alone if the other people are all full-time students.

Students living with their partner should be aware of the possibility of the 25 per cent discount, as full-time students are effectively 'invisible' when a local authority works out a Council Tax bill.

 More information on tax is available from the www. taxguideforstudents.org.uk website – a valuable resource on all issues relating to tax and students.

Managing Non-Priority Costs

So far we've been considering the essentials that must be paid for. But of course, we all like to spend money on non-essentials as well. Sometimes the difference between an essential and non-essential cost becomes much more subjective, but for the purposes of this book, the priority expenditure list is as we have defined – everything else is 'non-essential'.

The golden rule is to try and keep non-essential spending to a minimum – above all, beware temptation.

Try to set little goals for yourself. For example, if you keep within budget for a month, maybe you can reward yourself with an item you have been looking forward to (but don't undo your good work!).

Saving £2 coins can be a fun way of keeping some money aside for special purchases – and it can be surprising how quickly the amount can build up. Special occasions and parties can be expensive, and sometimes you may feel duty bound to let the budget go a little. Never underestimate how appreciated something home-made can be – and people usually understand your pockets are not lined with gold whilst you're studying. Holding a celebration at someone's house is a sure way of keeping costs lower, as it's going to be far cheaper to get food and drinks from the supermarket.

Seeking More Advice

Going to see an independent money adviser if you're in any kind of financial difficulty can be beneficial not only because they are usually able to give you some useful tips, but also because they can be an effective means of intervention when debts start to go bad.

A money adviser explores your finances with you, and engages with you in a confidential, non-judgemental and impartial discussion about how you have been using your money, and how you may improve your financial literacy. They can discuss your budget with you, and identify key areas requiring attention. Sometimes the conversation may be a difficult one, but the adviser will be acting with your interests at heart and seeking to identify options available to you.

If you're in debt, a money adviser can assess which debts need immediate attention, and which are not so urgent. They can help you draw up a financial statement which can be used as the basis of making revised offers of repayment to creditors – and by having an advice agency involved, the creditor isn't just taking your word for it, they're receiving information which has been assessed by a neutral agency (money advice is usually a free service!).

A money adviser:

- ✔ Identifies priorities
- ✔ Tries to maximise your income
- ✔ Discusses options to reduce your spending
- ✔ Suggests a strategy for your finances

On campus

Most universities have a money advice service available for students to use. This will either be located in the student services department or in the Students' Union welfare team. If you're unsure, just try one or the other and they can direct you to where you need to be. The services are usually run on a confidential, non-judgemental and impartial basis. This means you can go and talk openly about your situation, and receive information about the options available to you. The services are usually free.

If you're worrying about your money, go and seek advice as soon as possible: most situations have a better chance of being resolved if dealt with early – don't leave it until later.

Details of money advisers at universities throughout the UK can be found on the National Association of Student Money Advisers' website www.nasma.org.uk.

Off campus

Citizens Advice Bureaux are located in most major towns and cities in the UK and usually offer money advice. Their services are free, but open to the general public, so sometimes they can be very busy – for this reason you may be best served by exploring the services at your university in the first instance.

Online

Citizens Advice (www.citizensadvice.org.uk),
StepChange (www.stepchange.org), National Debtline
(www.nationaldebtline.org) and the Money Advice
Service (www.moneyadviceservice.org.uk/en) all
have informative websites giving free advice online. Their
resources can be a useful place to start when putting together
a strategy to deal with your finances.

Chapter 17

Maximising Your Income

· ·

In This Chapter

▶ Making sure you get the money you're entitled to

▶ Where to go for help with unexpected costs

▶ Alternative sources of student income

· ·

*Y*our student finance is worked out based on the information that you provide. You need to be sure that you've given all the necessary information and that it has been interpreted correctly in order to access the full amount of funding applicable to your circumstances.

Even if you've made sure that you're set to receive all the money to which you're entitled, there's still a chance circumstances may arise which you've not planned for, and this can upset any careful plans that you've made for managing your finances.

In this chapter, I provide some suggestions as to how you can maximise your income, both by checking your entitlement and exploring additional sources of student funding which could make all the difference in maintaining a healthy bank balance.

Ensuring That Your Assessment is Correct

Once you've applied for your student funding and received notification of how much you're going to be paid, you need to check whether the assessment has been done correctly. There are a number of ways that you can find out more information, depending on how hands on you want to be. A useful first step is to check your assessment against an online student finance calculator.

When applying for student finance, it's up to you to check the outcome of your application is correct. Don't assume the assessment is accurate – mistakes can occur.

The departments which process student funding handle huge amounts of information and occasionally things can go wrong. Getting your assessment checked by an adviser at your university can give you peace of mind that you're getting all that you're entitled to.

The advisory services at your university (usually found either in your Student Union or in the student services department) usually have plenty of experience in checking student finance assessments. After asking some fairly basic questions about your circumstances, they can usually indicate whether your student finance has been worked out correctly.

If you choose to contact an advice service, provide as much accurate information as you can to help the adviser make their calculations. If you've some additional information you feel is relevant, make sure that you bring it to the adviser's attention. Advice services are usually confidential, so you can be reassured your personal information will be secure (but do check so that you know for sure).

If you'd like to check the accuracy of your assessment yourself, additional resources are available on government websites. These are:

- Financial Memorandum
- Guidance Chapters
- The Education (Student Support) Regulations

Every year, the government publishes a *Financial Memorandum*, which sets out the rates at which student finance is payable. This document includes really useful tables which set out the amount of financial support available to students in various circumstances. It also gives details of the rates applicable to students living with their parents during anywhere else in the country. You can also see the difference between full and final year rates of loan. The tables are excellent at showing student finance available at various levels of household income. You can use these as a useful guide to give you an idea of how much funding is available to you once household income has been taken into account. The Financial Memorandum is published at `www.practitioners.slc.co.uk/policy-information/ student-support-information-notices.aspx`.

Guidance Chapters are published each year to provide interpretation of the regulations governing student funding. They tend to be useful for more complex scenarios and are much more straightforward than the regulations themselves. However, you would do well to check your situation with an adviser at your university if you find yourself consulting documents like this, as the information can sometimes be misleading without a good knowledge of the regulations it relates to. The Guidance Chapters are published in full at `http://www.practitioners.slc.co.uk/policy-information/guidance chapters.aspx`.

Also available in the public domain are the Education (Student Support) Regulations (available at `www.legislation.gov. uk`). These are the actual legislative measures which set out the basis of student finance in UK law. As you may expect, they're written in pure legalese and can be a challenging read if you are unfamiliar with documents of this type. If you need to consult these documents, your situation is probably a complex one, and so you should contact a student adviser at your university so that they can assist you.

Finding Additional Money to Apply For

Once you've made an application for your student finance, you can still consider a number of additional steps to ensure that you maximise the income available to you.

Make sure that you've applied for the maximum student finance available to you. Other sources of funding often expect you to do this, or even assume that you've done this, when they consider whether they can offer additional financial assistance.

Considering income-assessed support

Getting the maximum student finance you can means you should consider applying for income-assessed support. If you don't, you're automatically assessed for the basic (non income-assessed) package – and your circumstances may mean that you're entitled to more than that.

The student finance system at the time of writing provides support on the basis shown in Table 17-1 (which uses the 'Elsewhere' rate for students studying outside London and living away from the parental home during term-time).

Table 17-1	'Elsewhere' Rate
Household Income	*Type of Support*
£0 – £25,000	Income-assessed (maximum rate)
£25,001 – £42,620	Income-assessed (loan and grant)
£42,621 – £62,134	Income-assessed (loan only)
£62,135+	Non income-assessed (loan only)

These figures show the extent of the household income thresholds where income-assessed funding is available. Slightly different income ranges apply to the London and Parental Home rates, but the same basic principle applies. Don't dismiss the possibility of income-assessed support, particularly if there is the possibility of obtaining a grant (which does not have to be repaid). In the above example, some kind of income-assessed support is available on all household incomes up to £62,135.

Once you've checked that you've maximised the basic student finance package to which you're entitled, you should consider what other sources of funding may be available. A good place to start is to see whether your university has any additional funding that you can apply for.

Acknowledging that your priority expenditure must be paid for is important, but equally important is recognising that you don't always have to pay the most expensive rate for the essentials in your life. In the following sections I consider how it may be possible to pay less for the things you can't avoid purchasing.

Applying for discretionary funds

Most universities have additional funding for students who experience financial hardship on their course. They may use any number of criteria to determine whether a student qualifies for additional financial assistance, and if so how much. These types of funds are known as *discretionary funds*.

Each university decides what circumstances it considers to be a priority for assistance. Many use a list similar to this:

- ✔ Students who have previously been in Local Authority care
- ✔ Disabled students
- ✔ Student parents (especially lone parents)
- ✔ Students who are carers
- ✔ Students with pre-existing debts
- ✔ Students with priority debts
- ✔ Final year students

Whilst a list like the above may help universities prioritise the allocation of their discretionary funds, any student who meets some basic eligibility criteria can usually make an application. An application is judged on its merits and an assessment of the information provided determines whether any financial award is given.

Even if your circumstances are not reflected in the above list, then you can still make an application and see if you can get financial support. This is particularly the case if the reason you're applying is as a result of some unexpected circumstances. Examples include damage to your property, theft or as a result of a caring responsibility which you had not foreseen. Generally speaking, a university usually seeks to assist its students through discretionary funds if it can, as the purpose of the funds is to help the university retain its students and help them succeed in their studies. For this reason, it's well worth exploring the possibility of additional money from this source – and the great thing is, if your application is successful, you usually don't need to repay the assistance you're awarded.

When applying for discretionary funds, checking the following is really important:

- ✔ Are you eligible to apply for the funds?

- ✔ What information is required to support your application?

- ✔ Is there a specific application form, and is the one you have the current version?

- ✔ Have you answered all the questions relevant to your situation?

- ✔ Have you provided all the information you can about your circumstances?

- ✔ Have you signed and dated the application?

Discretionary funds are usually subject to regular audit. This means the university usually requires you to provide evidence of your situation wherever possible so that it can demonstrate it's providing financial assistance to those who deserve it most. You should always try to provide any documentation that is requested because doing so is likely to increase the chance of a successful application.

An application for discretionary funds may require you to provide personal documents (like bank statements) but the reason for this is simply to allow the university to show it has made a thorough assessment of your situation. If you're concerned about how your personal information is used, or stored, just ask about this. The departments that process applications for financial support usually observe data protection requirements to ensure that your details are secure.

Above all, you must satisfy yourself that you've given all the information that is relevant to your situation before you submit your application. You usually need to prepare a personal statement which describes your situation. Time spent on this part of the application can help ensure its success, as this is your opportunity to explain in detail how the evidence that you're providing supports your reasons for applying. Don't assume that the person who processes your application is able to pick up the relevant information from the various documents you've supplied – describing your situation in full is a far more effective approach. You can then be sure that the person processing your application knows exactly why you've applied.

Working towards bursaries or scholarships

Another very common source of additional funds from your university is through the bursary or scholarship schemes it provides. Since 2006, any UK university which charges more than £6,000 tuition fees a year for its courses has been required to provide additional financial support for students (particularly from lower-income backgrounds) – and this support has often taken the form of a bursary or scholarship.

Bursaries usually provide targeted support to students with particular circumstances or characteristics, whereas scholarships are usually made available based on a student's previous academic achievements. You may even find that some universities offer scholarships which become available depending on the level of achievement you attain during your university studies. Whilst bursaries are almost always paid as financial support to the student, you may find that scholarships are sometimes paid as discounts against tuition fees rather than a direct payment to you.

 Bursaries don't usually have to be repaid. Universities can choose their own criteria to determine who they target for additional financial support. These may include:

- ✔ Students from low-income families
- ✔ Students who are the first in their family to enter higher education
- ✔ Students from neighbourhoods with low participation in higher education
- ✔ Students who have attained a high academic standard (usually used for scholarships)

Bursary schemes vary from one university to the next – they depend on the priorities of the university as to what kind of student they target through the scheme, and the level of financial support available.

Universities often use information from the Student Loans Company to deliver their bursary schemes. When you make your application for student finance, look out for the question which asks you whether you give permission for your student finance assessment to be shared with your university. Allowing this to happen ensures that you're considered for the possibility of additional financial support through a bursary scheme.

Once again, making an income-assessed application for student finance is important because many universities use household income information from the Student Loans Company when working out if students are eligible for money from their bursary scheme. Students from low-income backgrounds are regularly targeted for additional financial support, and the information you provide when applying for student finance is key.

Some bursary schemes are more elaborate than others and may include several eligibility conditions. Make sure that you check whether you fulfil more than one of the eligibility conditions, as doing so may mean more funding can come your way.

Applying to educational trusts and charities

When applying for your course, do some research to find out whether any additional funding may be available to you from an educational trust even before you apply for your student finance from the government.

Identifying as early as possible the trusts and charities that may be able to help you is very important. There are two reasons for this:

1. Many trusts and charities operate on scheduled deadlines, so you need to make sure that you can make a timely application and not leave it too late.

2. The budgets these sources operate on vary enormously – if the trust or charity that you're applying to has a relatively small budget, you must ensure that you apply before the money has been allocated (whilst you may be eligible for a financial award, if the money has already been assigned to someone else, you won't be able to access it).

When you're doing your research, don't be put off if a trust or charity only has a small operating budget, or only makes small awards. Typically, these sources make awards of up to £500, although there are some that offer more. You should be aiming to make several applications to these sources to realise as much money from them as you can. Once you've made one application, you'll find it relatively easy to adapt the information for an application to another trust or charity.

There are thousands of funding schemes which have been set up throughout the UK, sometimes due to bequests from individuals, philanthropists or by organisations, all of which aim to help support students to achieve more through education. These schemes operate on many diverse criteria, and typically these may include:

- Location – by country, county, parish or electoral ward
- Occupation of parent(s)
- Subject of study
- Gender
- Disability
- Nationality
- Study overseas
- Level of study (undergraduate/postgraduate)
- Religious orders
- Profession

With so many different criteria, you may find that there are a number of avenues relevant to your circumstances which you need to explore.

Put as many irons in the fire as you can – it's unlikely that you'll find out if your application to any particular source of funding is going to be successful at an early stage. If more than one application ends up being successful, this is all the better for you.

In order to find out more about the trusts or charities which may be able to help you, you should contact the student services team at the universities you're planning to study at. They usually have resources available which can help you to identify some of the trusts or charities which are relevant to you.

You can also do your own research online, but do make sure that you're only using reputable websites, as they often ask you to submit some personal information to help narrow the search. A good place to start is the Turn 2 Us grant search (available via http://www.turn2us.org.uk). Turn 2 Us is a charitable organisation and its search facility includes trusts and charities relevant to higher education.

Working During Study

Earnings from employment are just as much a valuable source of financial support as your student finance, or any other additional funding that you're able to obtain.

A student's earnings from employment are not taken into account when the government calculates your student finance – so you can earn while you learn without it affecting the money you receive for your studies.

Recent research undertaken by the National Union of Students found that nearly half of students in the UK have a part-time job, with one third working during term-time to help with financial support for their studies.

There are a number of reasons why getting a job alongside your studies is a good idea:

✔ Working provides a regular income which is really easy to budget with (weekly, or monthly)

✔ Additional income from work means that you're less likely to require a bank overdraft, or other forms of credit

✔ Employment opportunities can help you add experience to your CV and increase your employability as a graduate

Finding work alongside study can have its challenges, but you can usually expect to receive some assistance from the careers service at your university. They have information and guidance on searching for jobs, and often keep lists of local vacancies suitable for students.

If you already have a job before starting your university course, it's always worth asking your employer whether you can change your hours of work so that they fit round your study. If you're moving away to university, and you work for a national company, check to see whether your post can be transferred so that you can carry on working – this is sometimes possible with employers like supermarkets.

Striking a balance

Finding the right balance between work and study is key. Remember your priorities when you find yourself working alongside study. Sometimes, you may find that your studies and your employment are in conflict with one another. For example, you may have several assessment deadlines which mean you are unable to keep to your usual weekly hours of work, or your employer may be short-staffed and may ask you to work more hours than you had originally intended.

Your studies are not just the hours timetabled in lectures and seminars – when considering how many hours you can go to work each week, you need to allow yourself time for private study, group work and planning for assessments and revision.

If you find yourself working because you've been struggling financially, don't lose sight of the time you need for study. Getting in as many hours of work as you can to improve your financial position is very tempting, but try to remember to plan so that your work and study are both sustainable.

Some employers are more flexible than others. You may find work on the university campus, or in a business that employs a number of students already – these employers are more likely to be aware of students' needs as well as their own. If you find yourself working somewhere less student aware, have a discussion about flexibility with the employer so that asking for time off around your busiest study periods doesn't come as a surprise.

First and foremost you are a student – any work you take on is to help you in your studies. If the number of hours you work starts to affect your studies, it's your responsibility to address the balance. Your university is unlikely to be sympathetic to any deterioration in the quality of your assessments due to you working rather than studying.

Reviewing Options that Work for You

Once you've taken the time to research all the opportunities available to you to maximise your income, consider which approaches you're going to take.

There may be reasons why you're unable to work during study, in which case you probably want to explore as many alternative sources of student funding as you can, such as discretionary funds or trusts and charities. Alternatively, you may be satisfied that the part-time hours you work are sufficient to support you in addition to your student finance, so you do not need to look for any further funding.

Take the time to review your situation and consider what options are available. You may find that the structure of your course changes from year to year, which can mean that there are additional opportunities arising from time to time, or further challenges, which may mean you need to explore further funding sources.

Chapter 18

The Credit Chapter (You knew it was coming . . .)

In This Chapter

▶ Understanding your credit options

▶ Being aware of credit to avoid

▶ Knowing where to seek assistance

*Y*ou may find that you need to consider exploring credit options during your time as a student. It's vitally important that you make the best-informed choices because the wrong kind of credit product can mean sending your financial situation on a downward spiral.

In this chapter, I provide information about the typical sources of credit that students might encounter, together with suggestions as to which might be more appropriate for you to consider taking on.

Always remember to shop around to see what options are available to you, and always seek advice in the first instance if you're unsure which option is best for you.

Deciding What to Do about Credit

A *credit agreement* is a contract in which a lender sets out the terms of a loan to you. By signing up to a credit agreement you are agreeing to the terms of the loan (the credit) being provided to you.

The first thing to ask yourself if you're thinking about entering into a credit agreement is 'Do I need to get into debt?' It's the most important question to ensure that you're taking proper care of your money – you need to be absolutely sure that you've explored all other options. Only when you're satisfied that the reason that you need the extra money is essential, that no realistic alternative exists and that the credit you're looking to use is suitable for you, should you take the next step.

Before you enter into a credit agreement make sure that you've applied for the maximum student finance available to you and that you've maximised your income from all other sources such as employment, relatives and savings.

An enormous range of credit is available in the UK, all made available in various shapes and sizes in a variety of financial products. The variety means that the options for credit can get confusing – especially when some products look remarkably similar at first sight. When you're using credit for the first time, the picture can become all the more puzzling.

Don't use credit unless you really need it AND can afford it. Credit is more expensive than cash.

Of course, some students enter higher education later in their life, and may bring existing credit agreements with them. In this case you need to consider how to manage existing credit during study. But the basic message remains the same, even where a student has existing debts, make sure that you limit the amount of credit you take on during your studies.

Working out your paying-back strategy

The reason why you need to be so careful around credit is quite simply that credit costs you money and the less burden you place on your future financial situation the better – particularly during the short period relating to your time of study.

If you find yourself in a situation where credit begins to look as though it could be a helpful way forward, the first thing you must do is to consider the types of credit available to you. Make an informed decision – don't just sign up to a product without researching the full range of options and the implications for you.

Work out a clear strategy to pay off the credit that you're taking on over a short to mid-term period – then you can be sure that your financial situation is sustainable.

Using credit effectively means that you're incurring a debt – but debt usually only becomes an issue when you can no longer afford to service it. Always take precautions to make sure that you do not overreach yourself with the credit you take on, otherwise you risk getting yourself into an unsustainable debt situation.

Check your credit score before you borrow – it can determine whether your application for credit is successful, and how much the credit is going to cost you.

Boosting your credit score

If you're thinking of using credit for the first time, consider what kind of credit score you have – lenders use a *credit score* to assess what level of risk you might be as a borrower.

Your credit score may be low if you've never used credit before, but you can take a few simple steps to help boost your score. Try the following when you're starting out in year one of your studies, as they can help you establish your credit score over time:

- ✔ **Open a bank account:** Having a bank account and managing it responsibly is the basic building block of your credit score – and can lead to further opportunities to add to your score.

- ✔ **Pay your bills by direct debit:** Direct debits help you build up evidence that you're capable of meeting your financial responsibilities on a regular basis. Ensuring that you've enough money in the bank to meet on-going commitments is a contributing factor to your credit score.

✔ **Consider using your overdraft:** This might seem like odd advice, but many student accounts come with interest-free overdrafts, allowing you a fairly safe first-time credit experience. Talk to your bank and ask them how to set up the facility to make sure that you use it without incurring any charges. As an overdraft is a form of credit, responsible use of it helps you to build your credit score – just remember that you'll be going into debt, and you need to pay off the overdraft in order to get back into 'the black'.

✔ **Make sure that you're on the electoral register:** The credit score is not solely built on your credit history – it also uses criteria such as where you live. Making sure that you're on the electoral register doesn't just mean that you're making sure that you're entitled to vote – it also means that you're visible to various authorities. The important thing here is to show you can be located should the need arise, giving you more points for your credit score.

Missing a payment can mean your credit score is affected – always ensure the credit you take on is affordable and consider setting up a standing order to make sure the repayments are made regularly.

Credit records, which show your credit history for the last 6 years, are managed by credit reference agencies. There are three main companies acting as credit reference agencies in the UK: Experian, Equifax and Callcredit. You can check your credit record online using any one of their websites. There is currently a £2 charge for the service.

Know how your credit record stands so that you can assess the likelihood of successfully applying for credit. Each time you make an application, a credit provider (creditor) usually makes a credit check on you. If the result is negative, this can be added to your record and may mean your next application for credit is affected. However, you can make 'soft' checks which do not affect your credit record – tools for doing so are available online, one example is at MoneySavingExpert.com (www.moneysavingexpert.com/eligibility).

Separating the Good from the Bad

If you find yourself needing to use credit during study, be sure to recognise the difference between the various types of credit products. Some are more friendly to use than others. This section focuses on the typical types of credit that you're most likely to encounter.

If you're thinking about using a product that doesn't fall into one of the descriptions here, always seek advice first – check with the advice service at your university.

Good debt

Is there such a thing as 'good debt'? Yes!

When considering your options for credit, the first places to look are those which have the least cost attached to them, both in terms of the levels of interest they attract (which determines the overall cost of what you have to repay) and the likelihood of serious repercussions if you have difficulty making the repayments.

Student finance

First on the list are the Maintenance Loan and Tuition Fee Loan available from the government via the Student Loans Company. The majority of students make an application for either or both of these loans more or less automatically as part of their preparations for study in higher education. However, some choose not to if they have other sources of income. If you're a full-time student and you haven't already taken a student loan out, look at this option first before any other forms of credit because it's likely to be the cheapest option available to you.

Even though student loans have interest attached to them, the additional terms and conditions governing when and how much you need to pay mean that they are often the most favourable option.

Hardship loans

If you already have a student loan, next on the list is to check whether your course provider has any kind of hardship loan scheme you might be able to apply for. Better still, they might direct you to sources of funding you don't have to pay back, so it's well worth making the enquiry. In the event of there being any loans you can apply for, they're likely to be interest-free and for a short-term period. How suitable this kind of credit is for you depends on how much money you're looking to borrow, and for how long.

Neither the government student loans nor money available to borrow from your course provider have any kind of credit checks attached to them – the money is made available to you based on some basic eligibility criteria. Making applications for these loans does not adversely affect your credit score, which makes them a good place to start.

Family

Having explored the above, the next option depends on your own family circumstances. If you can borrow from a relative, you should explore it. Borrowing from a member of your family can usually be done on a much more flexible and less costly basis than through a formal arrangement with a bank or other lender. This kind of borrowing also has the advantage of introducing you to the responsibilities of repaying credit without the risk of affecting your credit score.

Overdraft

Once you've explored all of the above, the next option is likely to be the overdraft attached to your student bank account. If you reach this stage, and you don't already have a student bank account, ask your bank about the option of switching to one. Most student accounts have an interest-free overdraft facility attached to them, so switching to one can be well worth the trouble. This arrangement means that, as long as you stick to the terms of the overdraft, you can get hold of some credit with no additional cost.

Student bank accounts do differ from one another, and so it's sometimes in your best interest to switch to a different bank altogether. Research the different options before starting your course by searching the Internet or by going into various high street banks and picking up leaflets on their student bank accounts.

Do be careful to discuss the arrangement of the overdraft with your bank, and familiarise yourself with the terms and conditions to avoid the possibility of incurring penalty charges or penalty interest. An overdraft is usually available on a short-to mid-term period – it might see you through to the end of an academic year, at which point your bank might be expecting you to gain employment during the summer to repay it before the start of the next year of your course.

Restrict yourself to just one student overdraft! You may even run the risk of being found guilty of fraud if you open more than one, and having two student overdrafts to pay back can be a considerable burden.

Credit card

This item is included in the 'Good debt' category with some heavy caveats. Only consider this option if you're disciplined with your finances and can repay any borrowing on your card by the end of the month. If you don't repay everything by the end of the month you *will* incur interest and using the card will have cost you money (see the later section 'Bad debt'). Because of this pitfall, this option really should be your last resort – not least because you need to have the money to repay the card within such a short period of time.

If you can't repay the card in full in one month, aim to do so as soon as possible before using the card again – otherwise the balance on the card increases. Always repay more than the minimal amount the lender asks you to pay on your monthly statement. If you only pay the minimum, you pay far more interest against the original amount you borrowed from the card.

Bad debt

The term *bad debt* is one used to describe the less favourable forms of credit available. Using the term in this way assumes your principal source of income is your student finance. If you have additional income, a greater number of credit options may become viable for you.

Bad debt simply refers to any sources of credit which are going to cost you money from the outset. If you're going to take on this kind of credit, you need to be fully aware that you are required to pay back more than the amount you borrowed. How much more depends on the type of credit you use and how well you stick to the terms of the credit agreement.

Of course, I'm using the term 'bad debt' to distinguish between cheap or free sources of credit and those which are available on more standard (costly) terms. A debt only really turns bad when you're not in a position to service it and it gathers additional charges over and above those in the original agreement. If you find yourself either in this position or approaching it, you should see an independent money adviser. Assistance is likely to be available via your course provider.

Tracking Down Sources of Credit

This section looks at the sources of credit which are less likely to be the best solution for you in the first instance. Have a read of each of the following sections to get an idea of how each of the products works so that you can see the comparison.

Credit cards

Credit cards are included in this category because it's far more usual to see people using them in a manner which has a cost attached.

You really need to be very careful about using this form of credit if you're not in a position to repay what you borrow immediately. Credit cards are an extremely convenient form of credit – you don't have to make an application every time you want to borrow, just use the card every time you make a transaction in a shop, restaurant or online. Easy! Of course, but maybe too easy.

You can apply for a credit card via your bank or online. If you do it online, you might find one of the price comparison websites helpful, as they list key features of each card – but pay closest attention to the interest rate the card charges.

Credit cards are issued under the Consumer Credit Act, so the card provider must give you full information about the rate the card charges, what your credit limit is, how to make payments and how to cancel the card (including the 14-day 'cooling-off' period). Make sure that you check the terms and conditions of your card. You may receive rewards for making certain types of purchases, and you may perhaps benefit from 0 per cent interest on some transactions. However, the golden rule you must follow is to ensure that you can repay the amount you borrow within a short period of time.

Figure 18-1 shows a simple example of how a credit card works.

Using a credit card with a 20% interest rate:				
AMOUNT BORROWED	MONTH 1	MONTH 2	MONTH 3	MONTH 4
£100 (repaid in 1 month)	Repayment = £100.00 Interest = £0.00 Total Balance = £0.00 Cost = £100.00	-	-	-
£100 (repaid £50 per month)	Repayment = £50.00 Interest = £10.00 Total Balance = £60.00	Repayment = £50.00 Interest = £2.00 Total Balance = £12.00	Repayment = £12.00 Interest = £0.00 Total Balance = £0.00 Cost = £112.00	-
£100 (repaid £25 per month)	Repayment = £25.00 Interest = £15.00 Total Balance = £90.00	Repayment = £25.00 Interest = £13.00 Total Balance = £78.00	Repayment = £25.00 Interest = £10.60 Total Balance = £63.60	Repayment = £25.00 Interest = £7.72 Total Balance = £46.32 Cost (to date) = £146.32

© John Wiley & Sons, Inc.

Figure 18-1: How a credit card works.

In Figure 18-1, it would take another two months to clear the debt at a rate of £25 per month. The examples show how a credit card can be useful if you pay the money back quickly, but costly if you over-extend and do not have the means to make large repayments each month.

You need to be aware that a regular payment needs to be paid every month and you should aim never to use the card until you get the repayments back under control. If you do use the card again, and add to the balance, you'll need even longer to pay the card off because of the interest.

If you miss a payment, contact the card provider at the earliest opportunity and make arrangements to pay. If you're in a position where you cannot make a full repayment within one or two months, consider setting up a standing order to make sure that payments are not missed. You also need to make sure that your payment is affordable but meaningful (and more than the minimal payment on the card).

If you miss a payment because you're in financial difficulty, the card provider should contact you with a default notice and a fact sheet (from the Financial Conduct Authority) which explains what you can do to put things right. Seek advice at this point – if you haven't already done so – to find out how you can get your finances back on track. If you don't respond to the default notice, the card provider may cancel your card so that you're unable to use it any more. They also usually take further action to recover any money that you owe, including the possibility of taking you to court.

Court action can usually be avoided if you stay in correspondence with your card provider. As soon as you pay the money owing under the agreement (note that this is not necessarily the full amount you owe, it could just be the payment(s) you missed), the credit card is usually activated again.

Personal loans

A personal loan is usually obtained from a bank or building society, and online options are available as well. A wide range of products is available, so using a price comparison site to compare products might be helpful. Do remember to check with your own bank as well – as an existing customer your credit score may be higher with them.

When offering you a personal loan, most lenders take you through a credit check. The outcome of the credit check depends on your credit score and indicates whether the loan is going to be available to you, and at what kind of rate. A lower credit score may mean a lender is unwilling to make credit available to you, or makes credit available at a higher than average rate.

Personal loans are governed by the Consumer Credit Act, so the loan provider must give you details of the terms and conditions including the amount you have borrowed, the rate of interest, the amount of payment you need to make and how often, and how to cancel the card (including the 14-day 'cooling-off' period).

A personal loan is usually offered at a lower interest rate than rates attached to credit cards – but they can be more difficult to obtain if your credit check shows you have a low credit score. The other difference with a credit card is that the amount you borrow is fixed at the time that you apply for the loan as well as the rate of interest and repayment terms. Personal loans also tend to last a mid- to long-term period, so you must be in a position to maintain the repayments over a longer period of time. A typical loan period is measured in months rather than years – a 60-month loan is one lasting 5 years.

As well as usually having a lower rate of interest, the personal loan has the advantage over the credit card of telling you exactly how much the credit will cost you over the period of the loan (this can vary on a credit card if you continue to use it and allow the balance to be unpaid at the end of the month). So, with a personal loan you can be much more sure of what you're taking on – you just need to be sure that you can meet the conditions of the agreement over its full lifetime.

If your only source of income is student finance, you're less likely to qualify for a personal loan than people who have income based on their job. Most lenders want to see evidence of some regular (monthly) income. If you work alongside your studies, then maybe this is an option you could consider – but remember you need to check the affordability alongside your other commitments such as rent, course costs, food and so on before you sign on any 'dotted line'.

If you miss a payment because you're in financial difficulty you should contact the loan provider as soon as possible. Just as is the case with a credit card, if you don't, the loan provider should contact you with a default notice and a fact sheet (from the Financial Conduct Authority) which explains how to put things right. Seek advice at this point, if you've not already done so, to find out how to get your finances back on track. If you don't respond to the default notice, the loan provider usually takes action to recover any money you owe, including the possibility of taking you to court.

Court action can usually be avoided if you stay in correspondence with your loan provider – as soon as you pay the money owing under the agreement, the loan provider may allow your repayments to continue as normal. (This is not necessarily the full amount you owe, it could just be the payment(s) you missed – the terms of your agreement will determine this.)

Pay day loans and doorstep lenders

These two types of credit share one very important characteristic – they are very expensive forms of credit. From the per-
spective of those working as money advisers, the usual advice
is that these forms of credit should be avoided, particularly
if you're on a low or irregular income. Nevertheless, both of
these types of credit are legal and, despite being so expensive,
should not be confused with 'loan sharks' who operate in an
entirely unregulated and illegal manner.

Pay day loans

The pay day loan industry has been very lucrative in recent
years, and adverts for various companies have swamped
commercial breaks during daytime TV. Some of these loans
have been targeted at the student market, with some online
products readily identifying themselves as being intended for
students to use.

My general advice is to leave pay day loans well alone. If you
have to use one, do so with great care after first checking out
all your alternative options. Make sure that you can pay it off
within the month – if you can't do so you really shouldn't be
taking the loan out, as it only adds to your financial difficulty.

The premise of the pay day loan is that you can borrow a relatively small amount of money and then pay it back in a short
period of time – ideally the end of the month, hence the term
'pay day loan'. Because the loan is made over such a short
period, the loan provider charges a higher rate of interest
than would be found on personal loans or credit cards – and
it is this, together with the fees and charges associated with
managing the loans, that usually makes a pay day loan a least-
favoured option when it comes to seeking credit.

When they first arrived on the scene, pay day loans were
responsible for some devastating debt situations for individuals stuck with a debt that they couldn't make any headway in
repaying. The government has since introduced some measures to curb the excesses of the industry, but you can still
end up owing twice what you borrowed.

Doorstep lenders (home credit)

The interest rates of doorstep lenders are comparable with those for pay day loans, so the first rule here is to avoid this form of credit if at all possible. Just as with pay day loans, these loans expect regular repayments – usually weekly. Repayments are usually made in cash to an 'agent' who comes to your house for the payment – hence the term doorstep lending. Just as with pay day loans, the interest rates charged on these loans are so high that they rarely make any financial sense and are best avoided altogether.

If you do use a doorstep lender, make sure you take time to read the terms and conditions of the loan before you enter the agreement. If you do find yourself having difficulty making the repayments, discuss this with the agent – they may be able to vary the repayment terms for you (although this is likely to make the loan even more expensive in terms of what you repay overall).

Knowing What to Do about Debt

Taking out credit doesn't automatically mean that you have a debt situation on your hands. You have a responsibility to repay the money you have borrowed under the terms of the agreement, but that doesn't necessarily make the credit a 'debt' if you're managing your finances responsibly and you can afford to make repayments on time and in a manner which reduces the debt over a planned period.

If you find yourself in a situation where the credit you've taken on begins to dictate your finances, then you need to start thinking about your credit in terms of it being a debt. It is important to recognise that you can still have a debt situation even if you haven't missed a payment on your loan or credit card. If you have to reduce the money you spend on essential costs such as food or travel, then you're in the beginnings of a debt situation – and you should seek advice at this point.

When seeking support with your financial situation, remember that usually more can be done to prevent a situation from getting worse if tackled in its early stages. If you think you might be struggling financially, seek assistance sooner rather than later. Doing so is usually far more productive and means cutting out a lot of the worry that a debt situation can bring with it. The advice service provided by your course provider can usually assist you directly, or let you know where free help is available.

Using Debt Strategies

If you find yourself in a debt situation, the first thing to do is to seek assistance. Free advice is usually available from a number of sources including your course provider, but also agencies such as your local Citizens Advice Bureau or the StepChange Debt Charity (www.stepchange.org).

Once you've accessed support, you need to discuss the strategy you're going to use to resolve your debt situation. Various options exist, ranging from negotiating repayment with your creditors, all the way through to submitting a petition for bankruptcy. Which strategy you use is determined by the type of debts you owe and the amount owing overall. Speaking to an adviser helps you to identify the most suitable approach for your situation.

Self-help approaches

If your situation is relatively straightforward you can possibly take direct action to resolve your debts. A good first step towards this is to discuss your situation with an advice service in the first instance, and ask if they have a 'self-help debt pack' which can equip you to deal with your creditors. Resources can also be found online with a simple search via the Money Advice Service (www.moneyadviceservice.org.uk). If you're able to follow a self-help route, you'll probably use the standard money advice procedure, which goes like this . . .

Money advice services are typically free, confidential and non-judgemental. They will offer you advice on the various options open to you, but it will be your decision as to which course of action you follow. The advice service will usually respond to your needs – so if you feel confident you can handle your affairs by yourself, they will usually have a self-service debt pack available for you to use. If you require assistance, they can usually help you out with pro formas and standard letters, and may even negotiate with creditors on your behalf. Money advice of this kind is a licensed activity requiring registration with the Financial Conduct Authority – you should check to ensure the service you use is registered and holds a current licence.

First, identify your priority creditors – usually your landlord/ mortgage provider, Council Tax (if any), utility bills and also your course provider (so that you can protect your status as a student). Check to see if you have any money owing to these and if you do, contact them directly to make arrangements for payment in the first instance.

Once you've done this, draw up a financial statement. This statement needs to record all sources of income, and also all of the items of priority costs you need to pay. These include basic needs such as the above list (rent/mortgage, food, utilities, clothing), travel costs and everything else that are essential costs you need to meet.

Take time to make sure that you're using consistent figures when you draw up the financial statement. On the income side, you might get paid termly for your student finance but monthly for your part-time job. Your expenditure might include monthly rent, but a weekly amount for food shopping. Make sure that all these amounts are easily compared by settling on a standard time period. If you choose to show monthly figures, you will need to divide your total annual student finance by 12 to get a monthly figure. A weekly food shop bill should be multiplied by 52 and then divided by 12 to get a comparable figure. Once you have identified all the figures, you can present them as an *income/expenditure sheet*, as shown in the example in Figure 18-2.

Your version of Figure 18-2 forms the first half of your financial statement. As well as showing individual items of income and expenditure, it compares the totals and indicates what income you have spare, if any. It is this spare income which will form the basis of the repayment offers you make to your creditors. If you do not have any spare income, you will need to demonstrate why this is and make a 'token' offer of payment. This could be as low as £1 per month. Creditors may accept this in the short term, but be aware that they will expect to see an improvement in your situation and an increase in the amount you are offering to repay. When you send in your offer of repayment, you should tell your creditor you're experiencing financial difficulty, and request they freeze any interest being added to the account – some may agree to do this for you.

INCOME AND EXPENDITURE SHEET

Name:	
Address:	
Additional Household Members:	
Date:	

INCOME	£/month	EXPENDITURE	£/month
Maintenance Loan		Mortgage/Rent	
Tuition Fee Loan		Council Tax	
Maintenance Grant		Water Charges	
Parental Learning Allowance		Gas	
Childcare Grant		Electricity	
Adult Dependants Grant		Tuition Fees	
NHS Bursary		Telephone	
NHS Grant		Housekeeping	
Social Work Bursary		Travel Expenses	
TA Training Bursary		TV Licence	
Child Benefit		Child Care	
Child Tax Credit		Buildings Insurance	
Working Tax Credit		Contents Insurance	
Incapacity Benefit		Clothing	
Income Support		Course Equipment/Materials	
Jobseekers Allowance		Health Related Costs	
Housing Benefit		Entertainment	
Wages		Court Fines	
Partner's Income		Other	
Other		**TOTAL EXPENDITURE**	
TOTAL INCOME		**AMOUNT AVAILABLE**	

PRIORITY CREDITORS	BALANCE	ARREARS	£/month

© John Wiley & Sons, Inc

Figure 18-2: Example income/expenditure sheet.

The second half of your financial statement is the *creditors' sheet*. This is where you list all your credit debts, giving names and addresses of each creditor, the account details, amount borrowed, amount owing and how much you propose to pay. A creditors' sheet looks like the example shown in Figure 18-3.

CREDITORS' SHEET

Name:
Address:

CREDITOR'S NAME AND ADDRESS	ACCOUNT NUMBER/ REFERENCE	BALANCE	ARREARS	MONTHLY OFFER

© John Wiley & Sons, Inc

Figure 18-3: Example creditors' sheet.

Once you have completed your financial statement, you should send it to each of your creditors, together with individualised letters setting out the reasons you're in financial difficulty, and how much you're offering to repay. Including the financial statement means that each of your creditors is able to see the other debts you need to pay, so they become aware of the full extent of your financial situation.

You need to follow a procedure to determine how much you offer to each of your creditors. This procedure is called the equitable distribution calculation, as detailed in the next section.

The equitable distribution calculation

When contacting your creditors with an offer of repayment, you need to demonstrate that you're treating them all fairly and on the same basis according to the income you have available. Your financial statement should describe your priority expenditure, any priority debts that you have and how much you intend to pay. Once these factors are taken into account, any remaining money is what you can afford to offer to your non-priority creditors.

In order to work out how much to offer each individual creditor, the following equation is used:

$$\text{Individual Debt} \div \text{Total Debt} \times \text{Available Amount}$$

The total debt figure is the amount you currently owe to all of your non-priority creditors – don't include any of the debts listed on your income/expenditure sheet, only the ones in the second half of your financial statement.

Once you have worked out an offer for each of your creditors, you're ready to contact them. A financial statement of this kind is usually expected to be reviewed on a 6-monthly basis. The real advantage of this approach is that it reflects the approach taken by county courts, and most creditors recognise this.

Legal matters

If a creditor contacts you and says that they're considering court action, you really need to contact an advice service at that point. They may possibly act as a third party on your behalf and bring the creditor back on side and avoid the need to go to court.

If your situation is more serious and the standard money advice procedure is not sufficient to resolve it, other strategies might need to be used. These can include Debt Relief Orders, Individual Voluntary Arrangements (IVAs) or even bankruptcy. Which of these routes is suitable depends on an individual situation, and you really should seek out advice from a specialist money adviser or solicitor if you're considering any of these routes.

Money advice services

Most course providers have advice services for their students, many of which provide money advice. The National Association of Student Money Advisers (NASMA) aims to promote best practice in advice services aimed at students in higher education – check whether your advice service is a member.

Advice services are usually confidential, impartial, independent and free. You can expect to be able to have a full and frank discussion about your situation without anyone sitting in judgement and pointing out where your finances went wrong. All the emphasis will be on finding a way forward, and using strategies to avoid the situation repeating itself in future.

Money advisers are not able to wave a magic wand (unfortunately) but they are a valuable resource which will help you to identify your options for a way forward, and who can provide on-going advice and guidance whilst you're seeking to resolve your situation.

In the event that your course provider does not offer money advisory services, be sure to look up local alternatives via your local Citizens Advice Bureau, or by contacting StepChange via their website.

Part VI

The Part of Tens

Find a list of ten great student finance resources available today at www.dummies.com/extras/student financeuk.

In this part . . .

- ✔ Check out the top ten do's and don'ts of applying for funding.

- ✔ A penny for your thoughts – ten tips for making money go further during your studies.

- ✔ Go myth-busting by dispelling ten common rumours about student finance.

- ✔ Access quick and easy information on how to make your finances work better for you throughout your studies.

Chapter 19

Ten Do's and Don'ts when Applying for Student Finance

*M*aking an effective application for your student finance is the key to getting financial support for your studies. Knowing what you're eligible for, and what kind of funding you can expect to receive, is vital.

Navigating the application process can be a challenge, so it's important to find out as much as you can about making an effective application.

In this chapter, I have highlighted aspects of the application process which are not readily apparent, but which are important to observe to ensure that you get the maximum funding available to you.

Apply OnLine

The way you apply for your student finance is important, and the first thing to remember is to apply online. The government's systems are designed to handle the receipt of electronic information through its websites.

Each nation in the UK has its own student finance application website. Use the site for where you normally live in the UK, as follows:

- **England:** www.gov.uk/student-finance
- **Wales:** www.studentfinancewales.co.uk
- **Scotland:** www.saas.gov.uk
- **N. Ireland:** www.studentfinanceni.co.uk

Keep your account details safe and secure – you'll need them every time you wish to check on your application's progress.

The online application usually takes between 30 minutes and an hour to complete, depending on how complex your circumstances are, so make sure that you set aside sufficient time. If you get interrupted, save your progress and return to the application later.

The core items of funding (Tuition Fee Loan, Maintenance Loan and Maintenance Grant) can all be applied for online. If you're making a more complex application where you need to demonstrate independence, or you're making an application for grants for dependants, it's likely that you'll need to send the relevant documents to be assessed alongside your application.

Always send documentation by recorded delivery so that you can track it – this is especially important if you're sending original copies of important documents like a birth certificate or passport. Copies are usually acceptable for financial evidence, and you should also write your name and customer reference number on every page of every document you send.

Apply Before Your Final Decision on Course/University

Your application for a place on a university course usually begins a year in advance of the start of your university studies with an online application to the University Courses Admissions Service (UCAS).

The UCAS application focuses only on your choice of course
and university – and can sometimes take several months to
complete, depending on the interview or other selection pro-
cedures your choice of university uses.

The UCAS system allows you to apply to several choices
of courses/universities at the same time, so your choice of
course may not be certain by the time the funding application
cycle opens (usually February for a course starting the following September).

In some cases, you might be applying to UCAS within a few
months of the start of your university course, particularly if
you make an application during Clearing.

This doesn't mean that you have to wait to be certain of your
course and university before applying for the money to support your study. The Student Loans Company is fully aware
of the flexibility within the UCAS system, so it has created its
online systems to be flexible too.

Always apply as soon as possible once the applications for
student finance open:

- ✔ Apply early
- ✔ Apply online
- ✔ Apply for income-assessed support
- ✔ Check the progress of your application

Use the details of the course and university where you feel
that you're most likely to study to get your student finance
application underway as early as you can – these details can
be changed later if required.

You have until 1 September to change details relating to
your choice of course – and you usually know your final
choice before then. As 1 September is the first day of the academic year for funding purposes (for courses starting in the
autumn), you're not allowed to change the details beyond that
date – ownership transfers to the university you have chosen.
You can still change university/course after that date, but
you'll need to get in touch with the university named in your
application so that they can confirm you'll not be studying on
the course in question.

Apply Even if You Think You Don't Qualify

You might think that you won't qualify for student finance so it's not worth making an application. Perhaps your family has a better than average income, or you have had credit refused in the past. Neither of these factors has a bearing on the availability of student finance. For example, you can be bankrupt and still qualify to receive student loans to support your studies.

The fact is the student finance system provides support to the vast majority of higher education students in the UK. Its principal aim is to support UK nationals with financial support to allow them an opportunity to engage in higher education study, usually to achieve an undergraduate degree (though some postgraduate opportunities are funded as well).

With this aim in mind, the funding is largely available as long as some basic eligibility requirements are met. Personal circumstances are then considered to work out how much *additional* financial support you might qualify for, rather than to work out whether you'll get funding or not. Whilst EU students are limited to Tuition Fee Loan support only, in limited circumstances, the full range of student finance is available to non-UK nationals – if you wish to find out more, you are advised to contact advisers at your course provider so that your individual eligibility can be checked.

It's also worth remembering that any earned income you receive during your studies is disregarded for student finance purposes – only *unearned* income is taken into account (for example, taxable interest on savings, or rent from property you let out to tenants). So, when working out whose income is taken into account, remember it's usually your parents (if you're under 25) or your partner (if you live with them and you're aged over 25, or you are married/in a civil partnership).

The student loan terms and conditions often compare very favourably with other forms of credit – so it usually pays to take out a student loan rather than use savings or other credit.

Check the Eligibility Requirements

Eligibility is an important consideration when working out how much student finance is available to you.

Student finance eligibility depends on:

- ✔ Where you have been living
- ✔ Where you will study
- ✔ What you will study
- ✔ Whether you have studied before
- ✔ Whether you have made required repayments on previous student loans

Where you have been living

Where you have been living prior to your studies is a crucial factor. Don't assume that because you hold a UK passport you have the 'right' to the financial fund to your studies.

The rules around ordinary residence are complex – particularly if you or your family has been living within the European Economic Area (outside the UK) during the three-year period. It's always worth contacting an adviser at the university you're applying to for advice.

Where you will study

Most universities in the UK qualify for student finance, particularly those which are deemed to be public institutions. Most long-established universities fall into this category.

When applying to study at a UK university, you also need to be studying a course which runs in the UK (some UK universities have campuses abroad!).

What you will study

The rules governing student financial support clearly define which courses qualify for student finance. Most of the common forms of undergraduate degree qualify, as follows:

- ✔ Foundation degree
- ✔ Certificate of Higher Education
- ✔ Diploma of Higher Education
- ✔ BA/BSc degree

The above list is not exhaustive – refer to Chapter 3 for more details.

Whether you have studied before

If you've already achieved a higher education qualification, the usual rule is that you cannot receive funding for a qualification which is equivalent to or lower than the qualification you already hold.

If you've studied in higher education previously, but didn't achieve a qualification, you should be aware that any years of study you were on the previous course are usually taken into account. These rules are strict – registration for one day on a previous course is enough for that to be counted as one year's study, and so reduce your future entitlement by one year.

If you studied on a part-time course and did not achieve a qualification, and you plan to study your next course full-time, your previous study will not be taken into account. The same applies vice versa if you plan to study part-time and have studied full-time previously.

An important consideration regarding previous study is the reason you left your last course. If this was because of health reasons or a caring responsibility, then you can qualify for 'compelling personal reasons', in which case that year's study will not be counted against any future funding entitlement (but you are still asked to repay any loans you received for that year).

Whether you have made required repayments on previous student loans

If you have existing student loans as a result of previous study *and* you were required to make repayments but didn't, you will not usually be able to receive any further loans *or* grants until the required repayments are made.

Student loan repayments depend on you having finished your time in higher education *and* earning income over the required threshold – if both these requirements are not met, no repayments are required. So, you may have student loans from previous study that you have never been required to repay, in which case any future student finance entitlement will be payable.

Apply For Income-Assessed Loans and Grants

Non income-assessed student finance represents the minimum support available to you if you are eligible to receive funding for your course. Non income-assessed support typically consists of a Tuition Fee Loan and a Maintenance Loan equivalent to 65 per cent of the maximum amount available for a particular year.

Income-assessed student finance provides financial support above the minimum levels. Applying for income-assessed support unlocks the possibility of receiving grants alongside the loans, as well as accessing the income-assessed portion of the Maintenance Loan.

An income-assessed application is a must if you are a student who is a care leaver, a lone parent, single and aged over 25, or single and have supported yourself financially for the three years before your course begins.

Don't Leave it Too Late

Make your application as early as you can before the start of your course. As a rule, applications for student finance made nearer the start of the course are less likely to be ready for payment when your course begins. Having said that, even if you apply early, you may still experience a delay in your funding being paid to you.

Applying early means you give the Student Loans Company the time it needs to process your application. The standard processing time is 6 to 8 weeks, but the process can take longer at busy periods of the year.

If your application is incomplete, more information is needed or an electronic data check goes wrong (for example, checking your National Insurance number with HMRC), then your application will take longer. Applying early allows you to make allowances for the possibility of something going wrong.

If you do leave it late, don't assume that you're too late! Deadlines vary depending on the type of finance you're applying for, but most can still be accessed after the start of the course.

Do Check Correspondence for Accuracy

When you receive a letter regarding your student finance, always make sure that you check the details are correct. Pay close attention to:

- ✔ The name of your course
- ✔ The academic year
- ✔ Your year of study (first, second, third and so on)
- ✔ The names of the loans and grants awarded to you
- ✔ The amounts of money for each loan and grant
- ✔ Dates of payment

Incorrect details can result in delays to your student finance being paid to you.

If you find details which don't look correct, or you're unsure about the accuracy of a letter, contact the agency you applied to (for example, Student Finance Wales) or your university.

Your online student finance account is regularly updated when correspondence is sent to you – you can see a letter that has been added to your account up to five days before it reaches you in the post.

Don't Forget to Check You Have Completed All You Need To

When you fill in your online application, take time to ensure that you have completed all that is required on each section. The form is designed so that you can review it, so it is a good idea to take advantage of this facility before sending it off.

If you are making an income-assessed application and someone else is sending information in support of your application, ask them to take the same approach.

If, at any point, you're not sure that you have provided the correct information, or don't know what to do in response to a question, seek advice. Contact the advice service at your university, or the agency assessing your application.

Even when you have clicked 'submit' on the online form, your application is not complete. Look out for your declaration form which should be available to download as soon as you hit 'submit'. Fill it in and send it off in the post as soon as possible – your application is not complete until it is signed and sent back.

Don't Assume Things Are OK if You Don't Hear Anything

The Student Loans Company does not have a reputation for being proactive when it comes to sorting out problems with applications. Normally, it's your responsibility to check on the progress of your application. If the usual processing time of 6 to 8 weeks has elapsed and you haven't heard anything, make sure you contact the assessing agency dealing with your application.

There are a number of common issues which can arise and disrupt the progress of your student finance application. The Student Loans Company cannot always identify these issues, so it's best to check that your application is making progress.

Do Contact Your University to Check Your Entitlement

Ask the advice service at your university to check the funding you're receiving. As well as checking your student finance entitlement, they can usually inform you of additional sources of funding, either from the university itself or from other funders such as educational trusts and charities.

Making sure that your funding request is correct and that you are getting all the entitlement you are due gives you the peace of mind that you have explored all the funding opportunities available to you.

Chapter 20

Ten Tips to Make Your Money Last

- -

In This Chapter

▶ Budgeting effectively

▶ Checking out money-saving tips

▶ Using useful strategies

- -

*O*nce you've applied for your student finance and taken steps to ensure that you have your full entitlement, it's really important to try and make your money work for you.

Managing your money on a limited income can be extremely difficult, particularly when it's paid in large, infrequent instalments – especially if you're managing your finances for the first time.

In this chapter, I suggest some ways you can plan to make your money work for you, and some strategies that can help you manage your money, including making sure that you don't end up paying more than your fair share of essential costs.

Drawing Up a Budget

The prospect of examining your budget in depth is unlikely to get your adrenaline rushing, but nevertheless, it's impossible to underestimate the importance of carrying out this basic reality check of your financial situation. There's no better way of getting an overview of your money in terms of what you have coming in, and where it gets spent.

Once you've made a budget, you know how much money you have available on a weekly or monthly basis after your essentials have been paid for – even if it means going back and checking the plan from time to time.

Successful management of your money during your studies is best achieved through gaining a thorough understanding of how much you have available to you.

Many budgeting tools are available on the Internet. These are really helpful because they prompt you to think of items of income and expenditure you may not have included otherwise. Brightside and the Money Advice Service provide the following budget planners which are free and easy to use:

✔ studentcalculator.org

✔ www.moneyadviceservice.org.uk/en/tools/
   budget-planner

Your budget plan needs to include all items of your income and expenditure. You also need to:

✔ Use a standard period of time (week/month) for each item you include in your list

✔ Prioritise your essential costs

✔ Be realistic about the amounts you put down

✔ Check that you include everything you spend money on

Take away your total expenditure from your total income to work out how much money you have left over.

You probably won't pay all your costs on a weekly or monthly basis, but you do need to pick one for your plan.

If it becomes apparent that your budget won't balance, even though you've taken steps to ensure it does, this is an indicator that you need some input from a money adviser – contact your university's student services team for confidential and impartial advice.

You can convert your costs from weekly to monthly amounts, or vice versa like this:

For a monthly amount:

Weekly amount $\times 52$ = Annual amount

Annual amount $\div 12$ = Monthly amount

For a weekly amount:

Monthly amount $\times 12$ = Annual amount

Annual amount $\div 52$ = Weekly amount

Completing a budget plan gives you a better insight of:

- ✔ Where your money comes from, and when
- ✔ Your essential costs
- ✔ What you spend your money on
- ✔ How much money you have left over

The key thing is that you can identify a 'ball-park' figure upon which you can plan your spending. So, if you've had an expensive week, you know that you need to reign in your finances over the next two or three. Knowing your budget allows you that flexibility – and it also means you're in a position to be in control.

Your student finance is paid in three, roughly equal termly instalments, but the three terms are often different lengths (the summer term is usually the shortest). This means that you may have less money than you expected for the majority of the year.

Resisting Temptation

The biggest threat to your budget plan is unexpected or unplanned spending. Whether you have a particular fondness for clothes, nights out or travelling, any instances of impulse spending are likely to have a lasting impact when you're on a limited income.

The ease of Internet shopping is a constant threat to you keeping your finances on track – resisting browsing for items is really important unless you really need them and you can clearly afford to spend the money.

Impulse buying can just as easily occur on cheaper items as well as more expensive ones – the thing is, if it's a frequent occurrence, it soon adds up.

Regular expenditure on a daily bottle of water from a corner shop can mean you spend over £300 a year – when you can use a refillable bottle and fill it at home.

Try to establish strategies so that you don't get overwhelmed by urges to spend your money on what you can't afford.

There are some quick and easy steps you can take to guard against spending on impulse:

✔ Limit the number of 'special' purchases you make each month

✔ Make a wish list and use it for your birthday and Christmas

✔ Make a list before you go shopping – this helps you keep to what you need rather than what you may want

✔ Use cash instead of plastic

✔ Use small amounts of cash in the interests of your safety and security

✔ Establish healthy spending routines and keep to them

To some extent, the success of the above is highly dependent on how effectively you can exercise your willpower – so if you're finding it hard to control your spending, it may help you to talk to someone about it. This may be something you could turn to your close friends about, but if you'd rather speak to someone in complete confidence, advisers at your university are usually available to offer helpful guidance.

Finding Ways to Save Money

Recognising that 'saving' is not just about putting money away in a savings account is really important. But equally important is how you can reduce your spending whenever the opportunity arises. Whilst putting money away as savings is extremely challenging when on a limited income, it's not entirely impossible, even if the amounts you save are relatively small.

Whenever you save money you're doing your finances a favour – but beware of saving opportunities which are a false economy. A two-for-one or an 'extra 50 per cent free' deal isn't a saving if you weren't going to buy the item in the first place!

If you remain within your budget at the end of a given period, you may consider rewarding yourself. Alternatively, you may just enjoy the satisfaction of having managed your money effectively – this is certainly the cheaper option!

You can make effective use of the traditional 'penny jar' idea by using any £2 coins you're given in change – always keep them for the jar! If you're feeling like it, you can always add the occasional £1 as well. You can get a useful sum together surprisingly quickly (but keep your nest egg in a safe and secure place!).

Keep a savings diary. Once you've started to make successful savings, a record of what you've done to save, as well as how much, can offer you further encouragement when you look back at what you've achieved to date.

Choosing the Best Time to Start Spending

Avoid spending on items that you don't really need. The best way to do this is by planning ahead as much as possible, so reducing the risk of buying on impulse.

Shopping for food when hungry is a classic example – filling your basket with food for instant satisfaction without thinking through your needs for the week ahead is very tempting. It's all too easy to get back home and find that you've a luxury meal for that evening but barely anything for the rest of the week, meaning you need to go out and shop again.

If you've a hobby or other regular activity, think about what you spend whilst you do it and what steps you can take to cut back on your expenditure. For example, do you really need to go for a drink after playing sport? Could you leave for home earlier, or meet somewhere cheaper than the usual place?

A regular review of your bank statements to examine your own spending habits helps you see if you can identify areas that you can improve upon. Any savings you can make on a regular basis add up to a substantial amount over time.

Household bills are an example where planning your expenditure means a bill isn't a shock to your finances when it arrives. Take time to explore the payment arrangements available when you open an account with a utility company – you may find there's an option that allows you to budget effectively and avoid worrying about how you're going to pay a bill when it comes through your door.

Taking Advantage of Discounts

Being a higher education student means you can sign up for an NUS card through your university's student union. Whilst there is usually an initial cost for the card, make sure you do get one because the NUS card can easily pay for itself over and over with the opportunities for discounts at numerous shops, restaurants, travel companies and more.

Always carry your NUS student discount card so you can take full advantage of it wherever you go. Details of current offers are available at `www.nus.org.uk`.

Don't forget to check out other opportunities for discounts as well. The NUS card is an excellent source of savings which are only available to students, but don't let that stop you exploring other opportunities to get money off what you need.

Many mobile phone companies provide offers to their customers on a range of goods and services. Supermarket reward schemes can be a useful source of savings – check out how the schemes work and what you can get from them. Keep a lookout for discounts wherever you can find them so you can save your money.

Discount offers can only usually be used one at a time, so don't assume you can use several for one transaction. Also, check for expiry dates, particularly on any voucher-based schemes you may use.

Spending on an Evening Out

Going out for a night's entertainment can easily turn into the most expensive activity you do in a single week. There are some steps you can take to try and bring down the costs.

Get your friends organised into small groups who can share a round – this is far more preferable to buying a round for a large group. You may find all your friends are there at the start of an evening, but then some move on to other things – so it's usually the person who has bought that first round who doesn't see the favour repaid.

Whenever you go out, always set yourself a limit as to how much you want to spend. Use cash so you can see what you're spending.

Don't go and get more from an ATM, or start using plastic in any other way during the course of the evening. Just like anything else you buy, you need to try to stick to your budget.

Of course, there's always the option of gathering with friends at home for special occasions, rather than going out. Shopping for food and drink is usually cheaper than paying for it in restaurants and bars. Preparing a meal with friends can be fun too, and even if you end up doing the cooking, your friends are likely to be highly appreciative of your efforts.

Shopping and Eating as a Household

Cooking for one can be quite tricky in terms of managing a weekly shop and making it as economical as possible. And when you share a kitchen with others, there are always the inevitable instances where ingredients get 'borrowed' or several bottles of washing-up liquid vie for attention around the sink.

Shopping as a household with your housemates helps overcome these issues, and by following some simple rules you can ensure that your weekly shop becomes a lot more manageable and effective:

- ✔ Agree a weekly budget

- ✔ Agree a basic list of essentials

- ✔ Check which essentials need topping up

- ✔ Negotiate a menu suiting everyone's tastes

- ✔ Agree a list of personal favourites (take note of costs)

- ✔ Check cleaning products and toiletries

Once you've got the basic approach in place, it should be easy enough to share the bill, allowing for additional contributions where 'special items' have been placed on the list. After a few weeks you may find that a couple of members of the household may be able to manage the weekly shop, rather than everyone going each time.

Shopping as a household means you probably share cooking – and this can mean more economical use of electricity and gas. As a household, you also make fewer trips to the shop, which can help to reduce travel costs as well.

Checking Whose Name is on the Bills

When sharing a house with others you should take some basic precautions to ensure that no one is at risk of bearing the full cost of living there.

Take steps to ensure that everyone's name is on:

- ✔ Utilities bills (electricity, gas and water)

- ✔ TV licence

- ✔ Phone bill

- ✔ Broadband/Internet bill

- ✔ Additional TV package

In some cases you should ensure that everyone's name is on the accommodation contract (where the contract mentions joint and several liability).

By including everyone's names on these documents, you're formally sharing the costs of living together. If someone has financial difficulty or refuses to pay, it becomes easier for the others who have paid to demonstrate who is responsible for the unpaid portion of the bill.

 When sharing accommodation, ensure all housemates exchange details of their email address, phone number and permanent address where they normally live outside term-time – this gives you the best chance of following up issues if any shared payment arrangements go wrong.

Shopping for the Supermarket Brands

When doing the weekly shop, always remember to check for supermarket 'own' brands.

Surprising as it may seem, in taste tests between leading brands and supermarket brands, the supermarket products often come out on top. This is not always the case, but a little bit of trial and error should tell you when the supermarket brand is a satisfactory alternative for the more expensive product – and, of course, some of this is down to your personal taste.

Some supermarkets offer two varieties of 'own' brand – one being cheaper than the other. Both are likely to be cheaper than leading brands (unless the leading brand is on offer, so remember to check).

 When buying fresh produce, remember to check 'loose' fruit and vegetables rather than just going for pre-packed, because they are almost always the cheaper option. If you want to make the greatest savings you can, consider going to your local market, as the prices there are usually lower still.

Getting About Without a Car

Travel costs can often be a significant outlay, particularly if you live some distance from your university, or if your course has placements or field trips you need to get to. Using public transport is a great alternative, because you only need to pay when you use the service.

Much as owning a motor vehicle is very desirable when it comes to offering a great deal of convenience and freedom, the down side is that they are a regular burden on your finances – even more so if you're a young driver because of the high insurance premiums you need to pay.

Maintenance and fuel costs add up over the year, so if you have a motor vehicle, ask yourself if it's essential that you bring it with you – even if you only pay insurance and tax over the year, it's still a substantial cost to take into account.

If you have to use your own vehicle, remember to find out from your university if there is any funding which can help with the costs.

Walking or cycling are great alternatives for saving money and keeping you in shape! Just remember to keep safe.

Chapter 21

Ten Myths About Student Finance

In This Chapter

▶ Avoiding common misconceptions

▶ Understanding repayments

▶ Keeping a clean nose in the student finance system

Student finance is not immune from myths being generated around it, some of which can seem very plausible or even likely.

Myths can, at their worst, have a negative effect and allow inaccurate information to dissuade you from engaging with the given subject – in this case the opportunity to maximise your income.

In this chapter, I focus on ten myths and clarify the truth. Reference to this list of myths hopefully helps you to combat those negative messages, both for yourself and your fellow students.

'Interest on My Student Loan Means I'll Have a Huge Debt to Repay'

You may think that the interest being applied to your account means that you'll have more loan to repay as a result. Not so.

Repayments are always calculated on your income, not what you owe. So, if your earnings mean you repay £60 per month – that remains the case no matter how much interest gets applied to your loan balance.

Pay attention to your repayments (9 per cent of your income over the repayment threshold) rather than your annual statements from the Student Loans Company (these need to be issued for legal reasons, but are for information only and are not a demand for payment).

'You Can Only Apply After You've Got a Place on a Course'

The process of applying for your higher education course typically involves two applications – one for your place on the course via UCAS (the university admissions service), and one for your student finance via the government's website (www. gov.uk/student-finance).

If you're considering higher education study, you can apply for your student finance no matter what stage your UCAS application has reached.

If you're not yet sure which university you want to study at, or which course you want to pursue, don't let this stop you applying for your student finance – use your best guess as to which university you'll be at and which course you'll be on. If it turns out that these details change, you have the opportunity to change the information on your account once your application has been processed.

Always apply for your student finance as soon as you can. The sooner you apply, the less chance there is that your funding will be delayed.

Chapter 4 provides more details on the application process.

'Grants Never Have to be Repaid'

A very brief mythbuster here.

Grants don't usually have to be repaid. *But* . . . if you leave your course early and you've received a payment of grant in respect of a period of time when you weren't in attendance on the course, this payment is treated as an overpayment and is regarded as immediately repayable.

'If You've Lived Outside the UK, You Can't Get Funding'

An often-quoted eligibility requirement is that you must have been 'ordinarily resident' in the UK and Islands for the three years before your course begins in order to qualify for living cost as well as tuition fee funding.

This is certainly a basic requirement. And you should note that for the purposes of the regulations which govern student finance, the start date of a course beginning in the autumn term is 1 September (even if the course doesn't actually start on that date). However, there are exceptions to the rule, as shown in the following sections.

If you're a UK citizen and have been abroad during the required three-year period, I recommend that you contact the advice service at the university where you intend to study – they can check your situation in detail and advise as to your eligibility for student finance.

Temporary absences

The concept of *ordinarily resident* involves a notion of permanence in terms of your residence in the UK. If you have a temporary absence abroad, then this could mean that you're still deemed ordinarily resident.

Short breaks abroad like holidays are not going to jeopardise your residency status. If, however, you or your family have been working or staying abroad for an extended period, you may still qualify if you can show the move abroad was never intended to be permanent.

Try to gather as much evidence as you can of your intention to return to the UK after a short period.

Key documents are travel documents or employment contracts, which show your time abroad was for a limited period. Also, if you can show you kept up a UK bank account, registration with a GP or dentist – all this is going to help show that you always intended to return.

Exercising right of residence abroad

In England, Wales, Scotland and Northern Ireland, where you or a member of your family has gone to work abroad in the European Economic Area (EEA) during the three-year period, you may still qualify as ordinarily resident if you return to the UK before the first day of the first term of the first academic year of the course, and if you have been ordinarily resident within the EEA for the duration of the three-year period.

'Well-Off Partners or Parents Equals No Student Finance'

If you consider your family circumstances to be 'comfortable' or even 'well off', don't make the assumption that there is no student finance available for you.

Both the Tuition Fee Loan and 65 per cent of the Maintenance Loan are available on a non income-assessed basis, which means as long as you satisfy the basic eligibility criteria for student finance, you can get all your tuition fees covered, and have the opportunity to obtain money to contribute towards your living costs.

The basic eligibility criteria are:

- ✔ Ordinarily resident in the UK and Islands for the three years prior to the start of your course

- ✔ Resident in the UK nation in which you're going to be studying on the first day of your course

- ✔ Studying a designated course

- ✔ Studying at a UK education establishment

- ✔ Not having arrears owing to the Student Loans Company

If you're eligible then you can usually count on funding in excess of £12,000 per year regardless of your household income situation.

Furthermore, you need bear in mind the income thresholds for student finance, as you might be surprised how much funding may be available to you.

In England, Wales and Northern Ireland, income-assessed funding is available on incomes in excess of £50,000 per year. The most extensive range of income covered is in England, with students studying in London with household incomes up to £67,000 per year still qualifying for an amount of income-assessed funding.

In short, you may be surprised to find you qualify for more than just the minimum funding available – and there's always likely to be some student finance available to you to support your studies – particularly if you're studying in higher education for the first time.

'No Welfare Benefits Are Available to Students'

Whilst there is a general rule that full-time students cannot access income replacement benefits from the welfare benefit system, part-time students can make a claim for means-tested welfare benefits, and all students can be considered for tax credits provided they meet the eligibility and means-test criteria.

Some full-time students DO qualify for means-tested benefits. If you fall into any of the following categories you can probably make a claim for welfare benefits at some point during your studies (seek further advice if necessary):

✔ A lone parent responsible for a child or young person aged under 20 who is a member of your household and in full-time non-advanced education; or

✔ A lone foster parent responsible for a child or young person aged under 20; or

✔ Have a partner who is also a full-time student and either or both of you are responsible for a child or young person aged under 20 in full-time non-advanced education; or

✔ A disabled person qualifying for a disability premium; or

✔ Treated as incapable of work for a continuous period of at least 28 weeks (two or more periods of incapacity with a break of no more than eight weeks counts as one continuous period); or

✔ deaf and qualifying for a Disabled Students' Allowance; or

✔ Aged 60 or over; or

✔ Entitled to Personal Independence Payment, Armed Forces Independence Payment or Disability Living Allowance.

'Paying Tuition Fees Up Front is Better than Taking out the Tuition Fee Loan'

You may be tempted to think that avoiding taking out a loan must work out as the better deal, but the terms of repayment on student loans mean you do need to make a very careful decision not to use the Tuition Fee Loan to pay for your studies.

Student loans don't need to be repaid until you're earning over the appropriate earnings threshold, and you have finished your time studying. Even then, the repayments are only based on 9 per cent of your income over the relevant threshold, and this usually makes repayments extremely competitive when compared to other forms of credit. Add to this the fact that loans have a maximum lifetime of 30 years, and your repayments stop if your personal income drops below the relevant threshold, and you may find that you aren't required to make repayments of all the money that may otherwise be due under the scheme. Even when adding up repayments over 30 years, you may possibly end up not repaying what you borrowed during your studies when considering the money in real terms over the time period.

Of course, if you find yourself heading towards a very well paid graduate career (a job with a starting salary of £38,000 p.a. or more, for instance) then you might consider that you don't need a Tuition Fee Loan – but in all other cases you need to take a long, hard look before taking the decision to pass up the loan.

'You Only Get Funding for Three Years'

Don't make the mistake of assuming that the funding you can access matches the length of your course. In fact, the usual scenario is that you can access full funding for the ordinary duration of your course plus one year.

If you're studying after having undertaken and gained a lower level degree qualification (such as a foundation degree or HND), you may even find that you can access student finance over a longer than usual period – this is to guarantee you're given the equivalent opportunity of being funded to first degree level.

'If You Go Abroad After Graduation, You Don't Have to Pay Back the Student Loans'

Another simple bit of mythbusting here. The answer to the above is very much a 'yes you do'. Whilst there's no denying recovery of the loan gets more difficult over a national boundary, the Student Loans Company will try to find you. And the thing is, whilst they are doing that, every letter they send, and every day that goes by, penalty charges and penalty interest are applied to your loan account.

'A Student Loan Debt Means You Won't Get a Mortgage'

Whilst suggesting that your student loan isn't taken into account by a mortgage provider isn't entirely correct – it is how it is taken into account which is crucial. Rather than being viewed as an item of credit, mortgage providers are more likely to treat your student loan repayments in a different way.

The reason for this is that the amount you repay is determined by your income, not by the usual terms of a loan agreement (requiring repayments at a fixed rate regardless of income). This means that if your income takes a turn for the worse, mortgage providers take into account the fact that your student loan repayments cease, meaning more of what income you have left is available for your mortgage – so a student loan is rarely likely to be a barrier to a mortgage.

Index

About the Author

Phil Davis has worked in the field of money advice since 1995 when he started his career at Middlesbrough Citizens Advice Bureau. He has worked in higher education since 1998, and his current role is Head of Student Advice and Learning Development at Bishop Grosseteste University, Lincoln. From July 2007 until October 2014, he acted in a voluntary role on the Board of the National Association of Student Money Advisers (NASMA), spending four years as company secretary, and the last two years of office as chairperson of the charity. Throughout his term of office he took part in policy meetings within government and with senior managers of the Student Loans Company – and continues to do so. He also regularly contributes to editions of BBC Radio 4's *Moneybox Live* on student finance matters.

Dedication

This book is dedicated to all the colleagues I have worked with within higher education and partner organisations, who have played a part in helping me develop my understanding of all things student finance and money advice. In particular, to Ian Summers Noble who has been a constant source of inspiration throughout my career, and to Lynne Condell MBE whose commitment to student money advice is second to none.

Author's Acknowledgments

I would like to thank my sister, Lesley and her husband Aelwyn for all their encouragement and a place of sanctuary in which to write. I would also like to thank my partner Suzi for helping me get to the end of this project.

Thanks to David Malcolm for his input and expertise on NHS matters (and encyclopaedic knowledge of student finance policy), and to NASMA and BGU colleagues who have provided me with encouragement along the way. Also, thanks to all members of the team at Wiley for their patience, understanding and support throughout this project.

Publisher's Acknowledgments

Acquisitions Editor: Annie Knight

Project Manager: Michelle Hacker

Development Editor: Word Mountain Creative Content

Copy Editor: Martin Key

Technical Editor: Laura Robbie

Production Editor: Kumar Chellappan

Cover Photos: ©YinYang/ iStockphoto.com

Take Dummies with you everywhere you go!

Whether you're excited about e-books, want more from the web, must have your mobile apps, or swept up in social media, Dummies makes everything easier.

Visit Us

Like Us

Follow Us

Watch Us

Join Us

Pin Us

Circle Us

Shop Us

BUSINESS

978-1-118-73077-5   978-1-118-44349-1   978-1-119-97527-4

MUSIC

978-1-119-94276-4   978-0-470-97799-6   978-0-470-49644-2

DIGITAL PHOTOGRAPHY

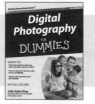
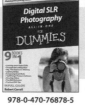

978-1-118-09203-3   978-0-470-76878-5   978-1-118-00472-2

Algebra I For Dummies
978-0-470-55964-2

**Anatomy & Physiology
For Dummies, 2nd Edition**
978-0-470-92326-9

Asperger's Syndrome For Dummies
978-0-470-66087-4

Basic Maths For Dummies
978-1-119-97452-9

**Body Language For Dummies,
2nd Edition**
978-1-119-95351-7

**Bookkeeping For Dummies,
3rd Edition**
978-1-118-34689-1

British Sign Language For Dummies
978-0-470-69477-0

Cricket for Dummies, 2nd Edition
978-1-118-48032-8

**Currency Trading For Dummies,
2nd Edition**
978-1-118-01851-4

Cycling For Dummies
978-1-118-36435-2

Diabetes For Dummies, 3rd Edition
978-0-470-97711-8

eBay For Dummies, 3rd Edition
978-1-119-94122-4

**Electronics For Dummies
All-in-One For Dummies**
978-1-118-58973-1

English Grammar For Dummies
978-0-470-05752-0

French For Dummies, 2nd Edition
978-1-118-00464-7

Guitar For Dummies, 3rd Edition
978-1-118-11554-1

IBS For Dummies
978-0-470-51737-6

Keeping Chickens For Dummies
978-1-119-99417-6

Knitting For Dummies, 3rd Edition
978-1-118-66151-2

A Wiley Brand

SELF-HELP

978-0-470-66541-1 978-1-119-99264-6 978-0-470-66086-7

LANGUAGES

978-0-470-68815-1 978-1-119-97959-3 978-0-470-69477-0

HISTORY

978-0-470-68792-5 978-0-470-74783-4 978-0-470-97819-1

Laptops For Dummies 5th Edition
978-1-118-11533-6

**Management For Dummies,
2nd Edition**
978-0-470-97769-9

Nutrition For Dummies, 2nd Edition
978-0-470-97276-2

Office 2013 For Dummies
978-1-118-49715-9

Organic Gardening For Dummies
978-1-119-97706-3

Origami Kit For Dummies
978-0-470-75857-1

**Overcoming Depression
For Dummies**
978-0-470-69430-5

Physics I For Dummies
978-0-470-90324-7

Project Management For Dummies
978-0-470-71119-4

Psychology Statistics For Dummies
978-1-119-95287-9

**Renting Out Your Property
For Dummies, 3rd Edition**
978-1-119-97640-0

**Rugby Union For Dummies,
3rd Edition**
978-1-119-99092-5

Stargazing For Dummies
978-1-118-41156-8

**Teaching English as a Foreign
Language For Dummies**
978-0-470-74576-2

Time Management For Dummies
978-0-470-77765-7

Training Your Brain For Dummies
978-0-470-97449-0

**Voice and Speaking Skills
For Dummies**
978-1-119-94512-3

Wedding Planning For Dummies
978-1-118-69951-5

WordPress For Dummies, 5th Edition
978-1-118-38318-6